MAKING SENSE, MAKING WORLDS

Nicholas Onuf is a leading scholar in international relations and introduced constructivism to international relations, coining the term constructivism in his book *World of Our Making* (1989).

This powerful collection of essays clarifies Onuf's approach to international relations and makes a decisive contribution to the debates in IR concerning theory. It embeds the theoretical project in the wider horizon of how we understand ourselves and the world. Onuf updates earlier themes and his general constructivist approach, and develops some newer lines of research, such as the work on metaphors and the re-grounding in much more Aristotle than before.

A complement to the author's groundbreaking book of 1989, *World of Our Making*, this tightly argued book draws extensively from philosophy and social theory to advance constructivism in International Relations.

Making Sense, Making Worlds will be vital reading for students and scholars of international relations, international relations theory, social theory and law.

Nicholas Greenwood Onuf is Professor *Emeritus*, Department of Politics and International Relations, Florida International University, Miami, and Professor Associado, Instituto de Relações Internacionais, Pontifica Universidade Católica do Rio de Janeiro.

The New International Relations

Edited by Richard Little, *University of Bristol*, Iver B. Neumann, *Norwegian Institute of International Affairs (NUPI), Norway* and Jutta Weldes, *University of Bristol*.

The field of international relations has changed dramatically in recent years. This new series will cover the major issues that have emerged and reflect the latest academic thinking in this particular dynamic area.

International Law, Rights and Politics
Developments in Eastern Europe and the CIS
Rein Mullerson

The Logic of Internationalism
Coercion and accommodation
Kjell Goldmann

Russia and the Idea of Europe
A study in identity and international relations
Iver B. Neumann

The Future of International Relations
Masters in the making?
Edited by Iver B. Neumann and Ole Wæver

Constructing the World Polity
Essays on international institutionalization
John Gerard Ruggie

Realism in International Relations and International Political Economy
The continuing story of a death foretold
Stefano Guzzini

International Relations, Political Theory and the Problem of Order
Beyond international relations theory?
N.J. Rengger

War, Peace and World Orders in European History
Edited by Anja V. Hartmann and Beatrice Heuser

European Integration and National Identity
The challenge of the Nordic states
Edited by Lene Hansen and Ole Wæver

Shadow Globalization, Ethnic Conflicts and New Wars
A political economy of intra-state war
Dietrich Jung

Contemporary Security Analysis and Copenhagen Peace Research
Edited by Stefano Guzzini and Dietrich Jung

Observing International Relations
Niklas Luhmann and world politics
Edited by Mathias Albert and Lena Hilkermeier

Does China Matter? A Reassessment
Essays in memory of Gerald Segal
Edited by Barry Buzan and Rosemary Foot

European Approaches to International Relations Theory
A house with many mansions
Jörg Friedrichs

MAKING SENSE, MAKING WORLDS

Constructivism in social theory and international relations

Nicholas Greenwood Onuf

LONDON AND NEW YORK

First published 2013
by Routledge
2 Park Square, Milton Park, Abingdon, Oxon, OX14 4RN

Simultaneously published in the USA and Canada
by Routledge
711 Third Avenue, New York, NY 10017

Routledge is an imprint of the Taylor & Francis Group, an informa business

British Library Cataloguing in Publication Data
A catalogue record for this book is available from the British Library

Library of Congress Cataloging-in-Publication Data
Onuf, Nicholas Greenwood.
Making sense, making worlds : constructivism in social theory and
international relations / Nicholas Greenwood Onuf.
    p. cm. – (The new international relations)
  Includes bibliographical references and index.
  1. International relations–Philosophy. 2. International relations–
Social aspects. 3. Constructivism (Philosophy) I. Title.
JZ1251.O58 2012
327.101–dc23   2012010802

ISBN: 978-0-415-62416-9 (hbk)
ISBN: 978-0-415-62417-6 (pbk)
ISBN: 978-0-203-09671-0 (ebk)

Typeset in Bembo
by HWA Text and Data Management, London

For my graduate students in Washington, New York, Colombo, Kyoto, Miami, Rio de Janeiro, Los Angeles and Geneva, 1966–2011

CONTENTS

FOREWORD

I always enjoy writing forewords to the books that appear in this series, but it is a particular pleasure and privilege to be writing this one. It is over forty years since I first began reading Nick Onuf's work. At that time, I was thinking about the idea of intervention as the topic for my doctorate, although it quickly became apparent that it is not possible to understand intervention without also taking account of the putative norm of non-intervention, and after I came to this conclusion I very quickly came across an early article by Nicholas Greenwood Onuf on non-intervention. In the subsequent years Onuf has developed into one of the most profound and original thinkers in the field of international relations. This book, which pulls together a range of material that he has produced over the last fifteen years, reveals very clearly not only the depth and originality of his thinking but also the way his thinking continues to evolve and, in the process, he perennially retains the capacity to challenge received wisdom.

Although Onuf is generally acknowledged as a major theorist in International Relations, it still seems to me that his body of work has not had either the level or breadth of recognition that it fully deserves. It would be gratifying if this book helped to rectify this situation. Yet, ironically, the book also illustrates why his work has never become part of mainstream thinking. Onuf is an uncompromising theorist who often works in unfamiliar terrain, reads texts very closely and thinks hard about them but at the same time he expects his reader to work hard too. It is not that he writes in a convoluted fashion, on the contrary, his style is remarkably direct and easy to follow. But he is almost always working outside the boundaries of conventional thinking and frequently draws on literature from outside of the field. Indeed, it can sometimes seem that he is not writing about international relations at all but that is only because he is anticipating that readers will be actively engaged with the text and identify for themselves the relevance of what is being said for the task of understanding international relations.

Even so, it might seem strange, at first sight, to suggest that Onuf is not part of mainstream thought. After all, a good case can be made that he was one of the very first theorists in International Relations to raise the idea of a constructivist approach to the study of international relations and there is little doubt that constructivism has now become one of the most dominant approaches to the subject. Yet as he makes clear in this book, the field has, in practice, veered away from the form of constructivism that he advocates. Whereas he favours what he calls a 'radical' form of constructivism, he acknowledges that mainstream thinking has come to favour what he describes as 'limp' constructivism. But he also recognizes that the message of his magisterial text *World of Our Making* was not easy to grasp and that its radical implications were not taken on board by mainstream thinkers when the book came out. From Onuf's perspective, the form of constructivism that has come to prevail in subsequent years considerably diminishes the very broad ranging and robust meta-theoretical framework which he put together. Limp constructivism fails to demonstrate the necessity for International Relations to take an 'ontological turn', one that acknowledges that international relations are not a unique type of relationship but one that must be folded into a common overarching framework that permits the analysis of any form of social relationship. In the opening section of this book, Onuf restates his original position in a way that aims to clarify its extraordinarily radical message. Indeed, for Onuf, *World of Our Making* effectively makes the field of international relations and its received theories 'superfluous'. It is not, as a consequence, really so surprising if the field and the creators of these received theories have not been entirely receptive to Onuf's approach.

It is also, perhaps, logical to place this first section at the start of the book, but I think that anyone who is coming to Onuf's ideas for the first time would be advised to read the chapters in the final section first because they reveal the implications of Onuf's conception of constructivism for how he thinks about both International Relations, the field of study, and international relations, the subject matter of this field. Having seen the very distinctive take that Onuf has on the theory and practice of international relations, it then becomes intriguing to see how this take and its attendant 'ontological turn' has been generated by the framework that is laid out in the opening section. Indeed, it probably makes sense to read the very final chapter first, because not only is it the latest chapter to have been written, but it also exposes so very clearly how constructivism informs how Onuf sees and interprets the world. It also reveals that Onuf himself is still in the process of exploring the implications of a radical constructivist view of the world. The chapter explores what it might mean to envision international relations from the 'periphery'. Of course, Onuf is quite clear that the dominant perspective for the field of international relations is from the 'centre'. Indeed, he frankly admits that within the last decade he contributed to a book that explored different visions of international relations and yet managed to ignore the existence of a vision from the 'periphery'. His approach to constructivism, however, does not then lead him to argue that analysts at the centre have a duty to explore the world from the perspective of the 'periphery'. On the contrary, he is quite clear analysts have no alternative but to accept that the 'centre of world power' is also the 'centre of world-making' but he also insists that, albeit within unknown limits, it is possible for scholars to systematically analyse social relations in the modern world without reverting to the ideas of 'centre' and 'periphery' as organizing concepts. Onuf goes on to illustrate this point and he reveals why he believes that these distinctively modern terms are in the process of atrophying.

Although profoundly critical of the prevailing 'discipline' of International Relations, there is nothing arrogant about Onuf's position. On the contrary, he is remarkably willing to acknowledge the strengths of theorists with whom he disagrees and amazingly adept at folding their theories into his own more encompassing and eclectic approach. This is very evident in the chapter on institutions that opens the final section of the book where his sympathetic reading of a wide range of theorists enables him to build on their insights and provide the most persuasive framework for studying international institutions that I have seen. Stanley Hoffmann wrote many years ago about the long road to theory, but I suspect that Onuf would argue that the road is necessarily never-ending. Certainly, he acknowledges the importance of transitional theorists, past and present, who help to throw light on those times when there is an ontological shift and history moves from one age to another – what Seldon Wolin views as a paradigm shift. Onuf believes that we are operating today at such a juncture and it is primarily for this reason that he argues that International Relations is projecting such an increasingly irrelevant image of the contemporary world. If he is right, then there is little doubt that Onuf will come to be viewed, although maybe only retrospectively, as one of the foremost transitional theorists of the era.

Richard Little,
Emeritus Professor, University of Bristol

PREFACE

Scholarship is a craft, a skilled activity. No less is it a creative undertaking. As Aristotle said, any such activity has "an end other than itself." Its *ends* are nothing other than our *goals*—terms I use interchangeably for our socially mediated, normatively freighted beliefs, wishes and desires. Being able to form and act on goals is a defining feature of the human condition. Language makes it possible for us—those of us who are scholars, all of us as self-aware human beings—to form and revise goals for ourselves, with others, for others. Forming goals is itself always goal-oriented—a means to an end other than itself—and it depends on language or some other skilled activity by which to manifest or represent what we have in mind.

To form goals and act on them skillfully (rationally, effectively, strategically, appropriately: terms that I use more or less interchangeably even if most of my colleagues would not), each of us must make some sort of sense of our circumstances. For scholars, this is an explicit, indeed a defining goal, a reason for being. It is our ardent wish to make sense of the world. Making sense means coming to terms with the complexity of the whole, the way that its innumerably many parts are evidently connected, the apparent contingency of events, the impact of what we do—by ourselves and with each other—on what we think we see. Our activities demand an audience, even if only imagined, whose approval we seek.

What scholars do deliberately, as a craft, all of us do all of the time, often (as we say) on purpose, even more often (as we also say) without a second thought. To make sense of the world is to engage in making the world what it is for each of us. Making worlds together gives meaning to what we think our senses tell us about the world each of us finds within ourselves. This is never a simple, subjective operation. Doing it together, we do it not just with others, but *to* ourselves and others—language has *two* functions, representational and performative. We do it *socially* but never all at once. Only as we give meaning to the world does it have meaning.

In striving to make sense of the world, we make ourselves whole in a double sense: as self-aware individual beings with multiple, not always reconcilable goals and variously developed skills, and as a number of beings (not necessarily enumerated) who take we-ness for granted. If the world is whatever we, in this double sense, can make sense of as a whole, then there are as many worlds as there are sensible wholes. Among possible worlds, there is one that we take for granted in the very process of taking we-ness for granted. It is *the* world within which we locate all those other worlds that we make for ourselves—as we say, the *whole* world.

This is my credo as a scholar. It informs this collection of essays, just as it informed my book, *World of Our Making: Rules and Rule in Social Theory and International Relations* (1989), now re-issued after many years out of print. That book emphasizes the processes and consequences of world-making—making together, making at cross purposes, making work, making over. Ruled by language and its rules, we make rules and instantiate rule, thereby making the world what it is for us. The world thus made will always work to the advantage of some at the expense of others. This book shifts emphasis, if not very much, to the twin tasks of making sense of the world that we are forever making, even as we take it for granted, and finding a sense of purpose in our strivings, even as we fill the world with rules and rule, pomp and privilege, and pain and misery.

I undertake these tasks by exploiting two senses of the term *sense*. Conventionally, we discriminate between sense as in perception and sense as in cognition. In my view, these senses of *sense* should be taken as a whole for most purposes. We make sense of the world that our senses somehow make available to us. We do this for each other by making sense when we speak. In these pages, "to make sense" and "give meaning" are familiar, effectively interchangeable ways of talking about the same operation. Despite my post-Kantian sensibilities (as presented in Chapters 4 and 6), I do not mean to suggest a phenomenological stance when I use the term *meaning*. To speak of tasks, or functions, as I just have, is to suggest an altogether different point of view, one that I expressly adopt and hope to do justice to.

We make sense of the world—*any* world—by assuming that parts working together constitute working wholes. The language of doing and making, of purpose and work, of parts and wholes is one that Aristotle more than anyone else gave sense and coherence to. Yet my point of view is not Aristotelian in one crucial respect. Aristotle's world of functioning parts, including ourselves, comes ready-made—it is there for us to find (see Chapter 4). From my point of view, we make the world make sense to us by making it work for us. These are inseparable activities: it is what we do together, with purpose in mind.

In my view, then, world-making is something like shipbuilding and even more like household management. These are Aristotle's examples of *making*—

sustained, goal-oriented, skilled activity (see Chapter 8). What we produce together may not conform to anyone's goals (or, to use term I use frequently in these essays (especially Chapters 1, 5, 7 and 10), one's *intentions*: goals and ends are presumably capable of being objectively reported; intentions can only be subjectively understood (see below). Making something includes a vast amount of discrete, readily executed, more or less routine operations such as using an awl, broom or calculator (Aristotle's *praxis*).

All such operations are functionally implicated in world-making as they become normativized through familiar processes (Onuf 2008: Chapter 28); craft depends on rules. What we produce is never a finished product. Goals change as work proceeds, rules change, and the world changes. Moment by moment, we make the world whole because we experience it as a whole, freshly made *and* never finished. At any given moment, what we see *in* the world, what we see that we have done, what we talk about together, we imbue with normative properties and inflect with esthetic judgments (again, an Aristotelian point of view; see Chapter 4).

In the process of selecting essays for this book and arranging them thematically, I had given the book the working title *World-Making*. As I prepared to write this Preface, I happened to read a review of Ulster-born Paul Muldoon's new collection of poems called *Maggot*. The reviewer, Nick Laird, himself a novelist and poet, addressed the question as to whether Muldoon's difficult poetry is poetry at all by quoting Muldoon's response when someone asked him this question at a reading of his poetry.

> It doesn't come naturally to me to defend these things as poems. As a concept, I see it like this: the word "poetry," as you know, means "making," so these are constructs in the world … One is trying to construct something that will help us to make sense of things, and a construct, or building even, let's say, a space, a clearing, a momentary stay against confusion (from Robert Frost's phrase), which, when we enter, we have some clarification, however slight, and when we leave it, something, however slight, has been clarified. We have been helped in some way to make sense of the world.
>
> (Laird 2011: 66)

.When I saw the words, "to make sense of the world," I saw them as a title for this book. Gradually, I came to think that these words left too much out: world-making as doing, as craft. Instead, I decided *Making Sense, Making Worlds* would give a fuller sense of what I was trying to do. I also saw in Muldoon's remark about poetry, making, constructs and buildings an impromptu defense of Muldoon's craft as a poet *and* my own as a scholar. Muldoon is what I called myself in *World of Our Making* and continue to call myself: a constructivist.

This book's subtitle, *Constructivism in Social Theory and International Relations*, says as much, at least about me. The subtitle has an additional goal. It gives my audience, which is so unlike Mudoon's, a frame of reference that Muldoon's poetry has no need for. It is, moreover, the frame of reference that I had earlier established for *World of Our Making*. That book's subtitle, *Rules and Rule in Social Theory and International Relations*, was, but for a late moment of inspiration, to have been its title.

Muldoon reminded his audience that the English word *poetry* derives from the Greek term *poiêsis*. Translated as making or production, this term suggests, if only by association, that any purposeful activity, such as speaking to or writing for an audience, has an esthetic dimension, however little acknowledged. In this respect, poets are a model for all of us who practice a craft. Craft is mystery, "to use that admirable English word meaning all information relating to the theory and practice of a craft, which we borrowed from the old French *mestier*," and which, "by carelessness amounting to genius," Rebecca West went on to say in *Black Lamb and Grey Falcon* (1941: 935—her magnificent account of her travels in Yugoslavia in the late 1930s) we "confused in spelling with the word we derive from the Greek for occult."

Writing is a craft, and so is speaking. Art is advocacy; we speak to persuade; we choose words for effect. If few of us have mastered the poet's craft, everyone who speaks, speaks in metaphors. As figures of speech, metaphors please us. It pleases me to think of craft as mystery. At the same time, metaphors do conceptual work (concepts *are* stock metaphors—see Chapter 3); they convey whatever sense we human beings can make of the world that we go on making for ourselves.

As it is with words, so it is with sentences, paragraphs, arguments, texts as a whole. Constructing a sentence, deciding when to end a paragraph, working through an argument, offering a text, such as a poem, or this Preface, or this volume, to an audience: these activities give form to the sense we, individually and collectively, make of the world. We "shape and shove" what we think we know and want to say about the world (cf. Chapter 6), and we do so with normative and esthetic considerations always in mind—even if it is in the metaphorical back of our minds. We generally want to feel good about what we say, for it to seem right and fitting.

On these occasions, such values as consistency and clarity guide what we say. We take turns speaking, and we try to be responsive to what others say. Indeed we have an extensive repertory of guidelines (principles, generally stated instruction rules—see Chapter 1) to help us make sense of the world: arc, balance, symmetry, opposition, proportion, sonority, rhythm, harmony, resonance, color and shading. These guidelines vary from culture to culture, craft to craft, as do their relative importance. That they are not always compatible acknowledges divergent goals, affords choice and fosters creativity.

There are occasions, of course, where we use words insincerely, to hide our feelings even from ourselves, deceive an audience or maintain appearances (here see Chapter 7). We repeat ourselves for reassurance. We revel in paradox, delight in puzzles, thrill at crescendos, hope for catharsis. All that we aver to be real, or true, seems never to be fixed. And we know that words and texts are only one of many media that we become skilled in using to achieve our ends. World-making is an art. In these pages I have much less to say, at least directly, about social theory than I did in *World of Our Making*. Social theory is, however, the name that I prefer for both book as works of art (I know: sounds pretentious), and for all of my scholarly work.

Yet this is not the whole story. To shift metaphors, world-making goes deeper than art. It reaches beyond the self-conscious application of craft, the arduous niceties of theory-making. World-making depends on more fundamental, involuntary processes that take place in our respective minds. What we think we see, hear, feel already has form that *we* have given it in the act of apprehending the allegedly real contents of the world.

This claim implies a metaphysical stance. What we take in this world to be directly accessible, materially manifest and reliably represented—even in the concrete circumstance of anyone's "here and now" (Chapter 5)—necessarily results from cognitive operations performed on whatever it is that we "sense" our senses "telling" us. This way of thinking owes more to Kant and his "Copernican Revolution" in epistemology than it does to Aristotle. For Kant, the mind must be equipped with an ability to sort out and simplify a vast multiplicity of perceptions by reference to space, time and cause, and render them whole, such that each of us has a self-centered unity of consciousness. Made whole in the mind and continuously refreshed, this selectively processed multiplicity insists on its reality.

Kant had quite a bit to say about the additional normative and esthetic operations that we, as individuals, actively perform on what seemingly comes to the mind as a seamless whole. He had less to say about the place of language in making this whole seem more or less the same for everyone; in his work human beings make their worlds one by one. If world-making is a process of *social* construction—"the social construction of reality" (Berger and Luckmann 1967)—then Kant needs updating. Or, considering the importance I attach to Aristotle in making sense of the world as a *social* reality, perhaps we should think of it as backdating. For a post-Kantian metaphysics, Aristotle's work is an indispensable resource.

Updating and backdating aside, Kantian metaphysics finds support in contemporary research on the multiple neurological correlates of consciousness—of reality-construction—all of which contribute to the human quest, or compulsion, or indeed the survival imperative "to make sense of the world" (see Baars 1997, for an accessible review; here I am quoting p. 162). Even when cognitive scientists such as Bernard Baars emphasize the adaptive value of consciousness in Kantian terms (and thus talk about "objectlike representations," p. 173, instead of objects), they cling to the notion of an objective reality (see pp. 94–7 for the usual talk about reality). More self-consciously, evolutionary psychologists have also found metaphysical Kantianism attractive (Tooby *et al*, 2005). Evolutionary success has depended on the mind's capacity to construct a workable representation of a world that we think must be "out there" on the other side of our senses.

Kant recognized that for practical purposes we are empirical realists in our daily lives—for the most part we can rely on what we think our senses tell us about the world as we immediately experience it. I see no contradiction, paradox or philosophical sin in this defense of Kantian metaphysics, at least once we update Kant and characterize world-making as simultaneously the result of cognitive processing in individual human brains and an art—a social activity. By contrast, most philosophers favor realism over Kantian constructivism. Their barely concealed normative concerns (see for example Devitt 1997, Boghossian 2006) suggest a certain literal-mindedness that Kant himself did not always exhibit. Constructivism is most certainly not a metaphysical stance that most people find congenial, perhaps because they, too, worry about constructivism's alleged indifference to common sense (Devitt) or embrace of relativism (Bohgossian). Once we rehabilitate Aristotle's holistic, functional way of thinking and fold it in with Kantian metaphysics, such worries should recede. They will not disappear because constructivism takes work.

In this context, "most people" refers to those of us who live in what we call the modern world. Aristotle lived in a different world, yet his texts have shaped our modern world to an extent that I did not fully appreciate when I wrote *World of Our Making*. Indeed, Aristotle's presence in these pages will strike some readers as altogether odd. After all, Kant's reworking of Aristotle's metaphysics effectively crowned a sustained effort over at least two centuries to dislodge the hegemonic influence of Aristotle's way of thinking about the contents of the world.

To many scholars today, the success of this project is the very definition of modernity as a world-transforming world. Aristotle himself gave us little reason to think that any world—here understood as the whole that some substantial number of people make, sustain and live in together—can ever change so much as ours has in so many evidently linked respects. It may indeed be the case that in no other world than our own have people ever thought of world-making as an end in itself. Nevertheless, Aristotle's way of thinking suggests that every world is forever remaking itself (so-called autopoiesis). Deep down, our world seems to work more or less as Aristotle understood, even if we have created new ways of making it work.

The metaphorical construction "deep down" suggests my position: for half a millennium, modernity has deposited successive layers of innovations in ways of thinking about ourselves, in apprehending what we take to be the world's contents, and in devising our social arrangements, on the bedrock of the classical world. Each layer covers up the layer below. The cumulative effect is to obscure what, more than two millennia ago, Aristotle and many others in his world had worked out for themselves, and what, so many centuries ago medieval priests and Renaissance scholars brought back to light. While this "archeological" conception of modernity derives from Michel Foucault (Chapter 12), it holds, as he did not, that old ways of thinking never fully disappear. Indeed, modernity's innovations make sense only in a world where change is continuous and partial, massive and unfinished.

The grand story of modernity, in all its novelty and complexity, is too grand, novel in too many ways, too complex and surely too normatively fraught to be told in this or any other single volume. Instead, two themes (topics, elements, foci, features—no one term is metaphorically adequate) thread their way through the pages of this book and weave into patterns as intricate as they are elusive. One theme is the modern preoccupation with the individual self—self-consciousness, self-expression, self-realization—and the metaphorical extension of self to our social arrangements. Agency and identity come to be seen as the subjective self's objective, socially situated realization (see especially Chapter 5); state and nation emerge in tandem as novel realizations of collective self-expression (here see Onuf and Onuf 2006).

The other theme is signaled in the book's subtitle and speaks to the particular contents of the modern world commonly called international relations. Scholars in the field of International Relations (routinely capitalized to distinguish the subject from its study) are actively concerned about their craft, indeed their identity, but hardly in agreement on what the field's contents properly include. Narrowly conceived, international relations include just two ostensibly related subjects. One consists of those activities that political leaders of nation-states direct toward other states and their leaders (conventionally called foreign *policy*—see Chapter 7). The second consists of all those stable patterns (conventionally called *structures*—see Chapter 6) or normatively fixed social arrangements (conventionally called *institutions*—see Chapter 11) that have an effect on the activities that state leaders direct toward each other. Any other conception cannot produce a discriminant set of activities and arrangements for scholars in International Relations to concern themselves with.

Such an outcome erases the conventional boundaries between fields of study and subverts the shared premises of a field-specific craft. The result is as predictable as it is unacceptable to most of my colleagues. The field of International Relations must have as its subject whatever large numbers of people in today's world do that scholars in the field take to be important—politically relevant and normatively consequential (Chapter 11). This is, as we say, a slippery slope. The field ends up being about modernity, taken as a whole, from a sustained point of view such as constructivism.

The very thought of a field this encompassing has long heartened me. Because it makes most of my colleagues uncomfortable, they take refuge in events, episodic bundles of activities, which they believe to be "out there in the world" and to which they attach *prima facie* importance because everyone else whom they know does the same. Readers of this book will find few events. Instead, as they must already realize, they will find me trying to make sense of what many other scholars have said about international relations, modernity, society writ large, ourselves, and the ways of world-making that define the human condition.

I have arranged the twelve essays making up this book into four parts reflecting the concerns that I have just identified. I have not revised any of the essays substantively or brought them up to date. There are two reasons. First, I believe the essays to constitute an integral whole, even if they were composed at different times for different purposes. More precisely, I have taken them as they are and ordered them in parts to work together in what I take to be a whole—this is world-making at work. Second, I have not revised the book's twelve essays because they are not driven by events in the world so-called or by the latest research on the state of the world.

It is always tempting to add yet another reference for support of some point, or another few sentences in the illusory pursuit of perfect clarity. Just for example, reading Stephen Turner on mirroring, "empathetic universalization," interactively achieved meaning, and normativity (2010: 175–80) set me wondering. Is empathetic universalization Kant's faculty of apperception? Should I extend my brief remarks on apperception in Chapter 7 and link them to Chapter 4's discussion of parts and wholes in Aristotle's metaphysics? In view of the rapidly diminishing returns on such activities, I have resisted such temptations—with minor exceptions such as deleting a few notes, correcting botched quotations (there were some) and re-writing an ill-crafted sentence here and there. Whether I should have taken the opportunity to rework the general argument or to reconcile inconsistency in my claims is another question. I have done neither in the conviction, perhaps self-serving, that the general argument emerges clearly enough in the many ways these essays converge, and that inconsistencies in the way I formulate my claims in no way undermines the coherence of the general argument.

I offer a single, simple illustration of the point. In Chapter 2 I advocate "constructivism in its strong form," and in Chapter 12 I vary this formula slightly by advocating "a robust theoretical framework." In Chapter 6, I speak of "post-Kantian constructivism," which I also call an "updated constructivism." Chapter 4, however, identifies my position as "radical constructivism." After assembling this book, I encountered Niklas Luhmann's "radical constructivism" (2002: 128–33). On philosophical grounds, I take his constructivism to be more radical than my own—contra-Kantian and not just post-Kantian—because it calls into question "not the external world but only the simple distinction being/not being"—a distinction that Western metaphysics has always insisted on (p. 133). Since no one is likely to confuse my position with Luhmann's, I see no need to find myself another label. The more general point is that readers are unlikely to be confused by my having used the terms *strong, robust, updated* and *radical* more or less interchangeably.

There is, however, a subtle distinction lurking in these choices. The three essays in Part I spell out my sense of what constructivism is in the context of International Relations as a field of study and how I as a craftsman think it can be used to make sense of the world, or worlds (Chapter 2), that we purport to study. The constructivism that I describe in this context is strong or robust when compared to what other scholars in the field have in mind when they call themselves constructivists. I make no such claim by comparison with other fields of study. Although scholars in many fields now talk about constructivism, my exposure to their worlds is episodic and my use of their work opportunistic.

Thirty years ago I "discovered" constructivism for myself when I realized, belatedly and with help from my feminist graduate students, that gender is a social construction. This realization changed my view of all things presumptively natural. They too are social in kind. Reality so-called is a social phenomenon. Indicatively, the three essays in Part II turn from the field of International Relations to what I have been calling the metaphysics of world-making. In that context, post-Kantian constructivism *is* radical, even if Luhmann's contra-Kantian constructivism is more so.

The three essays in Part III are devoted to the art, or craft, of world-making, as practiced not just by scholars, but by all of us all of the time. In these essays, I have less occasion to talk about constructivism either as a guide for scholars or as a philosophical challenge. Part IV's three essays turn to modernity, but only the last essay resumes any discussion of International Relations as a field of study. Only then do I distinguish my constructivism from my colleagues', in this case by using the adjective *robust* as a synonym for *strong*. For some time, I have addressed much of my attention to modernity and its novel properties—most thoroughly in work that my brother, Peter Onuf, and I have undertaken together (2006). In doing so I have felt little need to spell out the constructivist premises upon which my craft depends.

All but one of these essays has been published previously, some in highly visible or readily accessible places, some not. The first essay (Chapter 1, "Constructivism: A User's Manual") has been around the longest and has undoubtedly been more widely read than anything else in this volume. Published in 1998, it marks my return to the main themes and arguments of *World of Our Making*, which I had put aside in favor of other interests. Vendulka Kubálková had suggested that she and I organize a group of colleagues and students to meet regularly and discuss our scholarly work (the Miami Group, as it came to be known). In this context she prevailed on me to prepare a concise, simply written précis of my book—something which, quite independently, Kurt Burch had also urged me to do. I am grateful to them both for reminding me of my responsibilities as a scholar and teacher and for giving a second life to the constructivist framework that I had presented in *World of Our Making*.

The second essay (Chapter 2, "Worlds of Our Making") appeared in 2002, thanks to Charles Kegley and Donald Puchala, who had commissioned me to write the book that became *World of Our Making* many years before. This essay says more than I had previously about the several worlds of international relations. It also attempts to explain why *World of Our Making* made, at least initially, such a slight impression on my colleagues in the field. Finally it reflects on the swell of scholarship that so many of my colleagues had begun to call constructivist.

The third essay (Chapter 3, "Fitting Metaphors") is quite recent, having appeared in print only in 2010. My earlier interest in metaphors having waned, I hold Eric Blanchard personally responsible for its revival. Some other constructivists have also brought metaphors to attention, including Petr Drulák, whose work on the subject I considered in a paper he invited me to present at the Institute of International Relations in Prague. Given the importance of metaphors in social construction on any scale, this essay endeavors to show what a well-crafted constructivist inquiry should look like.

Part II probes the metaphysics of world-making. Leading off is a long essay (Chapter 4, "Reading Aristotle"), only parts of which have been previously published. I presented the bulk of it at a conference in Belo Horizonte in 2006. Translated into Chinese, a severely abridged version appeared in 2006. Translated into Portuguese, the original text is forthcoming in a symposium volume.

Still deeply preoccupied with Aristotle's metaphysics, I augmented the 2006 paper with some material taken from a symposium volume to which Eric Heinze and Brent Steele had graciously invited me to contribute (Onuf 2009). I presented the essay more or less in its current form at the European Consortium on Political Research General Conference in 2009. I thank Benjamin Herborth and Oliver Kessler for making an extended, very useful discussion possible. Chapter 4 now covers predication, drawing distinctions, metaphorical language, classification, valence and much more. On reading it yet again—with fresh eyes, as we say—I find myself saying that Aristotle gave us tools "to put our thoughts in order and make sense of the world."

The second essay in Part II (Chapter 5, "Parsing Personal Identity") made its first appearance as a presentation to the Miami Group. Published in a symposium volume of the Miami Group's work in 2003, it is a response to the surge of scholarly interest in identity. Then and since, self-proclaimed constructivists in International Relations have taken such an interest to be an integral feature of constructivism's identity, in the process displacing agency as the locus of action taken on behalf of some object, with identity as a summary description of that object's properties. The object in question is typically a social collective already subject to unwarranted metaphorical personification.

Instead constructivists should focus their attention on agency in relation to structure, understood as a summary description of recurring, evidently stable features of the world in which any given agent is located. The problem here is the propensity of most scholars in the field, and not just constructivists, to assume that structures, as observers' constructs, directly affect agents even if those agents are not the observers in question. When Ken Booth invited me to a conference in Aberystwyth to celebrate Kenneth Waltz and his work, I took the opportunity to examine this problem and its metaphysical ramifications. The resulting essay (Chapter 6, "Structure? What Structure?") was published in 2009 in a special issue of the journal *International Relations* and in a symposium volume in 2011.

With Chapter 7, "Speaking of Policy," the book turns to the art of world-making (Part III). This essay originated in a presentation to the Miami Group and was published in another of its symposium volumes (2001). My goal was then (I find myself saying) the same as it is now: the goal of "making sense of the world." More specifically, in the many years I had lived in Washington, I had heard a great many people talk confidently about policies as if they were objects whose properties were obvious to any observer. Instead I talk about policy statements, along with professions of commitments and agreement, as instruments through which agents act on their goals. Consequently this essay shifts attention to the properties of performative language (any utterance or "speech act" by which we intend to affect what others do by that act alone), thereby continuing a line of inquiry launched in *World of Our Making* and reprised in Chapter 1.

In the earlier book and again in Chapter 1, I had focused my attention on what I have argued is a necessary relation between individual speech acts and rules which, whether we choose to follow them or not, simultaneously constitute and regulate our social arrangements. In the next essay (Chapter 8, "Rules in Practice"), I examine more closely the way rules work together in making our skilled activities effective in accomplishing our goals. As with identity (Chapter 5), I evaluate claims that practice is a collective phenomenon endowed with the properties—in particular, causal powers—that we customarily attribute to agents. I first presented this essay to the Miami Group in 2004 and tinkered with it off and on until its publication in a *Festschrift* for Fritz Kratochwil, who has thought more about rules in practice than anyone else in the field.

The last essay in Part III (Chapter 9, "Friendship and Hospitality") had its source in an intuition that one could speak of kin, neighbors and strangers just as Alexander Wendt did of friends, rivals and enemies (1999: 257–9), but that these two formulas do not "speak" to each other. I was prompted to ask why this was so when Anthony Lang invited me to participate in a conference on international political theory, the agenda for which specified friendship and hospitality as major themes in an emerging subfield. Aristotle is the classic point of reference for discussion of the former and Kant for discussion of the latter, with Jacques Derrida looming over recent discussion of both. My essay, published as a journal article in 2009, recapitulated what they had to say in order to show that friends and strangers figure in fundamentally different kinds, or basic forms, of social relations.

Part IV looks at the modern world—a world that we have made different from any other world both adventitiously and on purpose, a world that has made us what we are, a world that may be less different from other worlds than most of us would like to think. I can hardly claim that Part IV's three essays do anything more than scratch the surface, the everyday "reality," of this extraordinary world of ours. The first essay (Chapter 10, "Institutions, Intentions, and International Relations") considers the relation between intentions and institutions in modern liberal thought in order to assess conceptions of institutions among liberal scholars in International Relations. Since this essay appeared in the *Review of International Studies* in 2002, international institutions have gained enormously in importance and scholars in the field have responded accordingly. Indeed the rise of interest in "global constitutionalism" makes my lament that few scholars have given any thought to the constitution of international society quaintly dated.

If I were to revise any essay in this volume, it would be this one, but not because it is dated. My concern is one of craft: I have grown increasingly skeptical about the widespread, unexamined tendency to treat intentions as objective states that we, as observers even of ourselves, can reliably document. (For an overview and similar conclusion, see Steele 2011: 2606–10.) This tendency is also found in Chapters 1, 5 and 7, but it is perhaps most conspicuous in Chapter 10. All four of these essays date from the same five year interval—a decade ago. In the years since, I have come to think that intentions are subjective states (and largely subconscious states at that). They lack form (here see Chapter 6).

Since intentions, even our own, cannot be assessed directly, I prefer a less heroic activity. On the evidence, we can—and regularly do—formulate motives or reasons for conduct (what we, as observers, see agents, including ourselves, actually doing). These formulations stand in for intentions, and we judge conduct accordingly. By the same token, I would now speak of "unplanned consequences," and not "unintended consequences"—as I do at some length in this essay. (Chapters 5 and 7 grant some attention to plans and planning, as does Chapter 12 from an entirely different perspective.)

I adapted the second essay in Part IV (Chapter 11, "Civil Society, Global Governance") from a more elaborate paper I prepared for a conference on global civil society, which Randall Germain and Michael Kenny had invited me to attend. Idyllically set in Wales, the conference happened to coincide with 9–11, as we in the United States call one of the most memorable events in my lifetime, and the paper was duly published in a symposium volume (Onuf 2005). Meanwhile, I presented most of the material in the paper at Ritsumeikan University in Kyoto, where I had previously been a visiting member of the faculty and then, with permission from the conference organizers and their publisher, prepared this essay for a journal published at the university. In this essay, I resume an earlier interest in the political theory of civil society (Onuf 1998a: Chapter 10) before turning to the (mis)construction of globalization and modernization in late modern discussions of modernity.

The last essay in the book (Chapter 12, "Alternative Visions") is also the last to be published. It dates, however, from 2005 when I presented it at the Pontifica Universidade Católica do Rio de Janeiro; I revised it four or five years later, but not drastically, and adapted parts of it for other projects. The conference theme prompting the paper—visions of international relations from the modern world's periphery—also prompted in me a continuing preoccupation with what the modern world looks like not just from the periphery, but, insofar as can be plausibly envisioned as a whole, from outside itself. While the vision sketched here puts modernity into a familiar temporal sequence, its emphasis on conditions of possible knowledge follows Foucault in reaching back to Kant's constructivism. With craft in mind, I would like to think that this essay brings the book to a satisfactory conclusion.

This book is not the one that I had been planning for several years to write. *That* book was to have been drawn from many of the same papers as this one but reworked into a whole. It was to have been relatively short; the last of its several working titles was to be *The Metaphysics of World-Making* (now the title of this volume's Part II). By that late date, Chapter 4 would have formed its first two chapters. I abandoned the book in favor of the volume in front of you only reluctantly and only after presenting a considerable mass of undigested material (not all of it reprinted here), to the best possible audiences. In 2008, I subjected Fritz Kratochwil's students to this cumbersome text at a workshop that he sponsored at the European University Institute. I am grateful to Fritz and his students for their help. Jens Bartelson, Oliver Kessler and Edward Weisband later did me the considerable favor of reading the disjointed entirety. Finally, in 2011, I tried out an even larger mass of my recent work, published and unpublished, in a class I taught in 2011 while I was a visiting professor at the Graduate Institute in Geneva. With encouragement from David Sylvan, then head of Political Science, I called this class "World-Making."

After weeks of sustained discussion with two dozen willing, capable but often baffled students, I came to realize that I was not going to be able to turn this disjointed mass of material into the well-crafted book that I had in mind without making it unduly difficult for any imaginable audience to make sense of it—as a working whole in itself and as a companion volume to *World of Our Making*. The students were surprised when I told them this. They were even more surprised when I told them how much they had helped me, in ways that I could not easily express, in thinking through what I could hope to achieve as a craftsman. And so I told them that my graduate students had taught me far more cumulatively about my craft than I had been able to teach any one of them.

Along with friends and colleagues, quite a number of these students have had a far more direct impact on the essays previously published and collected here; I have already acknowledged them specifically and in print.[1] Other students of mine (including those not technically mine but with whom I have worked closely) will occasion to pick up this book and read these words as an acknowledgment that they otherwise never received. In the forty-five years that I have been teaching, a vast number of my graduate students have gone on to lives not even remotely linked to my own—a life that they have enriched in ways beyond what I can even begin to assess. To you, the whole lot of you, I dedicate this book.

---

1   Here, however, I should acknowledge Victor Coutinho Lage, Harry Gould, Stefano Guzzini, Patrick Jackson, Sandra Keowen, Oliver Kessler, Vendulka Kubálková, Ned Lebow, Cecelia Lynch, Renée Marlin-Bennett and Jon Strandquist for their advice specifically on this Preface, and/or their advice and encouragement on getting this project into print. At Routledge, Heidi Bagtazo, Alex Quayle, John Hodgson and Holly Knapp handled matters with good cheer and efficiency.

PART I
Constructivism

1

CONSTRUCTIVISM: A USER'S MANUAL

(1998)

CONSTRUCTIVISM is a way of studying social relations—any kind of social relations. While it draws from a variety of other ways of studying such a broad and complex subject, it stands on its own as a system of concepts and propositions. Constructivism is not a theory as such. It does not offer general explanations for what people do, why societies differ, how the world changes. Instead, constructivism makes it feasible to theorize about matters that seem to be unrelated because the concepts and propositions normally used to talk about such matters are also unrelated.

As presented here, constructivism applies to all fields of social inquiry. In recent years, dissident scholars in many fields have selectively used the language of social construction to criticize existing social arrangements and scholarly practices. A great deal of discord has ensued (also see Kubálková *et al.* 1998). When constructivism is used systematically, it has the opposite effect. It finds value in diverse materials and forges links where none seemed possible.

Full of discordant voices, International Relations is the field to which this particular system of concepts and propositions was first applied. While this manual is intended for the use of anyone with methodical habits of mind, its users are most likely to have an interest in the subject of international relations. They may have also had some exposure to the field's scholarly controversies. If this is indeed the case, they will soon discover that the subject is less distinctive, but more complex, than they have been led to believe.

Overview

Fundamental to constructivism is the proposition that human beings are social beings, and we would not be human but for our social relations. In other words, social relations *make* or *construct* people—*ourselves*—into the kind of beings that we are. Conversely, we *make* the world what it is, from the raw materials that nature provides, by doing what we do with each other and saying what we say to each other. Indeed, saying is doing: talking is undoubtedly the most important way that we go about making the world what it is.

Countries such as France, or the United States or Zimbabwe are among the social constructions, or societies, that people make through what we do. Countries are self-contained worlds because people talk about them that way and try to keep them that way. Yet they are only relatively self-contained. Relations among countries—international relations—constitute a world in its own right (see further Chapter 2). This is a self-contained world for the simple reason that it covers the earth, but it is still nothing more than a world of our making—a society of relatively self-contained societies.

Constructivism holds that people make society, and society makes people. This is a continuous, two-way process. In order to study it, we must start in the middle, so to speak, because people and society, always having made each other, are already there and just about to change. To make a virtue of necessity, we will start in the middle, between people and society, by introducing a third element, *rules*, that always links the other two elements together. Social rules (the term *rules* includes, but is not restricted to, legal rules) make the process by which people and society constitute each other continuous and reciprocal.

Rules are statements that tell people *what* we *should* do. The "what" in question is a standard for people's conduct in situations that we can identify as being alike and can expect to encounter. The "should" tells us to match our conduct to that standard. If we fail to do what the rule tells us to, then we can expect consequences that some other rule will bring into effect when other people follow the rule calling for such consequences. All of the ways in which people deal with rules—whether we follow the rules or break them, whether we make the rules, change them or get rid of them—may be called *practices* (on practices, see Chapter 8). Even when we do not know what a rule says, we can often guess what it is about by looking at people's practices.

Among much else, rules tell us who the active participants in a society are. Constructivists call these participants *agents*. People are agents, but only to the extent that society, through its rules, makes it possible for us to participate in the many situations for which there are rules. No one is an agent for all such situations.

Ordinarily, we think of agents as people who act on behalf of other people. Considering the matter more abstractly, rules make it possible for us to act on behalf of social constructions, which may be ourselves, other human beings, or even collections of people, along with the rules, practices and the actual things that we make and use. Conversely, agents need not be individual human beings to be able to act on behalf of others (here referring to agents in the third person to emphasize that the terms *people* and *agents* are not completely interchangeable). Agency is a social condition. Thus the government of a country is a collection of people and a social construction. According to the relevant rules, these people act, together and in various combinations, on behalf of that country as a much larger collection of people.

Rules give agents choices. As we have already seen, the most basic choice is to follow the rule—to do what the rule says the agent should do—or not. Only human beings can actually make choices, because we alone (and not all of us) have the mental equipment to consider the probable consequences of making the choices that are available to us. Nevertheless, we always make such choices on behalf of, and in the name of, social constructions, whether ourselves, other people or collections of other people, practices and artifacts.

Agents act in society to achieve goals. These goals reflect people's needs and wishes in light of their material circumstances. Every society has rules telling agents which goals are the appropriate ones for them to pursue. Of course, there are situations in which people are perfectly aimless. For example, when we freeze up in fear or fall asleep from exhaustion, we are no longer agents or, for that matter, social beings.

When we, as human beings, act as agents, we have goals in mind, even if we are not fully aware of them when we act. If someone asks us to think about the matter, we can usually formulate these goals more or less in the order of their importance for whomever we are acting as agents, starting with ourselves. Most of the time, agents have limited, inaccurate or inconsistent information about the material and social conditions that affect the likelihood of reaching given goals. Nevertheless, agents do the best they can to achieve their goals with the means that nature and society (together—always together) make available to them. Acting to achieve goals is *rational* conduct, and agents faced with choices will act rationally. Viewed from outside, these choices may appear to be less than rational, but this is due to the complexities of agency and human fallibility.

Agents make choices in a variety of situations. Rules help to define every such situation from any agent's point of view. In many situations, rules are directly responsible for presenting agents with choices. Agents have made or acknowledged these rules in the belief that following rules generally helps them reach their intended goals.

In these situations, rules are related to agents' practices, and to each other, through the consequences that agents intend their acts to have. Whether by accident or design, rules and related practices frequently form a stable (but never fixed) pattern suiting agents' intentions. These patterns are *institutions*. As recognizable patterns of rules and related practices, institutions make people into agents *and* constitute an environment within which agents conduct themselves rationally. While it is always possible, and often useful, to think of agents—all agents—as institutions in their own right, we more commonly think of agents as operating in an institutional context that gives them at least some opportunities for choice.

Exercising choices, agents act on, and not just in, the context within which they operate, collectively changing its institutional features, and themselves, in the process. Nevertheless, from any agent's point of view, society consists of diverse institutions that seem, for the most part, to be held in place by rules linking them to other institutions. Any stable pattern of institutions (including agents of all sorts) is also an institution. Agents are aware of the institutions populating their environments, and not simply because the rules forming these institutions directly bear on their conduct. To the extent that some agents make choices, and other agents are affected by these choices, institutions produce consequences for other agents that they cannot help but be aware of and respond to.

In a complex world, agents often make choices that have consequences, for themselves and others, that they had not anticipated or do not care very much about. Unintended consequences frequently form stable patterns with respect to their effect on agents. A perfect market provides a compelling illustration of this phenomenon. One by one, a large number of sellers and buyers are incapable of affecting the supply of, and demand for, a good. Collectively, their rational choices have the unintended consequence of setting a price for that good which they must individually accept as fixed (for more on institutions and unintended consequences, see Chapter 10).

Anyone may notice such stable patterns of unintended consequences. In the case of a market, no one could fail to notice it in the form of a good's price, over which no agent seems to have any control. Sometimes, agents will choose to prevent changes in such patterns by adopting rules that are intended to have this effect. A rule fixing the price of a good under certain conditions is only the most obvious example.

Any stable pattern of rules, institutions and unintended consequences gives society a *structure*, recognizable as such to any observer (Chapter 6). Agents are always observers. Insofar as they observe consequences that they had not intended, and accept them, such consequences are no longer unintended in the usual sense of the word. If agents decide that these consequences are bad for them, they will act to change them, perhaps with other unforeseen consequences resulting.

Outside observers (agents from a different society) may recognize a more complex structure than agents do as observers. Outsiders can stand back, so to speak, and see patterns that insiders cannot see because they are too close to them. As agents on the inside become aware of what observers have to say, observers become agents, whatever their intentions. When agents in general take this new information into account in making their choices, an even greater complexity of structure results.

Scholars who think of themselves as constructivists have given a good deal of attention to the "agent-structure problem" (see Gould 1998 for a thorough review of these discussions). The term *structure* is the source of much confusion (an *ontological* confusion), because scholars cannot agree on whether structures exist in reality or only in their minds. The important point to remember is that structure is what observers see, while institutions are what agents act within.

Nevertheless, structure can affect agents. We are often affected by phenomena, natural and social, that we do not or cannot see, but we then respond as agents by putting what has happened to us in an institutional context. When agents do this, they *institutionalize* structure by bringing rules to bear on their situations.

Generally speaking, scholars today tend to think that the structure of international relations is not institutionalized to any great degree. This is so even for some scholars who think of themselves as constructivists. They believe that countries are highly institutionalized as *states*, but that states, through their agents, conduct their relations in an anarchic world. The term *anarchy* points to a condition of *rule* among states in which no one state or group of states rules over the rest. It also implies that there is no institution above states ruling them. When we say that states are *sovereign*, we are saying the very same thing.

By calling international relations anarchic, scholars are not saying that there is an absence of rule. This would be chaos, not anarchy. Instead, they seem to be saying that structure—and especially a stable pattern of unintended consequences—rules the day. In the same sense, we might say that the market rules the behavior of sellers and buyers.

Starting with rules, as constructivists often do, leads quickly enough to patterns of relations that we can only describe as a condition of rule. Usually this condition is sufficiently institutionalized that we can recognize specific agents as rulers. Sometimes there is very little evidence of institutionalization, as in mob rule, but there is also little reason to think that this condition will persist as a stable pattern without institutions emerging. In other words, where there are rules (and thus institutions), there is rule—a condition in which some agents use rules to exercise control and obtain advantages over other agents. Rule is a stable pattern of relations, but not a symmetrical one.

Anarchy is a condition of rule in which rules are not directly responsible for the way agents conduct their relations. To be sure, there are rules in the background. They make sure that the unintended consequences of agents' many choices, and not rulers, do the job of ruling. If unintended consequences *seem* to rule, it is because some agents intend for them to do so.

Some agents want to be ruled in this indirect sort of way because it suits their goals more than any other arrangement would. Other agents have little or no choice in the matter. Perhaps patterns just happen, but agents make arrangements. Arranging for anarchy is just one possibility.

Constructivists should seriously consider dropping the word *structure* from their vocabularies. *Social arrangement* is a better choice. Appearances aside, international anarchy is a social arrangement—an institution—on a grand scale. Within its scope, many other institutions are recognizably connected. In every society, rules create conditions of rule. The society that states constitute through their relations is no exception.

Whether we, as constructivists, start with agents or with social arrangements, we come quickly enough to particular institutions and thus to rules. If we start with rules, we can move in either direction—toward agents and the choices that rules give them an opportunity to make, or toward the social arrangements that emerge from the choices that agents are making all the time. Whichever way we go, we ought to keep in mind that rules yield rule as a condition that agents (as institutions) can never escape.

The practical problem is that, as constructivists, we want to move in both directions at the same time. Yet if we try to do so, we come up against the staggering complexity of the social reality that we want to know about. It is impossible to do everything. The practical solution is to start with rules and show how rules make agents and institutions what they are in relation to each other. Then we can show how rules make rule, and being ruled, a universal social experience.

The remainder of this user's manual is dedicated to these two tasks. To make points as clear and understandable as possible, it repeats most of what the reader has now had a taste of. In the process, it introduces many additional concepts and propositions, expressed in the simplest terms that its author can think of. Used consistently and systematically related, these concepts and propositions constitute a comprehensive framework for understanding the world in constructivist terms.

Rules make agents, agents make rules

Rules make agents out of individual human beings by giving them opportunities to act upon the world. These acts have material and social consequences, some of them intended and some not. Through these acts, agents *make* the material world a social reality for themselves as human beings. Because agents are human beings, acting singly or together on behalf of themselves or others, they act as they do for human purposes—they have goals reflecting human needs and wishes. The tangled connections between agency (who is acting on whose behalf?), goals (whose goals are affected by what acts?) and circumstances (which features of the world actually matter?) make it difficult for agents to explain fully and convincingly why they act as they do. Even if they seem confused, observers can often figure the reasons for their conduct from the evidence at hand.

Agents use whatever means that are available to them to achieve their goals. These means include material features of the world. Because the world is a social place, at least for human beings, rules make the world's material features into *resources* available for agents' use. Some resources are not directly material— rules also constitute agents and institutions as resources. Whether agents are able to spell out their reasons for using the resources available to them, or observers figure them out from the evidence, recognizable patterns in the results constitute agents' *interests*.

Agents need not know what their interests are to act on them. Once they learn more from other agents (as observers) about their own interests, they may act differently. Indeed, human beings do not need to think about themselves as agents to be agents. While being an agent does not require the degree of self-consciousness that we associate with having an *identity*, agents are usually aware enough of their identities, singular and collective, to have an interest in fostering those identities. (I say more about identity in Chapter 5.)

As agents, people can make other people into agents by giving the latter the opportunity to act on the former's behalf for particular purposes. The former may do so individually or collectively, and the latter may be one or more individuals acting on the former's behalf. Agents acting collectively become a singular agent. By using resources, they acquire a material existence, and, as the previous paragraph suggests, they become objects of identification.

Agency is always limited. Agents are never free to act upon the world in all the ways that they might wish to. Many limits have a material component. We need air to breathe; we do not have wings to fly. No rule can readily make things otherwise, even though rules allow us, agents, to use resources to alter these limits, for example, by fashioning scuba gear and airplanes. Rules that give any agent an opportunity to act create limits for other agents. Rules in general limit the range of acts that other agents are free to take.

It follows from this proposition that no individual human being, as an agent, has full *autonomy*. By the same token, agents acting together never have full *independence*. As noted, agents are always limited by rules that give other agents opportunities to act. Agents acting together are additionally limited by the very rules that give them the opportunity to act collectively. Rules allowing other agents, individual and collective, to act on their behalf limit them even further.

When a very large number of people collectively operate as an agent, when they have agents acting for them, when they have some considerable measure of identity (including some place identified as theirs), and when they are free to act within very wide limits, these people constitute a country. For several centuries, agents have had a consistent interest in talking about countries as if they are independent of each other and any other social construction. This is made clearest by defining sovereignty as absolute independence and describing countries as sovereign states. As constructivists, however, we should always bear in mind that full independence is a useful fiction, and sovereignty is a matter of degree.

The freedom that agents do have depends on their ability to recognize the material and social limits that apply to them. They must also be able to evaluate the consequences of exceeding those limits. To be an agent requires the mental equipment that individual human beings normally develop over the course of their social lives. Agents exercise their freedom by choosing to act one way, or another, in an unending series of situations that make choosing unavoidable. It hardly needs saying that *not* choosing is a choice, presumably taken, as all choices are, to advance agents' goals. Agents make choices in light of the skills that they possess and the resources that they have access to, for reasons that they are more or less able to articulate. In short, they make choices in pursuit of their interests.

Rules offer agents the simplest kind of choices. They may choose to follow a given rule, or to break it. Compared to most situations in which agents make choices, the choice of following a rule, or not following it, involves consequences that are easy to calculate. While unintended consequences are always possible, rules give agents the opportunity to make rational choices—choices dictated by reference to goals—with some assurance that they are making the best choices available to them.

A rule makes rational choice relatively easy by telling the agents to whom it refers what they should do in some sort of situation that they might find themselves in. These agents may act on the contents of the rule without realizing that the contents form a rule. In principle, however, any agent (including any observer with enough information) can formulate contents of a rule in the form of a rule. There is nothing tricky about this. Saying what a rule is—putting its contents in the right form—is exactly the same as speaking in a form that gets anyone who is listening to respond to whatever we are saying. The point of speaking in this way is to have something take place—to accomplish something with the assistance of someone else.

The act of speaking in a form that gets someone else to act is commonly called a speech act. The form that a speech act must have will be clear from the following examples: (1) You assert that duck season has begun (you might actually say, "Duck season has begun!"). (2) She demands that we all go duck hunting (she might actually say, "Let's go duck hunting!"). (3) I promise to cook roast duck for dinner (I might actually say, "I'll cook!"). The generic form for a speech act is: I (you, etc.) hereby assert (demand, promise) to anyone hearing me that some state of affairs exists or can be achieved. The three examples suggest that speech acts fall into three categories, here called assertive speech acts, directive acts and commissive speech acts (see Chapter 7 for further discussion).

Whether speech acts accomplish anything depends on whether others respond to what they hear. The response to your assertion about duck season was obviously positive. I, at least, accepted her inclusive but imperative demand to go hunting when I promised to cook. We may surmise that both of you accepted my offer, and we all three went duck hunting, perhaps after we checked the newspaper to be sure that duck season had indeed begun.

Whatever category a particular speech act falls within, particular speech acts imply nothing about future situations. We start all over again when deer season begins. A speaker may assert the existence of some state of affairs and others agree, or request something and others comply, make a commitment that others accept, without any necessary consequences in the long run.

If, however, speakers frequently repeat a particular speech act with the same general effect, everyone involved begins to think that the repetition becomes significant. We end up hunting with each other all the time because we go through the same cycle of speech acts whenever the hunting season begins. Constantly repeated, the same old speech acts turn into *convention* as everyone comes to believe that the words themselves, and not the speakers mouthing them, are responsible for what happens. Hunting together is what we do at certain times, whether any of us even has to say anything much about it anymore.

Conventions come close to being rules. Recall that rules tell agents what they should do. A convention reminds agents what they have always done. The borderline between knowing that we have always done something and probably will continue to do it, and believing that we should do it because we have always done it, is exceedingly fuzzy. If a convention prompts agents to think that they should do something that they have always done, then the convention is indeed a rule. We should consider the rule in question a weak rule because it is *normative*, which means that agents accept the "should" element, only to the extent that the regular pattern of conduct (such as hunting together) continues.

As agents begin to realize that they should act as they always have, and not just because they always have acted that way, the convention gains strength as a rule. Rules keep the form of a speech act by generalizing the relation between speaker and hearer. Within the general form of a speech act, given rules make hearers into agents to whom those rules apply. Finally, agents recognize that they should follow the rules in question because they are rules and for no other reason.

Rules can take the general form of speech acts in each of the three categories presented above: assertive speech acts, directive speech acts, and commissive speech acts. Rules in the form of an assertive speech acts inform agents about the world—the way things are, the way it works—and inform them what consequences are likely to follow if they disregard this information. The information contained in such rules may be stated in very general terms, in which case we might call it a *principle*. The principle of sovereignty is a conspicuous example.

At the other end of the spectrum of possibilities, rules in the form of assertive speech acts may be stated in very specific terms. Instructions for operating appliances, or filling committee seats, or presenting diplomatic credentials, are useful examples. Wherever rules in this form fall on the spectrum, they are *instruction-rules*. Providing information is not normative, but telling agents what they should do with that information is. Agents always know what they should do because the rule tells them something useful about their relation to the world.

Directive speech acts are recognizable as imperatives. If the speaker says that you must do something, the speaker wants you to believe that you should do it. Rules in the form of directive speech acts, *directive-rules*, are emphatically normative. By telling agents what they must do (no hunting!), these rules leave no doubt as to what they should do. Directive-rules often provide information about the consequences for disregarding them. Having this information (sixty days in jail!) helps rational agents to make the right choice in deciding whether to follow these rules or not.

Commissive speech acts involve promises. Speakers make promises that hearers accept. Commissive speech acts give form to rules when hearers, as speakers, respond with promises of their own. Once these webs of promises become sufficiently general, generalized and normative in their own terms, they become *commitment-rules*. Agents are most likely to recognize these rules in their effects. These effects are the *rights* and *duties* that agents know they possess with respect to other agents. Any given agent's rights constitute duties for other agents (private property—no hunting!).

Rights may entitle the agents possessing them to specific benefits. Rights may also empower agents to act toward other agents in specific ways. Obviously, powers and limits on powers turn people into agents. More generally, rights and duties turn people into agents by defining opportunities for them to act upon the world. Instruction-rules and directive-rules also turn people into agents for exactly the same reason.

Speech acts fall into three categories because they perform different *functions*—they get things done for speakers and hearers together in three, and only three, ways. The same three categories hold for rules because they work in the same three ways that speech acts do—they get things done by instructing, directing and committing agents. As observers, we see rules in each category performing different functions for society. Quite a few scholars in such fields as law and sociology have worked out variations on this functional scheme, but they have never used all three categories, and just these categories, at the same time.

Philosophers have devised a different scheme for categorizing rules, and a number of constructivist scholars have adopted it. On functional grounds, there are two categories of rules: constitutive rules and regulative rules. Constitutive rules are the medium of social construction. Regulative rules are the medium of social control.

While this scheme might seem to be constructivist, it is actually a source of confusion. From a constructivist point of view, all rules are always constitutive *and* regulative at the same time. By definition, rules regulate the conduct of agents because rules are normative—they tell agents what they should do. Furthermore, the regulation of conduct constitutes the world within which such conduct takes place, whether agents intend this consequence or not. Acting in the world means acting on the world, often as an unintended consequence. Intentions might be a useful way to categorize acts, but it is never a decisive basis for categorizing rules.

Even when agents intend that a particular rule serve only to regulate conduct (an intention that other agents may thwart by choosing, for example, to disregard the rule), the conduct in question will have the effect of strengthening the rule or (if agents choose to disregard it) of weakening the rule. In the same way, a rule that agents intend be constitutive will have to affect conduct if it is to succeed. Often agents intend rules to be simultaneously constitutive and regulative. To give an obvious example, when agents called players take turns in playing a game, the rule instructing them to do so constitutes the game as one in which players regularly take turns.

As we have seen, rules serve three possible functions. Agents make rules and use them for instruction, direction and commitment. Within each of these three functional categories, rules differ in the extent to which they have been formalized. Rules are formal if agents encounter them as fixed and unavoidable features of their world. Rules also differ to the extent which they are linked to other rules. Agents often discover that particular rules are linked to other rules telling other agents what to do in the event that the relevant agents disregard the particular rules in question. Formal rules that are effectively backed up by other rules are *legal*.

Formality strengthens a rule by making its normative character clearer, in the process separating it from rules that are normatively more ambiguous (conventions, for example). A rule supporting another rule strengthens the latter by increasing the chances that agents will choose to follow the latter rule. The more frequently agents follow a rule, the stronger it will be normatively (and the easier it will be to make it formal). For example, the principle of sovereignty is a highly formal instruction-rule constituting the society of states. It is supported by commitment-rules empowering states, as agents, to bring new members into this society. These supporting rules, which we know as rules of recognition, are supported by instruction-rules that spell out a number of social and the material conditions that must be satisfied before statehood is possible.

Agents are inclined to make rules legal and to follow them if they are legal because they know what the rules are, how much they matter to other agents, and what consequences they can expect from not following them. When agents find themselves in a legal environment, it is rational for them to follow rules as a general proposition. It costs them less than careless conduct will. International relations is a peculiar environment in this respect, but still a legal environment. While there are very few formal directive-rules to be found, there are large numbers of other, quite formal rules intricately linked in support of each other. Relevant agents are perfectly aware of the situation and proceed accordingly.

Rules form institutions, institutions form societies

Rules are linked to each other in content as well as function—both by what they say and what they do. Standing back, agents can easily identify the ways that rules reinforce each other in what they say and do. Speaking figuratively, we might say that rules come in families, and that some families of rules come with rules documenting the family pedigree. Other families of rules depend on observers to document family resemblances. These and many other practices help to give families of rules their distinguishing features. Rules and related practices are almost impossible to separate in practice, because every time agents respond to rules, whether by making choices or observing the choices that other agents make, they have an effect on those rules and their place in families of rules.

By recent convention, scholarly observers of international relations call these families of rules and related practices *regimes*. At an earlier time, they called them *institutions*, and this remains the usual term for most scholars who devote their attentions to social relations. In practice, the two terms are indistinguishable. International regimes are said to consist of principles, rules, norms and procedures. By whatever name, these are all categories of rules. Principles and procedures anchor the two ends of a spectrum of possibilities distinguishable by how general they are in content. Rules and norms are distinguishable by how formal they are, norms being sufficiently informal that observers are not always sure that they are rules until they see how other agents respond to them.

International regimes differ in size. They have rules that work in different ways (assertive-, directive-, and commitment-rules) in different proportions. Additionally, regimes differ in the extent to which they have rules backing up other rules. Institutions differ in exactly the same ways. They are made up of rules that vary, not just in generality and formality, but also in number and arrangement.

Some simple institutions consist of a small number of rules whose content makes them a family, even if the rules seem to give little support to each other and get little support from other institutions to which they are connected. In the world of international relations, the balance of power is an example of such an institution. (Also see Chapter 10.) Instruction-rules constitute, and regulate, the balance of power. These rules tell the great powers what to expect when they choose allies and go to war. Yet even the balance of power, as an institution, is not as simple as it seems. Treaties give allies rights and duties. Rules limiting the conduct of war help to keep the balance from being permanently upset.

In the context of international relations, spheres of influence are also simple institutions made up of informal directive-rules. These rules direct weak states within the sphere to carry out a much stronger state's wishes. When these rules are backed up by principles justifying such arrangements, the sphere of influence is no longer quite so simple an institution. As formal equals, states may also adopt treaties distributing rights and duties that have unequal consequences within the sphere. Treaties are themselves simple institutions minimally consisting of formal commitment-rules that apply only to the states adopting such treaties. The principle that treaties are binding, and therefore legal, automatically provides them with support from other, highly formal rules.

Institutions such as the balance of power, spheres of influence and treaties are simple only because observers can easily pick them out of an institutional environment characterized by a large number of linked rules and related practices. Agents act as observers when they recognize any institution as such, no matter how complex it is. Scholars often think of international regimes as something that they alone can see, while agents can only see the simpler institutions making up the regime. Yet observers become agents, and regimes become institutions, when other agents learn what observers have to say.

International regimes are hard to see because the rules connecting the institutions that make them up tend to be informal. Agents take them for granted. Formal rules make things clearer, and agents need not stand back. For a long time in the context of international relations, agents have had access to a legal institution, conventionally known as the sources of international law, through which they can make legal rules and thus institutions whose existence no one can doubt. Treaties are one such institution, thanks to the legal principle that treaties are binding on the states adopting them.

Agents respond to rules with goals in mind; institutions serve their interests. As a general matter, simple institutions have a more straightforward relation to agents' interests than more complex and more difficult to recognize institutions do. We think of relatively simple institutions as performing distinct functions for agents and other institutions. Depending on what these relatively simple institutions do, they give priority to rules in one of the functional categories that I have already identified.

When instruction-rules are most in evidence, agents are situated in *networks* of rules and related practices. The balance of power is an example. Its rules assign an elevated *status* to a few great powers (ideally five states) that must act as if they are roughly equal in the resources available to them. If states' agents act as instructed, the consequences are supposed to be an ever-shifting and relatively peaceful balance of alliances among the great powers, whatever the immediate intentions of their agents might be. Recognizing the balance of power as an institution whose function suits their interests, agents intentionally foster those same consequences in the name of the balance.

When directive-rules are most in evidence, agents are situated in a chain of command, firm, or *organization*. A sphere of influence is a rudimentary institution of this sort. Its very informal rules assign each agent to an *office*, as we would call them in more formal organizations. Officers report up the chain of command and carry out orders that come down the chain. By this logic, the top officer decides what the organization's function is. In practice, most organizations are more complex than this. Nevertheless, a sphere of influence is so rudimentary in an organization that its function is nothing more than to fulfill the wishes of a leading power, as top officer, over the weaker states within the sphere.

Finally, when commitment-rules are most in evidence, agents end up in partnerships, or *associations*, with other agents. In the institutional context of international relations, the principle of sovereignty and supporting rules of recognition make states into formal equals. When two or more states adopt a treaty, they act as members of an association giving them at least some rights in common, including the right to commit themselves to each other. Under the terms of the treaty, all parties take on additional rights and duties with respect to the others. In this situation, states are formally equal because they all have the same *role*. The function of any association is to distribute roles to agents though its commitment-rules.

Only states (and the associations that they have created by treaty) can adopt treaties because there is a commitment-rule assigning this role to them exclusively. To return to an earlier example, markets function by assigning agents either of two roles—they are either sellers or buyers. Every seller is formally equal in possessing the right to buy, and so is every buyer. Note, however, that neither sellers nor buyers have a right to a fixed price. Formally speaking, agents in these roles are free to compete with each other, presumably for the good of every agent in the association. The function of this, or any, association is implied by the commitments that agents have made to a given distribution of roles.

It is important to note, however, that an association's roles are not generally equal in the rights and duties that they create. Think, for example, of the roles that members of most households have (on households, see also Chapter 9). For that matter, agents holding the same status (for example, white males) are equal to each other within the terms of that status, even if different statuses are unequal in relation to each other. This is no less true for agents holding the same or similar offices are (for example, foreign ministers). Nevertheless, commitment-rules are especially useful for making large numbers of agents formally equal for limited purposes.

Agency consists of statuses, offices and roles. Depending on the institutional context, every agent must have a status, office or role. Most, perhaps all, agents have all three in some combination. This is because most people are agents in a variety of institutions, and many institutions combine features of networks, organizations and associations.

Institutions such as these are complex in function and structure. Instruction-, directive-, and commitment-rules are all present, even if the proportions differ from institution to institution. Observers usually have no difficulty picking out the pattern of rules because institutions are social arrangements that always reflect agents' interests. From an observer's point of view, institutions have purposes. It seems this way even if the observer is an interested agent.

A complex institution will have general instruction-rules, or principles, telling agents what the purposes of that institution are. Detailed instruction-rules may provide support for these principles by spelling out all relevant statuses. Directive-rules may also repeat and elaborate on what these principles have to say and then support them by demanding that officers do what these rules say that they should. In situations where there are no conspicuous instruction-rules or directive-rules supporting principles, commitment-rules create roles for agents that have, from any one agent's point of view, the unintended effect of supporting the institution's principles.

Rules in all three categories often work together to support an institution's principles. Sometimes, however, institutions develop in such a way that rules from one or even two categories are scarce or not to be found at all. If we consider international relations as taking place within a single, overarching institution, its rules constitute a conspicuously lopsided arrangement. Thanks to the principle of sovereignty, there are few, if any formal, directive-rules. Observers will discover informal directive-rules in practice, even if some agents routinely deny that such rules exist.

Considered as a complex institution, international relations take place in a context where agents and observers find a large number of formal commitment-rules (rules of international law), behind which there are an even larger number of instruction-rules. These latter rules differ enormously in formality (quite a few are legal rules), detail and the degree to which they are linked to each other. They support the principle of sovereignty and a few other principles more or less directly and effectively. Thanks again to the principle of sovereignty, states are complex institutions within which formal directive-rules allow agents to act on behalf of states in their relations.

The context within which any institution functions as an agent is itself an institution. Society is a complex institution within which many other related institutions are to be found. Agents are likely to act as if their society's boundaries are clear and accepted, even if observers, including agents, have a hard time specifying those boundaries to anyone's satisfaction. States are societies that have exceptionally clear boundaries as well as highly developed institutions for conducting relations with other states.

The complex institution within which states function as relatively self-contained societies is itself a society. Within *international society*, states function as primary agents simply by conducting relations with each other. International society includes many other, more or less self-contained institutions. Some of them add secondary agents, such as officers of international organizations, to that society. The sum total of institutions and their relations add up to a society of staggering complexity and constant change, even though its large patterns seem at least to some observers to call for generalization (see Chapter 11).

Rules yield rule

We have seen that institutions consist of related rules and practices. It is possible to think of a single rule as an institution. As a practical matter, we never find a single rule standing by itself. Every rule gives the agents to whom it applies the choice of following the rule, or not, with more or less predictable consequences.

Most of the time, agents choose to follow the rule. The pattern of agents' choices has a general consequence, whether it is intended by particular agents— it has the effect of distributing material and social benefits among agents. An extremely important category of such benefits is control over resources and control over other agents and their activities. Some agents benefit more than other agents. Over time, institutions work to the advantage of some agents at the expense of other agents.

As rational beings, those agents who benefit the most from the rules that apply to them are the most inclined to follow those rules. Agents who benefit less are still inclined to follow the rules because doing so still benefits them more than not doing so. Nevertheless, agents may proceed to break any given rule after weighing the consequences of either choice for themselves. As a general consequence, rule-breaking is likely to involve a loss of benefits to other agents.

Agents who are negatively affected by the breaking of a rule also have a choice. They may accept the consequences (including a weakened faith in the broken rule and a greater chance of its being broken again). Alternatively, they may choose to follow a rule that has the consequence of presenting the rule breaker with a loss of benefits, which the rule breaker is either prepared to accept or had thought would not be likely to occur. The second choice, which we think of as enforcing the rule, involves using resources which might otherwise have been put to beneficial use. This loss of benefits is still less than the loss that comes from not enforcing the rule.

Instead of breaking a given rule, agents who do not benefit from following it may choose to use whatever resources are needed to change that rule and thus the distribution of benefits that results from the rule's existence. If some agents try to change the rule, other agents who would benefit less from the changes may choose to use the necessary resources to keep the rule from changing. Furthermore, those agents who benefit the most from a given rule will probably have to use fewer of the resources available to them to keep the rule from changing than will agents who want to change the rule. Clearly, rules say what they say, and institutions are slow to change, because agents make rational choices in circumstances that always give the advantage to some agents over others.

The general consequence of agents responding to rules with the resources available to them is that some agents exercise greater control over the content of those rules, and their success in being followed, than other agents do. In other words, rules yield rule. By making agents and society what they are, rules make rule inevitable. Rule is something that agents do to, and for, other agents, and they do it by following rules. Rule is something that happens to agents when they follow rules or when they suffer the consequences of not following rules.

Specific institutions may formalize rule by seeming to limit its exercise to a particular agent or set of agents—to rulers. Just because we can identify rulers, we should not conclude that they alone do the ruling. Wherever there are informal rules (which is everywhere), there is informal rule, either supporting or undercutting formal institutions of rule, or both (probably in a complex and hard to observe pattern). Even if the formalities of rule are nowhere to be found, rule remains a pervasive condition for that society. Loaded with rules but lacking rulers, international society is a case in point.

Rules in different functional categories yield different forms of rule. Where instruction-rules are paramount and status is a defining feature of society, ideas and beliefs seem to do the ruling. Despite appearances, agents actually do the ruling by getting other agents to accept their ideas and beliefs. They do so by example and by indoctrination. Rule in this form is *hegemony*.

Any society where principles get most of their support from detailed instruction-rules is hegemonially ruled. Caste societies are examples. Each hegemonially ruled caste has clear boundaries and a fixed position in the network of castes constituting the society. Membership in a caste gives agents so much of their identity, defined as a set of ideas about self and position in society, that caste identity seems to rule the society as a whole. Hegemonially ruled institutions exist in societies where other sorts of institutions and a mixed form of rule can be identified. The professions offer an example. Detailed instruction-rules, ordinarily learned through a long apprenticeship, support professional standards and rule agents to their advantage in their relations with clients needing their professional services.

In institutions where directive-rules are paramount and office is a defining feature of society, offices are vertically organized in a chain of command. Officers at each position in the chain use resources that their offices make available to them to carry out the rules that their offices require them to. From top to bottom, such an arrangement of offices is called a *hierarchy*, and so might we call the form of rule that results when officers carry out directive-rules. The state as a legal order exemplifies hierarchical rule.

When directive-rules are legal, hierarchy is formal. Despite the minimal description of the state as a legal order, formal hierarchies rarely stand alone. Hegemonial ideas typically reinforce formal hierarchy. The result is *authority*, conventionally defined as legitimate control. Military officers possess authority according to their rank, which is their status and office formally joined together in mutual reinforcement. Finally, informal hierarchy may reinforce hegemony that has achieved a relatively high level of formality.

After World War II, the so-called *pax Americana* may be thought of as a condition of rule in which the United States ruled, in the name of freedom and prosperity, by intervening whenever and wherever it chose. Proclaiming principles had the effect (perhaps initially unintended) of formalizing the status of the United States as leader of "the free world," while acting on those principles gave it an informal office.

Where commitment-rules are paramount and role is a defining feature of society, agents hold a variety of roles that are defined by reference to the roles that other agents hold. No one role, or institution, even comes close to making particular agents into rulers. On the contrary, formal commitment-rules mostly seem to reinforce formal hierarchy. They do so by granting officers well-defined powers to help them issue orders and carry them out, and by granting agents well-defined rights to help protect them from officers abusing their powers. The result is a constitutional state, in which the constitution formalizes commitment-rules that limit the government of the state and make it responsible.

Taken as a whole, roles may yield rule on their own, and not just because they reinforce other forms of rule. Agents in association are the rulers—all of them together—even if none of them have the status or office to make them rulers. Ruled by association, agents do not see rule in their roles. As agents, they are mostly concerned with their roles and what they are free to do within them. To return once more to the example of a market, agents participating in it generally have the sense that this is an institution free of rule. As sellers and buyers, they are nevertheless ruled as an unintended consequence of the exercise of their right to buy and sell. Adam Smith's invisible hand is a hand that rules, and it rules to the advantage of some agents over others.

As we saw, quite a few scholars describe international relations as anarchical. Anarchy is rule by no one in particular, and therefore by everyone in association, as an unintended consequence of their many, uncoordinated acts. Recall that agents who observe a general pattern of unintended consequences can no longer be said to act without intending consequences, even if they continue to act as they had. They intend to be ruled for good reasons, and if they did not have good reasons, they would make other choices.

If anarchy is a condition of rule unrelated to any agent's intentions, then international relations is no anarchy. We need another term to indicate the form of rule in which agents intend that they be ruled by what seem to be unintended consequences of exercising their rights. *Heteronomy* is a better term. Autonomous agents act freely, while heteronomous agents cannot. Both terms refer to agents, not society. From a constructivist perspective, however, agents are always autonomous, but their autonomy is always limited by the (limited) autonomy of other agents. The exercise of autonomy makes heteronomy a social condition, which agents accept as apparently unintended consequences of their individual, autonomous choices.

International society is heteronomously ruled because states exercise their independence under the principle of sovereignty and a number of commitment-rules granting them rights and duties with respect to each other. One state's independence is a limit on every other's, and all states' agents accept the unintended consequences that result from their many individual choices. Within this general condition of rule, a large number of institutions can be found contributing to rule in a variety of ways. Agents (and not just states' agents) constantly work on these institutions and work within them. Despite their number, variety and the complexity of their relations, they are arranged as they are on purpose, by agents' intentions, to serve their interests—including their shared interest in being ruled.

2

WORLDS OF OUR MAKING

(2002)

World, worlds: each of us lives in a world of our own; all of us live together in the same world. If this seems like a paradox, it is easy enough to resolve. All of us experience the world actively. Living in a world means acting on the world, and not just acting in it. We are agents, not actors—agents of change, bulwarks against change—in worlds that are always changing and always resistant to change. Together we have made the world what it is now, and we go on making the world what it shall become. As we make the world, it makes us individually what we are and it makes our worlds uniquely what they are.

For any of us as agents, the world is the whole of our experience. Once we stand back and become observers, we see many worlds, worlds within worlds, some of which we belong to, some not. By definition, the whole world that we live in is boundless. The boundaries of almost any world are easier to discern as we move away from it. Conversely, we are obliged to move closer to see very much of what is happening within that world. The closer we stand, the more likely we are to have an effect on what we see. Agents, observers: the distinction is analytic perhaps but indispensable in practice.

It is, of course, a metaphorical commonplace to speak of worlds as I do here. For those of us who are students of international relations, the metaphor *world* is exceptionally evocative and usefully ambiguous. We speak of worlds—*any world*—in the usual way of observers in every world. We also speak of *the world* more concretely as the Western world—a geographically bounded world of societies related by culture and history. Finally we speak of this world as having taken on planetary proportions. For the most salient properties of this world, we often use the adjective *global*.

We take this last world to be geographically inclusive, not to mention culturally invasive, thanks to the success that Western societies have had in spreading certain of their practices and institutions. None are more important than the practices and institutions that we put together and call international relations. The globalization of the Western world is recent, rapid, laden with ramifications for so many other worlds, and uncertain in its consequences for international relations. Some students of the subject seem to wallow in denial: the old world lives on. Others find themselves at a loss for words: suggestive metaphors substitute for systematic assessment.

A decade ago, I put the metaphor *world* to use—good use, I continue to think—when I titled a book *World of Our Making* (Onuf 1989). My goal was to provide scholars with a framework for the assessment of social relations in any world, including the world of international relations. In pursuing this goal, I paid no particular attention to the metaphor that I used to convey my chief claim, a claim that I repeat at the beginning of this essay. Looking back on a decade of global change, I am convinced that the constructivist framework, as I called it, makes better sense of international relations than any of its rivals. This essay revisits that framework and reviews its reception in the scholarly world that I inhabit. The intervening years, with their manifold changes and multiplying uncertainties, suggest another task. This essay is also something of a meditation on what it means to say that international relations constitute a world.

We might better say that there are many such worlds of our making. In the first section of this essay, I identify five of them. First is the ordinary, unbounded world of events, a world that we all know ourselves to live in, even as we stand apart from it. Second is a small, intense world of standing and statecraft, a world that has changed very little over several centuries. Third is a grandly formal world of relations undertaken in the name of states. The fourth of the worlds is a large, shadowy and rapidly growing world of technical activities and public services. The last of them is the world of scholars whose vocation is to observe any other world that they might choose to call the world of international relations.

The second section of the essay considers the unsettled situation in the scholarly world a decade ago. In that context, it introduces constructivism as a framework for studying social relations in general and international relations in particular. Claiming to be inclusive is one way to answer the first question that the editor of the volume in which this essay first appeared, Donald Puchala (2002), asked contributors to consider: What do we denizens of the scholarly world actually study? The answer should already be obvious. We study those social relations that we take to constitute some world of international relations, however uncertain we may be as to the contents and boundaries of any such world.

The third section of this essay is a brief account of the way that the world of scholars has changed in the last decade, in part because of changes in the world of events. Scholars increasingly use the term *constructivism*, yet most of them do so with little awareness of its history and even less discrimination. In the fourth section of this essay, I catalogue what I consider to be enduring strengths for the sort of constructivism that I had in mind a decade ago. These claims also serve to answer the second question that the editor asked contributors to consider: How should we conduct our scholarly studies?

The last section returns to the metaphorical language of worlds. By asking how worlds relate to each other, I conclude the essay with some thoughts on the editor's last question: Do, or should, we students of international relations work within a paradigm? Does indeed constructivism constitute a paradigm? That it does *not*, in my opinion, strengthens its claim as an inclusive framework for the study of social relations—of any and every world that we make for ourselves.

The many worlds of international relations

The world that we live in is a place, both physical and social. We are physical beings capable of living in, and acting on, the world only as social beings. Agency is a social condition. The world that we make for ourselves consists of social relations that make sense, and use, of our physical circumstances.

For any of us as agents, the world is, as I said, the whole of our experience. As Aristotle might have said, it is sufficient in itself. Were it not sufficient for our needs, we would make it so or we would cease to be. As agents, we may participate in making our world what it is, and have it make sense to us, without recognizing ourselves as agents, somehow apart from that world and acting on it.

Conversely, we are quite capable of detaching ourselves from our world and observing it, our places in it and the consequences of our acts upon it. Once we stand back and become observers, the world ceases to be the seamless place that we take for granted. We see social relations to which we have little or no connection. We make them into worlds in which we do not see ourselves as agents.

While each of us lives in a whole world that is uniquely our own, we share worlds by speaking about them to each other. Worlds that we speak of can only be partial and highly selective representations of what we see. We make these representations more or less compatible by telling each other not just what we (want them to) see but what we want them to do, and why they should do it. Speaking about worlds is always normative. By speaking, we narrow down the number of worlds that we are collectively able to identify.

To the extent that some number of observers commonly represent some set of social relations as a world (whether they belong to it or not), then they have made a world for themselves collectively, but not necessarily for the agents whose world (they say) it is. Moreover, they have made it normative (whether consciously or not). They hold themselves to this representation of the world, and they would have other observers adopt it. Indeed, they would have those agents whose relations (they say) make up this world stand back as observers, accept the world as represented to them and act accordingly.

By becoming agents in any world, observers make boundaries even harder to discern. Such is the case with a world for which the familiar name is *international relations*. The world of international relations has many observers. They include ordinary people who are quite sure that they have little effect on whatever they see. They also include a relatively small number of us who make the study of *International Relations* a vocation. We know full well that what we see, and say about, the world of international relations has an occasionally significant and cumulatively substantial effect on it.

For ordinary people, what they observe are events—wars, world leaders holding summits, the rise and fall of stock markets, extradition hearings. Behind these events are social relations largely taken for granted. While some few of these relations are highly conventionalized and always in view, others are shrouded in secrecy. Most are invisible to ordinary observers because they are so far removed from daily experience. This world has no discernible boundaries.

Even for scholarly observers, the world of international relations does not have obvious boundaries. If we look deep into its history—which is to say, deep into the history of the Western world—we see a remarkably small world of set practices. The main agents in this world act on behalf of political societies that we only gradually came to call states (Onuf 1998a: 2–20). Centuries ago these agents were rulers whose realms were indistinguishable from their selves and whose relations were simultaneously highly stylized and intensely personal. As political societies dissociated from royal *personae* and agents came to represent states as abstractions, relations among agents—heads of state, their ministers, diplomats—remained much as they had always been.

In this still small world, agents are preoccupied with the many signs of standing, both personally and with respect to their states. They attach great significance to ceremony. Most of their ceremonies involve the reciprocities of respect and the acknowledgment of relative position. Agents remember slights and they are quick to take offense. They are always ready to commit societal resources on a massive scale for vindication, and they are prone to believe in organized violence, not just as a last resort, but as an edifying spectacle. Rules matter, for these agents live by an unwritten code of honor, some version of which is to be found in every small world that is left to itself (Onuf 1998b).

The world that I just sketched—for lack of a better name, the world of standing and statecraft—survives more or less intact despite great changes in the world of events because of its relation to yet another world—the world of states. Paradoxically, this world is a large world spatially but much smaller socially. Membership in it is restricted to states, which are large worlds in their own right but few in number. On the one hand, states are the product of long histories of arduous social construction. On the other hand, they exist only in formal relation to each other, and the ways in which they conduct their relations are also formally limited.

Consider how the defining properties of statehood impose formal limits. To be states, other states must recognize them as such. Sovereign in principle, their rights and duties make them equal and apart. Furthermore, states are subject to general, formal rules, conventionally known as international law. These rules classify relations of states in categories as confining as they are familiar (starting with peace and war), and they give rise to a large number of voluntarily incurred obligations (treaties) and institutions (international organizations), all in the same general form (also see Onuf 1998a: 183–8).

States formally deal with each other through agents whose status as such is also formally determined. So too are the venues for the conduct of their relations. Because the formalities of statehood so severely limit the number of state agents and the exercise of agency, the grandly formal world of states supports a small world of state agents whose relations are at once stylized and intense—much as they were before states took form. Neither world could continue to exist without the other.

State agents take the formalities of their relations exceedingly seriously. They are always careful to justify their conduct by claiming to act on behalf, and in the interest, of their states. By doing so, they make the preoccupations of their small world weighty and impersonal. They have access to resources not otherwise available in any world. Their importance is unequaled, in their own eyes and in the eyes of many others. Every deed confirms them as indispensable, and the world of states as overwhelmingly, immediately real—perilous perhaps but irreplaceable.

The world of states has a remarkable capacity, through its agents and through its effect on observers, to reproduce itself in a form that has changed very little over the last two centuries. Form is the key, once we grant this world its formality and thus its limits. Bounded out are all sorts of social relations that have direct and lasting effects on a global or near-global scale. Conversely, a world that would encompass most such relations would have to relegate states to the background. A variety of other institutions would come to the fore, and the number of agents whose world it is would increase dramatically.

For centuries, institutionalized practices of the Western world have had global effects—and not just incidental effects, as many scholars find it convenient to think. Nevertheless, designing global institutions and insulating them from the pattern of relations characteristic of the mutually constituted worlds of states and state agents only began in earnest with the rise of industrial capitalism. With industrial capitalism, there also arose an interest in issues of technical facilitation and responsiveness to human needs. In what amounted to a design principle, state agents approached these issues one at a time, each time creating a specialized organization to complement rapid bureaucratic growth and differentiation within their states.

In these developments, observers saw a world in which states and their claims on agents mattered far less than the efficient performance of technical tasks. These observers supposed that technical successes would cause the new world to grow as state agents surrendered ever more responsibility to specialized organizations. The world of states would shrink, and the small world of statecraft and standing would become increasingly irrelevant. Eventually, a single, benign and encompassing world of technical services would supersede all those worlds that seemed to impede human progress.

While the passing years proved this "functionalist" prophecy to be wildly mistaken, the growth of technical organizations with global missions proceeded unabated. So, too, did technical task expansion within states. The long-term result is a vast, intricately organized world of services that depends on the formal relations of the world of states even as the former's many successes indirectly support the latter. Meanwhile, the prodigious scale and complexity of the world of services defy most observers' efforts to find its boundaries and put the whole of it in clear view. Indeed, much of the current rhetoric of globalization suggests a still inchoate sense of what that world has finally become (also see Onuf 1998a: 263–73; Chapters 11, 12).

Observers of international relations who see beyond the world of events impose boundaries and emphasize some sorts of social relations over others in order to make sense of what they see. By consensus, the world of international relations is a world of worlds—by definition, a world of states. Considerations of physical and social scale yield three plausible versions of this world. As opposed to the world of events, which matters to a great many people in a variety of ways, the world of standing and statecraft is a world whose few agents matter a great deal to each other. The world of states also matters to the agents of states because it perpetuates their own lived-in world. The world of services would matter to a great many people if they knew very much about it.

As an observer, I could no doubt propose any number of possible worlds of international relations by introducing additional considerations to the limit of my imaginative and linguistic resources. Nor will any other observer see the four worlds enumerated here quite as I do. As observers, we never stand in the same place, and we never see matters from the same angle. As agents, we can only experience our world from the inside.

Lived-in worlds have an immediacy and normative density that no observer can fully appreciate. Observers see that world from a distance and render it in drastically simplified terms, but they also live in other worlds. For those who make observing international relations a vocation, one of these worlds consists of observers like themselves. That lived-in world (which is my world) constitutes yet another world of international relations. Its agents collectively make the world of states into an important and distinctive subject of study commonly called International Relations. In doing so, they respond to normative demands that are too close, too immediate, for them to recognize. The world of scholarship exerts a normative pull over the world of states—pulling it away from both the world of standing and statecraft and the world of services, all the while pushing and pulling with the world of events.

Unsettled times

The worlds that we make for ourselves as observers look the way that they do because of the ways that we go about the business of seeing. Gaze fixed on some world or another, scholars figure out ways of seeing it better. We could just as well say—and often do say—that we draw maps and blueprints, devise tools and procedures, build models and frameworks, all of which make that world what we see it to be. Different worlds call for, and depend on, different ways of world-making.

Scholars have always raised questions about accepted ways of seeing. Beginning in the 1970s, their numbers increased, in the 1980s dramatically. Some critics came to the radical conclusion that we know not what we see, and delude ourselves into thinking that we do. A few others began to see worlds as never-ending construction projects involving even themselves as agents, and realized that they needed new and different tools—tools for making worlds and not just for seeing them.

Let me put these developments in more conventional, less obviously metaphorical terms. The 1980s were unsettled times in the social sciences. The positivist quest for reliable, cumulative knowledge about *the* world came under assault, along with the positivist assumption that, deep down, nature and society have the same "nature." Critics held positivist science, whether applied to nature or society, to be a central feature of what they called "the Enlightenment project" or, indeed, "modernity." Looking back, we can see that this assault did not come out of the blue. Ennui had beset positivist social science, and so had a measure of smugness.

Critics decried positivist science as an emblem of modernity, understood as the rationalizing, aggrandizing path that the Western world has taken over a period of several centuries and especially since the Enlightenment. Their critique did not proceed over matters of method—over the ways that we might acquire reliable, commensurable knowledge of the world. Positivists were always prepared to discuss such matters and likely to prevail on their own terms—terms that emphasize the measurable properties of things (positivities) and their relations. Instead, the assault began over prior matters: how are we capable of knowing anything at all about the world or able to convey what we think we know to anyone else? Suddenly the term *epistemology* displaced the term *methodology* as the signal that controversial matters were under discussion. So did the neologism *post-modern*, and the term *modern* itself took on an unaccustomed resonance (also see Kubálková *et al.* 1998: 12–20).

Epistemological radicals doubted that we can know anything for sure. Language deceives us. No matter what, how much, or well, we think we are communicating with each other, no language, natural or formal, is capable of representing the world as it is. Instead, what we think we know is the product of provisional agreement only relatively fixed in time and place, and these radical critics mocked the vain Enlightenment quest for firm foundations or an objective vantage point. Obviously, I mean vain in both senses of the word.

Positivists saw this assault as willfully destructive, even nihilistic, and not at all the liberating, playful, celebratory occasion that its advocates took it to be. Not only were these unsettled times. No one held out any hope for settlement, if only because post-modern critics interpreted any effort to settle matters as a symptom of the Enlightenment's rationalist pathology. The world of scholarship, long ordered into worlds (disciplines, fields) ostensibly corresponding to the diverse worlds of ordinary experience, found itself, and quite a number of its constituent worlds, torn in two.

As a field of study, International Relations was hardly exempt from these unsettling developments. Here Richard Ashley warrants particular mention. In a series of highly visible essays spanning the 1980s, each more slashing than the one before, Ashley left his audience gasping—whether in dismay or delight (Ashley 1981, 1984, 1987, 1988, 1989). Others followed suit. As the decade turned, dissidents joined in celebration (Ashley and Walker 1990).

Retrospectively, these developments seem far less surprising than they did at the time. Already in the 1970s, positivists showed signs of fatigue brought on by the demands of normal science. Fatigue made it all the more difficult to cope with dwindling resources as the Vietnam War came to an end, and fatigue did nothing to dull the disappointments due to the meager results that normal science had posted. By the end of the 1970s, realists had begun to reassert themselves. International Political Economy consolidated its position at the field's center; theory returned to prominence, and formal analytic skills earned instant prestige. It soon became clear that publication of Kenneth Waltz's *Theory of International Politics* (1979) was a defining moment for the field.

By the end of the next decade, International Relations was deeply divided— more deeply than K.J. Holsti had imagined when he called it the "dividing discipline" (1985). One response was to domesticate these disturbing developments. This was Robert Keohane's clear intention when he edited *Neorealism and Its Critics* (1986). No less was it Yosef Lapid's when he sought to bring these developments "into focus as an intelligible 'debate'" (Lapid 1989: 238)—the third great debate to punctuate the field's brief history.

A second response was my own. I announced it in *World of Our Making* (1989), and I named it *constructivism*. (I had first used this term in Onuf 1987—an article few scholars in my world had occasion to see.) The term betrays its origins in the 1980s and the influence of social theory at that time. Anthony Giddens (1984) and Jürgen Habermas (1984) were particular sources of inspiration. By building a bridge across the divide (Onuf 1989: 55–61), I aimed to provide for myself and other scholars a way between positivist social science and assaults on modernity then rampant (pp. 36–43).

This third way holds that *ontology* is the key to escaping the impasse between positivist complacency over epistemological matters and the wholesale post-modern dismissal of methodical pursuits. Ontological discussions refer to the world—any world—*as if* we could take its existence for granted, but *not* its properties. Constructivism, as I presented it in 1989, grants ontological parity to things and their relations. Conceptually speaking, neither agents as members of society, nor society as the totality of agents and their relations, come first.

On ontological grounds, constructivism challenges the positivist view that language serves *only* to represent the world as it is. Language also serves a constitutive function. By speaking, we make the world what it is. Nevertheless, in making the world, we do not just make it up. Constructivism takes the "linguistic turn" but only so far (Onuf 1989: 78–94; Shapiro, 1981, was particularly helpful as my guide into the turn).

Nevertheless, constructivism as presented is *not* post-modern because it does not challenge the Enlightenment belief in the possibility of meaningful knowledge about the world we live in. Constructivism treats such knowledge *as if* it were independent of the language that we use to represent the world, but only provisionally so. As for method, constructivism is eclectic. Ontological openness warrants methodological diversity. The constructivist is a *bricoleur*— one who makes what is needed out of available materials (Lévi-Strauss 1966: 16–22 inspired my use of this term). All such materials are necessarily social, the result of continuous *bricolage*: world-making is *bricolage*.

Three premises structure my systematic rendition of constructivism in *World of Our Making*.

1 Society *is* what it *does*. Any coherent set of social relations (including international relations) is also, and always, a process in which agents and their worlds constitute each other. Co-constitution accounts for pervasive change and the appearance of constancy in social relations.
2 Speech and its derivatives (rules, policies) are the media of social construction. People become agents by living in a world of language. They depend on language to express their wishes, to translate their wishes into goals, and finally to act on their goals. Performative speech is the basis of, and template for, normative conduct. Social construction is always normative.
3 As media, rules transform available materials into resources, eventuating in asymmetric opportunities for control and the asymmetric distribution of benefits. This is rule, and rule is to be found in every society—including international society.

Not coincidentally, 1989 is the same year that Friedrich Kratochwil's important book on *Rules, Norms and Decisions* appeared. Though widely cited as constructivism's foundational texts, neither his book nor mine has had a great deal of substantive impact. Indeed neither has had the impact of two papers (Wendt 1987; Dessler 1989) that also deserve to be considered foundational. In an account of what I hope to show has been a strange career for constructivism, it is entirely relevant to ask why this should have been so.

Both Kratochwil's book and mine are "technically demanding" (as I have acknowledged in my own case; see Kubálková *et al.* 1998: 20). As for whether they are needlessly so, let me point out first that both books take most readers into unfamiliar worlds. Adjusting to the unfamiliar always takes work. Both of us engage in a great deal of conceptual clarification, thereby calling on readers to do their share, so to speak, by reading closely. *World of Our Making* adds to the cost of careful reading, though very little in my opinion, by asking readers to supply some of the relevant connections to the worlds of international relations. After all, these are familiar worlds for most readers, and connections will come readily to mind.

Close, often critical reading of diverse texts is the method that I used in the first place to propound my version of constructivism. This method yielded a large number of assertions whose source readers will recognize even after I reformulated and assembled them systematically. Pedigrees matter, especially to scholars. For other, less demanding readers, I recently outlined constructivism's essential propositions with no reference whatsoever to anyone else's work (now Chapter 1).

Unlike *World of Our Making*, this unadorned but systematic exposition is, I believe, easy to read. Whether its systematic arrangement discourages just the sort of *bricolage* that I engaged in myself, and that social construction always involves, remains to be seen. Here I might note that Harold Lasswell and Abraham Kaplan's *Power and Society* (1950) provided me with an explicit model for all of my systematizing efforts. However much I continue to find this magnificent book suitable for selective appropriation, others seem not to, for it is long out of print and rarely cited.

There are (at least) two other reasons why *World of Our Making* failed to have a greater impact than it did. In the first place, its emphasis on the connection between rules and rule disturbs liberals. I define *rule* as a condition in which some people use rules, which are never neutral in content, to control the conduct of others. The condition of rule always confers advantages on those who exercise it. International relations have rules, as any liberal would agree. Few liberals would further agree with me that these rules can only be understood as resulting in a condition of rule, whether or not we choose to call it this.

Instead, liberals imagine that rules need do no more than establish the conditions of agency. Anarchy—rule by no one—is the presumptive result. If anarchy confers advantages on particular agents, it does not do so with the consistency that the concept of rule suggests. Most students of international relations, including realists, hold this view, which makes them liberals by my reckoning. It also makes them wrong. Insofar as these same students think that international relations are endemically anarchic, and distinctively so, then they are doubly wrong.

Second, *World of Our Making* starts with the claim that International Relations is a field lacking a distinctive subject. Rather more implicitly, Kratochwil made the same claim. Any such claim is deeply threatening to those who have made their careers on the premise of distinctiveness. This quest for distinctiveness— an "elusive quest" for a general theory of international relations (Ferguson and Mansbach 1988)—is indeed one way to write the field's history. As a field, International Relations is no less a world because it lacks a distinctive subject to validate its claim to autonomy. *This* world exists because we, who are its agents, say it does, and because observers by and large defer to what we say about ourselves.

Changing worlds

Long centered in the United States, the field of International Relations has experienced a number of changes necessarily related to changes in the world of events, not to mention other worlds of scholarship. I have already commented on the declining vitality of positivist social science. By the 1980s, rationalist theory, not positivist science, dominated the field. This tendency toward formalization culminated in the twinning of neorealism and neoliberalism (Baldwin 1993). If the twins stood astride the field, around the margins there had assembled a ragtag crowd of dissidents.

As the Cold War ended, the twins had almost nothing to say about the scale of change (see Kegley and Raymond 1994; Lebow and Risse-Kappen 1995 for useful discussions). National identity emerged as a large issue of interest. However loosely conceived, social construction offered an explanation for the formation of identities. It is in this context that Alexander Wendt (1992) popularized the term *constructivism*. Suggesting that "the basic 'sociological' issue" of "identity- and interest-formation" gives constructivism its identity, he deliberately dissociated himself from "recent epistemological debates" (p. 393). With dissidents sent to the sidelines, many young scholars saw the way open for contextually enriched, normatively aware scholarship.

Though described as constructivist, much of this work is reminiscent of the liberal institutionalist scholarship that had fallen out of favor decades before. Wendt's turn away from philosophical issues turned out to be a mixed blessing. As the field gained from an expanded agenda, constructivism lost what should have been its most distinctive features. Any concern with language was left to the dissidents; as a derivative of performative speech, rules ceased to matter; without rules as media of social construction, the co-constitution of agents and structures became an airy abstraction, needlessly subject to just the sort of debate that Wendt seems to have had enough of. Ironically, Wendt holds some of the responsibility for making "the agent-structure debate" so confused and pointless that most scholars (I among them) will have nothing to do with the subject (see Gould 1998 for the whole, ugly story).

In due course, well-established scholars began to identify themselves as constructivists. Peter Katzenstein became a leading figure as editor of *The Culture of National Security* (1996). Soon thereafter John Ruggie (1997: 11–13) announced that he had been a constructivist all along. Although Ruggie is something of an exception, most of the late-joiners had no interest in the social-theoretical and philosophical backdrop of constructivism as I had presented it in *World of Our Making*. In keeping with Wendt's "sociological" inclinations (1992: 393), the new constructivists drew on the new institutionalism in sociology for inspiration (see Finnemore 1996a for an overview). Routinely positivist and conceptually anemic (see for example Scott *et al.* 1994: 1–112), this literature served mostly to reinforce a deplorable tendency to talk about culture in the vaguest terms imaginable.

Constructivism today is still construed as a third way, or "middle ground," between positivism and post-modern epistemological radicalism (Adler 1997: 321–3; Checkel 1998: 327). In practice, however, many scholars increasingly treat it as the main alternative to the neo-twins, which, after all, have very little separating them (Ruggie 1997: 9–11, aptly called them both "neo-utilitarian"). Post-modern scholars must be surprised to find themselves thrown together with constructivists (see Jepperson *et al.* 1996: 46; Ruggie 1997: 35 for examples of this practice). If indeed the third debate that Lapid announced in 1989 "can now begin" (Adler 1997: 348), it is only because so many scholars believe that there are only two ways to proceed. If they are not rational choice theorists, then they must be constructivists. Either way, empirical research will suffice to settle differences. Indicatively, two recent surveys bear the exact same section title: "A Constructivist Research Agenda" (Adler 1997: 341–7; Hopf 1998: 186–92).

The end of the Cold War induced another significant change in the scholarly world of international relations. As Marxists declined in influence, many European scholars joined this world, but not without reservations. They resented the longstanding dominance of scholars in the United States, whose predilection for a narrow construction of international relations as a world of states they did not share. Constructivism offered an attractive alternative. While taking off in a number of directions (see for example the Aarhus-Norminde Papers 1998), European constructivists are generally more sensitive than their counterparts in the United States to the links between language, rules and rule. In this respect, Maja Zehfuss's discussion of constructivism (1998, in German) is far better than other surveys and review essays recently published in English (Adler 1997; Checkel 1998; Hopf 1998).

As the field globalizes, constructivism is everywhere, perhaps in danger of becoming all things to all scholars, finally suffering the fate of all fads. Symptomatically, talk of constructivism has seeped across the always leaky boundary between International Relations and International Law as a field of study (Slaughter *et al.* 1998). No less symptomatic are the flurry of essays sizing up constructivism (cited in the preceding paragraph), not to mention acknowledgment in general surveys (Dougherty and Pfaltzgraff 1996: 162–3; Knutsen 1997: 279–82) and journals of opinion (Walt 1998: 38, 40–1). Perhaps the greatest measure of constructivism's iconic value is the juxtaposition of "rationalist approaches" and "constructivist approaches" to organize the monumental special issue of *International Organization* sizing up its fifty years of publication (Katzenstein *et al.* 1998).

There are signs that constructivism can survive all this attention without slipping into blandness. Feminist and post-colonial studies have managed to do so. Furthermore, there are significant opportunities for reinforcement among the survivors, all of which share a concern for rules in relation to language on the one hand and rule on the other. Indicatively, Elisabeth Prügl (1999) drew on feminist theory, and Lily Ling (2002) on post-colonial theory, to do just this.

Constructivism's enduring strengths

In the decade since I introduced the term *constructivism*, it has come to be used in ways that I had not foreseen and, more to the point, in ways that vitiate what I meant to convey by the term. Notwithstanding constructivism's strange career, I see no need to revise the premises that guided me initially, nor even to change very many of the systematically related features of the text that appeared in 1989.

If I had been a better salesman, I would have spent the years since extolling constructivism as I continue to understand it. Belatedly, let me offer *five* reasons why any scholar should seriously consider working within this framework. These are the enduring strengths of constructivism in its strong form. They derive from, and further substantiate, the basic premises of constructivism, as I presented them above.

First, the strong version of constructivism fosters a sensitivity to language as *doing*. It fosters a disposition to use metaphors of *work*, as against *drama* (cf. Harré 1993: 148–85, on "Social Action as Drama and Work" [chapter title]). I do not want to suggest that the metaphorical language of play does not have its uses. Actually, I use this sort of language all the time—any *bricoleur* would. Nevertheless, there are two reasons why I think that we should prefer the metaphorical language of work.

Realists prefer the language of play, most emphatically in reference to war. The deployment of theatrical tropes and the terminological conventions of game theory help constitute a world that realists claim merely to observe, but further claim is distinctive—indeed uniquely set apart from the mundane world of ordinary people and the way they carry on with their lives (also see Fierke 1998: 31–43). Just as theater creates a world of elemental simplicity to which an audience responds with heightened awareness, so too does the realist rhetoric of struggle, violence and fear. I have already indicated why I think that the quest for distinctiveness is a mistake. I would add here that success in this respect has the effect of making the world of international relations distinctively terrifying but, paradoxically, a further step removed from the immediate world of experience that we routinely call "reality."

I might also note that the post-modern penchant for play, spectacle and narcissism—for theatrical posturing—betrays a deep connection to realism. More precisely, both betray a common heritage in the Romantic impulse of the nineteenth century. It is just this impulse that neo-realism would banish through the disciplining effects of formal language nevertheless dependent of the metaphors of work. The term *structure*, which is so conspicuously central to Waltz's refurbishment of realism (1979), illustrates the point (here again see Fierke 1998: 47–50).

The language of work and the language of play do have one feature in common. Both convey a sense that human activity is intentional. The language of play emphasizes the "role" of language (notice the metaphor) in representing the world—in mimicking it. In a complementary way, the language of work, of doing, underestimates the importance of speaking as a "tool" (again, notice the metaphor) for getting on with the tasks that we set for ourselves. Once we grant that speech is the most powerful tool available to us, then metaphors of work tell us how pervasive social construction is, even in the absence of immediate intention and conscious design.

Let me turn to a second strength of constructivism in its strong form. It suggests due attention to process, and thus to social construction as an element in any social process. In turn, social construction points to the work that rules do. By presenting agents with choices, rules affect conduct. Conversely, the pattern of choices affects rules, strengthening those that agents choose to follow and weakening those that they do not. In aggregate, rules perform regulative and constitutive functions because each and every rule simultaneously produces both kinds of effects. This is so whether rules are informal—so informal that many scholars call them *norms* and *conventions*—or highly formal—so obviously set apart from other rules that, by convention, we call them *law* and divide them by function.

In the context of international relations, constructivists soon discover that informal rules are ubiquitous but that their properties and effects are infuriatingly difficult to pin down. The constructivist emphasis on rules also validates scholarly attention to the formal rules making up international law and international organizations (cf. Adler 1997: 335, but note Martha Finnemore's unconsidered complaint, 1996b: 139, that constructivists give international law insufficient attention). Whether regulative or constitutive in intent, these rules affect agents in a variety of ways and through them a variety of rules, formal and informal. As Harvey Starr has reminded me, it is hard to study international law and not become an intuitive constructivist. Furthermore, the constructivist emphasis on rules leads to a consideration of the ways that agents justify their choices and thus to the place of ethics in international relations (Onuf 1998b).

Constructivism in its strong form has a third strength that few self-styled constructivists will recognize as such. Constructivism undermines the liberal tendency to ignore rule (asymmetries of control and privilege) as a constant feature of social relations. If, as Michael Smith suggested to me, constructivism is little more than "hard-headed liberalism," then few liberals manage to be hard-headed in the systematic way that constructivism encourages them to be. While I have more to say about the limitations of liberalism below, here I want to make my point about constructivism more affirmatively.

Constructivism fosters appreciation of rules that turn "raw" materials into resources and make rule possible. In the first instance, rules constitute resources by making material conditions generally intelligible. Linking material conditions to human needs and goals is an integral part of this process. Rules also constitute resources by defining the terms of agency. They tell us which agents, under what circumstances, have access to materials that other rules have assigned uses to.

Among agents whose goals and circumstances inevitably differ, differential access confers advantages unevenly. For that matter, so does the analytically prior process by which rules make material conditions intelligible, though perhaps more subtly. It is important not to be misled by the fact that rules always give agents choices, along with some indication of the benefit that they may expect to gain from following the rules and the cost that they should expect to incur from not doing so. Whatever choices agents make, rules cannot distribute consequences neutrally because of their content, and not because of the way that they work.

Finally, rules constitute resources by giving some agents the opportunity to use the materials to which the rules give them access to make and support still other rules that benefit them. For example, agents can use materials at their disposal to influence the choices that other agents make with respect to following rules. Enforcement and deterrence describe this process, which characterizes a familiar form of rule. If resources make rule possible, rules make resources what they are. They also make rule in some form an unavoidable feature of social relations.

As a fourth, somewhat related point, constructivism in its strong form holds that material conditions always matter, but they never matter all by themselves. On the one hand, constructivism abjures the vulgar materialism that realists are allegedly prone to. Wendt, for example (1995: 73), charged neorealists with a "desocialized view" of material capabilities. The charge is unfair. In responding to Wendt's many charges, John Mearsheimer (1995) simply ignored this one. Ever since Harold and Margaret Sprout (1965) vetted the relevant issues with exceptional thoroughness, few realists construe "capabilities" in the "brute, physical" sense that Wendt supposed them to.

On the other hand, constructivism is *not* philosophically idealist. As for Wendt's claim that "constructivism has an idealist (or 'idea-ist') view of structure" (Wendt 1995: 73), I concur with this view only because I believe that structures are nothing more than observers' descriptions of the stable patterns that rules and practices exhibit in any world (see further Chapters 1, 6). As soon as agents act on these descriptions (which may indeed stem from their own observations), structures enter the world, so to speak—they enter into the process of social construction. The process itself has the effect of *institutionalizing* structures, including the terms of agency. Any world, and every institution, is always and necessarily dependent on socially mediated material conditions.

Wendt has affirmed that material conditions are necessarily social, but not the converse. As a consequence, capabilities interest him less than "structures of shared knowledge" (1995: 73). Such a view ends up reducing the social world to mental states, and social construction to the diffusion of ideas. Identity becomes the main preoccupation of agents, as if they had nothing else to do. Norms are everywhere, but they seem to do very little besides granting agents their identity.

This sort of idealism is a perennial tendency for progressive liberals. It is also a particularly striking feature of the limp constructivism of recent fashion (Katzenstein 1996, is chocked with examples). No term illustrates this tendency more graphically than *norm* (also see Onuf 1998b, 2008: Chapter 28). Taken as more or less synonymous with "shared expectations," norms exist outside minds only incidentally. That norms cannot be shared without taking the form of linguistic statements brings them into the world of artifacts. As such, they are rules, if not directly linked to material circumstances, then linked to other rules that are. Agents use rules in their social relations for a variety of purposes, most, if not all, of them with material implications.

In strong form, constructivism's last strength is its methodological openness. Consider Hayward Alker's mastery of diverse methods to advance his wide-ranging concerns, many of which center on the uses of language (Alker 1996). Constructivism is perfectly consistent with rational choice theorizing, high positivist quantitative analysis, "thick description" and whatever else most of us actually do in the name of scholarship. Constructivism *cannot* be reconciled with claims that any particular set of scholarly activities are the only ones admissible.

Many such claims mark the divide between positivism and its critics. Stationed on one side or the other, most self-styled constructivists fail to see any way to reach across the divide (cf. Hopf 1998: 181–5 on "critical" vs. "conventional" constructivists). The reason, I suspect, is the widely shared belief that one's position on the fact-value distinction compels a choice between incompatible methodological allegiances. Either one accepts the conventional positivist position that facts and values are always separable in principle and that being neutral on matters of value is an important scholarly value. Or one takes the position that facts are always laden with values and that one can never be neutral on matters of value.

Constructivism acknowledges the fact-value distinction. From an observer's point of view, values *are* facts. As such, they are identifiable in what agents do (and saying *is* doing). Once identified, values as facts are capable of being separated from other kinds of facts, at least in principle. Indeed, moral reflection depends on just such an operation.

Constructivism also holds that, in practice, values pervade social relations. For any agent, speaking is, as I said above, always normative. Speaking is inextricably related to the achievement of the speaker's goals, and thus it is always laden with value. As soon as the observer (or perhaps I should say auditor) talks about, or otherwise acts on, the facts, however ascertained, then that observer becomes an agent, and those facts take on value (also see Onuf 2001: 252).

While observers and agents may occupy separate worlds (this is a positivist ideal), observers usually participate, as agents, in a world that they stand apart from only provisionally. As a consequence, any distinction that they make between facts and values (as facts of a different kind) is also provisional. It is no less useful for the fact of being provisional. As with people in general, constructivists have it both ways: they have no particular difficulty dealing with values, as facts, when they stand aside to do so, and they know what happens to these facts when they proceed to act upon them.

Worlds apart?

Throughout this essay, I have argued that worlds have porous boundaries, that all of us belong to many worlds and constantly traffic among them, and that a world of worlds is subject to constant social construction. It is possible to overstate these claims. Some worlds baffle observers from other worlds. To the extent that they succeed in making sense of what they see, what they say makes little or no sense to the agents whose world it is. In turn, observers acquire only the most limited agency for themselves.

On occasion, we hear talk of paradigms as if they were incommensurable worlds. If this were so, then most other talk about paradigms misses the point: there is nothing that we as outsiders *can* say about worlds so utterly different from our own. We might better say that paradigms resemble distant worlds that have little need for each other. They coexist in mutual disregard, their agents caught up in concerns too different to attract each other's attention.

We might also ask if constructivism (which is to say, my construction of constructivism) is a paradigm in this more limited but still quite general sense. My answer to this question—a negative answer—calls for a fuller consideration of the term *paradigm*. If constructivism is not a paradigm in any general sense of the term, then what indeed is it? I conclude the essay with a partial and perhaps not very satisfactory answer to this second question.

World of Our Making identifies three senses of the term *paradigm*. One is relevant to the book's central premises, another to its systematic properties. Neither draws inspiration from Thomas Kuhn's familiar use of the term (Kuhn 1970; see generally Onuf 1989: 12–27), which I called *puzzle paradigm* and which, I believe, is the one in general use. If International Relations could indeed be said to have built a paradigm around a central theoretical puzzle—for example, how is anarchy tenable over any period of time?—then indeed we might want to concede the disciplinary claim of distinctiveness. The price of doing so, I might add, is a field of such modest proportions and limited prospects that few among us would be content to work within its confines.

Borrowing from Sheldon Wolin (1980), I prefaced *paradigm* with the modifier *operative* to capture the sense of the term as it relates to constructivism's central premises. An operative paradigm is an ensemble of rules and practices, which agents speak of in world-defining terms and respond to as normatively compelling. Liberalism and the liberal world are aspects of a single operative paradigm. Liberalism as a way of talking about social relations makes the liberal world a coherent whole. At the same time, the evident coherence of the liberal world confirms the normative force of liberalism.

Seen from the outside, the liberal world lacks the coherence that liberals take for granted. Liberals prefer to think that rules in the form of rights minimize the need for rule. I would say instead that an ensemble of rights and duties constitutes an enduring form of rule, often styled "the rule of law." Thanks to the rules, some agents benefit beyond their due—they rule without the vestments of rule. Liberal societies exhibit this form of rule to a degree unmatched in other societies. Yet they combine this form of rule with others in complex arrangements that hardly make sense if liberalism is the only way of talking about social relations. For the observer, there is more to the liberal world than its operative paradigm can ever convey.

As I remarked earlier, liberals describe the world of international relations in the terms that they know best—liberal terms—because their liberal beliefs prevent them from seeing the way that rule works. The world of international relations is a world of rules and rule, even if no one ever claims to rule. No world is ruled by no one: the very idea of anarchy is a contradiction in terms (recall Chapter 1). Insofar as this world consists of states bound together by rights and duties, it is a liberal society ruled to the benefit of some states over others, despite the apparent absence of rule. Yet the world of international relations is more complex than this. Insofar as it displays features that I identified with functional institutions (the world of services) and status-conscious agents of state (the world of standing and statecraft), other forms of rule coexist, as do other operative paradigms.

Agents rule the world of international relations as they rule in every world. They rule with rules that other agents must take into account in their conduct, the paradigm that I see operating wherever there is rule I called *political society*. Within this paradigm is a place for the operative paradigm that liberals take for granted, not to mention places for other operative paradigms that liberals take little interest in. The world of international relations is a political society in the first instance. Thanks to the operative paradigm that makes it so, it works pretty much as any political society does.

Most worlds do have porous boundaries, forms of rule blend together, operative paradigms overlap. As observers make some things clearer, they must impose order on what they claim to know. If constructivism is to do its job, it has to be systematic in a way that worlds made by many and diverse agents can never be. Drawing on Robert Merton (1968: 64–72) and Talcott Parsons (1978: 352–3), I used the modifier *codificatory* to capture the sense of the term *paradigm* as it relates to the systematic features of *World of Our Making*. A codificatory paradigm is a fully worked out system of categories, a world made whole. As a tool, it helps any observer bring order to messy worlds.

It was surely a mistake to adopt the term *codificatory paradigm*, and not just because it sounds pretentious—which it does. Dealing with three discrete senses of the term *paradigm*, two of them unfamiliar, undoubtedly taxed readers' ability to keep all the relevant distinctions in mind. My systematic intentions might just as well have been served without invoking the term *paradigm* in the third sense, and possibly in any sense. This is not to say that I have second thoughts about the writing of a book that does function as a codificatory paradigm, if only for myself and a few other like-minded souls.

Constructivism is not a paradigm in the general sense of the term, even if it draws attention to meshed worlds as operative paradigms. Instead, constructivism is a way of studying any world of social relations (Chapter 1). My labeling it this "way" is deliberate, but perhaps unduly vague. Better to call it a framework, as I did earlier in this essay (also see Kubálková *et al.* 1998: 19, and note the subtitle of Lasswell and Kaplan 1950: "A Framework for Political Inquiry"). Indeed, constructivism offers an inclusive framework for the study of social relations. Notice that this claim suits my metaphorical inclinations, and it tells us broadly what constructivism is in functional terms—what we can use it for.

As a framework, constructivism makes it possible for observers to propose any number of theories, or general explanations, for what happens in any world, and it allows observers to fit theories together. Constructivism is *not* a theory itself (Onuf 1998a: 188–9), although I confess that I may have confused the issue recently by calling it a "theoretical stance" (Onuf 1997: 7). Few self-proclaimed constructivists seem to be confused; they do not seem to treat constructivism as a theory even if, as *bricoleurs*, they talk the language of theory. Wendt is an exception.

More precisely, Wendt has become an exception in his recent work. "Constructivism is a structural theory of international politics": "intersubjective structures" explain much of what happens in a world of states (Wendt 1994: 385; 1996: 48). Early on (1987), Wendt emphasized the co-constitution of agents and structures, not as an explanation, but as a description of how any world works. By the mid-1990s, we find him having abandoned this position (expressly in Wendt 1996: 48–9), evidently on the mistaken belief that this description denies the possibility of explaining anything in general terms. Because co-constitution is a comprehensive description, and constructivism a capacious framework, there is plenty of room for Wendt's structural theory. There is room too for any number of other theories—theories that start with social relations and end up with agents, theories that run in the other direction, theories that start with rules as the media of social construction and run both ways.

Wendt's commitment to building theory is commendable. If, by calling *World of Our Making* "meta-theory" (Wendt 1991), he meant to criticize me for not developing a theory, structural or otherwise, then this sort of criticism misses the mark. Frameworks come first. I put together a large and sturdy framework from the diverse "theoretical" materials of many disciplines because I thought that International Relations needed one. Insofar as the term *meta-theory* has become an epithet for self-indulgent epistemological posturing, I am even less inclined to accept it. Let me shift metaphors. Constructivism finds a way between epistemology and methodology by taking the ontological turn—a turn that opens up the road to theory.

3

FITTING METAPHORS

(2010)

Across many fields of study, scholars have turned to metaphors as a key to understanding some aspect of the human condition that has resisted or eluded their investigations. Many of these scholars offer ritual acknowledgment of Aristotle for defining and elaborating on metaphor in *Rhetoric* and *Poetics* but do not read these texts closely. In this essay, I start with Aristotle as if I were engaged in an archeological undertaking.[1] Yet I do so not simply to bring some ancient, unfamiliar concept, or way of thinking, to the light of day.

Aristotle saw the ornamental value in metaphors, and more. We use metaphors as one of many means to persuade others to accept or act on what we say. In effect, Aristotle anticipated the view that speech is performative—all speech. Representing the world, naming its contents, sorting things out: these are performative acts (see further Onuf 1989: Chapter 2). Some names for things that seem to be alike (some concepts) fit better (as representations) and work better (as performances) than others; things change and so do conceptual vocabularies. Metaphors are concepts in the making; concepts are metaphors we no longer recognize as such.

Aristotle never went this far. He did say that things have names and metaphors are names. "Metaphor consists in giving the thing [any thing] a name that belongs to something else" (*Poetics* 1457b7–8, Barnes 1984: 2332). Even if every metaphor names a concept, Aristotle did not say that all names are metaphors. In my opinion, he could have, had he considered the use of metaphor as an act of predication (here see Chapter 4), and not just persuasion. Through predication, new concepts acquire names already in use, and they give their names to yet newer concepts. I would call this process metaphorical extension.

---

1   For a much fuller statement of what I think this undertaking involves, see Onuf (2010a).

In Aristotle's view, we can invent a name for some kind of thing that may or may not be new or different instead of using the name of some other kind of thing. The new name works the way a metaphor does and therefore has the same effect as metaphorical extension. While we do find occasion to invent new names for new concepts, we more frequently borrow names already in use and put them to a new use. I suggest we do this because it is easy—there is always an inventory of names at hand—and because what we take to be new nevertheless reminds us of familiar things. It is also frequently the case that things we take to be new are not. Already named, they end up renamed. Metaphorical extension is an inevitable consequence of predication—of speech itself—and the engine for changing what we think we know.

Not all metaphors are equally persuasive. If we use metaphors to persuade listeners (or readers) that what we say is worth listening to, then those metaphors must seem right. As Aristotle said, they should help us "get hold of something fresh," and they "must not be far-fetched, or they will be difficult to grasp, nor obvious, or they will have no effect" (*Rhetoric* III, 1410b13, 32–3; Barnes 1984: 2050–1). To get at something fresh may take a fresh metaphor—one that is arresting because it is unfamiliar yet fitting—or it may take a familiar metaphor to make what is fresh easier to grasp. Either way, a metaphor must be fitting to be effective. Persuasion takes skill and practice in using metaphors.

The Romans assiduously practiced the art of persuasion but, with so much else, *ars rhetorica* (also the Latin title of Aristotle's work on this subject) fell into the trash heap of history (to use a familiar but still effective metaphor). When Renaissance humanists finally recovered this art, their foremost concern was the many figures of speech to be deployed for ornamental or stylistic effect in a literary culture where plain speech was little valued. Modern egalitarianism gradually undermined the social value and persuasive effect of highly ornamental speech, and thus any incentive to ask what metaphors are and how they work.

Thanks largely to post-modern scholarship, there has been a renewed interest in texts and textuality, discourse and the social uses of rhetoric (see White 1973 for an influential example). In my view, this kind of scholarly work exhibits a certain ambivalence. Figures of speech are ornamental, yet discourse in the most general sense, and not just clever word play, constitutes social reality. The publication of George Lakoff and Mark Johnson's *Metaphors We Live by* (1980) had an enormous impact in many fields of study, I would suggest because it uses plain language to show that metaphors suffuse the plain language we use every day. In the decades since this fresh and accessible book appeared, there has emerged a new field of metaphor studies, in which Lakoff and Johnson continue to play a significant part. In this essay, I draw selectively on some of the major works marking the rapid development of this new field (Lakoff and Johnson 1999; Gibbs 2005, 2008). A major theme in these materials is importance of our daily experience, as "embodied" beings, in our choice of metaphors.

Most contemporary students of metaphor hold the view I have advanced here that (all) metaphors are concepts and, perhaps more controversially, (all) concepts are metaphors. While they may not say this in so many words, they often talk about conceptual metaphors. By doing so, they deny, at least implicitly, the sharp distinction between substance and style, concept and metaphor, that defines the humanist heritage in the study of rhetoric. To soften this distinction, we need only say that so-called literal concepts are generalized, conventionalized and naturalized metaphors. Fixed by repetition, concepts are metaphors that are no longer fresh but all the more fitting in naming some kind of thing. As metaphors become naturalized, they tend to acquire affective and evaluative weight and, when they are used in with modal auxiliaries, they also acquire normative weight.

"Metaphors," according to Aristotle, "must be fitting, which means they must fairly correspond to the thing signified" (*Rhetoric* III, 1405a10–12, Barnes 1984: 2240). I would further say, metaphors are fitting when we believe they correspond to the thing signified, which they do because we have already used metaphors to make that thing what it is. No such correspondence is perfect. In saying that "metaphors are similes" (*Rhetoric* III, 1413a14, Barnes 1984: 2255), Aristotle was expressing the same position, if indirectly. To be similar is to be different in some small degree.

Many contemporary students of metaphor agree with Aristotle, even if they do not realize it. Performative language undercuts the possibility that our representations of the world, however fitting in the moment, are ever fully and finally fixed. Yet this existential uncertainty has important cognitive consequences. Similes encourage us to make comparisons. When we compare things that we take to be alike in one respect with things we take to be alike in another respect, we draw analogies and assign kinds of things to more inclusive kinds. By classifying things, we impose an order on the world that our representations depend on if they are to do the work we need them to.

Scholars in the new field of metaphor studies often say that effective metaphors are directional. In Aristotle's language, names are given, but not given back, even if the thing thus named already has a name. Take, for example, this metaphor: THE EU IS (LIKE) A HOUSE WITH MANY ROOMS (here following the convention of using capital letters to indicate some metaphor under consideration).[2] We are unlikely to say that A HOUSE WITH MANY ROOMS IS (LIKE) THE EU. Yet we could well say, BOTH A HOUSE AND THE EU ARE (LIKE) CONTAINERS, in which case directionality goes from the more general kind to the more specific kind. Moreover, metaphors of the same kind will lose their directionality as they become conventionalized. For example, social fraternities on university campuses in the United States have houses, and *fraternity* and *house* are interchangeable names (A FRATERNITY IS A HOUSE/A HOUSE IS A FRATERNITY).

---

2   The metaphor EUROPE IS A HOUSE is often used. See Hülsse (2006: 412–4) for discussion and citations.

Some metaphors are more durable than others and more widely distributed across cultures. They would seem to be basic or, as many scholars now say, primary, because they reflect, or represent, the experience we all have, as embodied beings, in dealing with the world. Even though it is frequently acknowledged that a large, indeterminate number of such metaphors are likely to exist, there has been some effort to assemble a list of primary metaphors, so far without any system or plan. Few scholars in the new field of metaphor studies are social scientists, and few of the primary metaphors any of them put forward have a social content or context.

With this in mind, I suggest that any such list should include three kinds of metaphors, all of which will have strong affective and evaluative associations. One kind represents our experience in orienting ourselves in space and time. A second kind represents our awareness of our bodies. A third kind arises from having learned that there are other embodied beings in the world. As we experience close relations with other embodied beings, we also learn that they have relations with each other. Primary metaphors constitute the world as a social place, even as they remind us that our bodily selves occupy that world.

Metaphors in the field of international relations

Only in the last twenty years have some few scholars in the field of International Relations given serious consideration to metaphors. The large majority of scholars in the field believe that the function of language, and therefore concepts, is to represent objects, their properties and relations. They take metaphors to be stylistic flourishes often impeding the clear statement of literal concepts. Only those scholars who have taken the "linguistic turn" are inclined to consider figures of speech as integral to the way people construct an intersubjectively meaningful reality for themselves. In my own case (Onuf 1989), I endeavored to show how metaphors (along with other figures of speech) work in shaping a world shaped in turn by our choices of words. To whatever extent my peers could relate to my larger argument about social construction, my more specific claims about figures of speech fell on deaf ears (to use another fitting metaphor).

Among those scholars in International Relations who have taken the linguistic turn, a growing number, starting with Friedrich Kratochwil (1989), have given their attention to discourse and argument. Yet they tend to disregard Kratochwil's important discussion of rhetoric as persuasive speech and thus have little to say about metaphors. Of course, there have been studies of the way metaphors are used in the conduct of international relations and of their constitutive effects (Lakoff 1991; Chilton and Ilyin 1993; Chilton 1996; Mutimer 1997; Marks 2001; this list is hardly exhaustive). Not all of these studies are due to scholars in the field, and they showed little in the way of constitutive effect themselves. There are, however, recent signs of gathering interest (Beer and Landtsheer 2004; Hülsse 2006; Slingerland et al. 2007; Carver and Pikalo 2008; Kornprobst et al. 2008). On of the more conspicuous signs is the appearance of

Petr Drulák's "Motion, Container and Equilibrium: Metaphors in the Discourse about European Integration" (2006) in a leading journal.

Drulák (2006: 503) adopted a constructivist approach to metaphors. "Rather than just describing pre-existing similarities between two subjects, and objectively mediating between them, metaphors actually contribute to the establishment of similarities and, thus, to the construction of our knowledge of the world" (2006: 503). Implied here is the Aristotelian position, recently reaffirmed by scholars in the new field of metaphor studies, that metaphors are indistinguishable from similes. While Drulák pointed to Lakoff and Johnson (1980) as a source of inspiration—an early version of Drulák's 2006 piece tells us this book offers "a radical elaboration of the constructivist perspective" (Drulák 2004: 6)—he has had little to say about the relation between metaphor and bodily experience, which Lakoff and Johnson have continued to emphasize.

In this respect, Drulák has much company, perhaps because the philosophical idealism of discourse studies and constructivist International Relations does not fit well with materialist tendencies in the new field of metaphor studies. Drulák is himself an unabashed constructivist. "Of paramount importance here is the idea that language is not only a simple mirror of social reality, but ... contributes to the very constitution of social reality" (Drulák 2006: 501). This claim would seem to make Drulák a language-oriented constructivist. Since he has credited Alexander Wendt (1999) as an influence on his work (even though Wendt is notoriously indifferent to language), we might think Wendt's "rump materialism" would have pointed Drulák toward Lakoff and Johnson's more thoroughgoing materialism. There is, however, no evidence that Drulák has, as a constructivist, come to grips with this nettlesome issue.[3]

Drulák has foregone any effort to define metaphor precisely. He did quote Kenneth Burke's classic work on literary theory (*A Grammar of Motives*, 1945): "Metaphors ... can be broadly understood as devices 'for seeing something in terms of something else'" (Drulák 2006: 502, quoting Cameron 1999: 13, quoting Burke 1945: 503). Drulak's choice of the metaphor A METAPHOR IS A DEVICE is related to what I would call a primary metaphor, DOING IS MAKING, and usefully points up his constructivist affinities. Burke's ocular metaphor (KNOWING IS SEEING) points to Aristotle's conception of metaphor as using the name of one thing for another but away from Aristotle's emphasis on predication and thus the constitutive power of language.

Drulák emphasized that "a metaphor first emerges as a novel and unusual statement, and then gradually loses its metaphoricity by intensive usage to eventually become part of plain thought" (2006: 506–7). Much as I endorse this claim, its formulation is ambiguous. The term *metaphoricity* suggests that a metaphor has some essential properties which, if they were to disappear, would mean that the metaphor ceases to exist. Aristotle's belief that metaphors must

---

3   Of course, the same can be said of my own Kantian constructivism. In recent work, I try to show in different ways (Chapters 4 and 5) that constructivist idealism and a materialism more expansive than Wendt's can be reconciled.

be fresh but also fitting does not make these properties essential if we treat "metaphors as necessary conditions of speaking and thinking, rather than as mere rhetorical deviations from normal language" (Drulák 2006: 502).

In the early version of Drulák's piece, he invoked "the traditional distinction between 'dead' and 'live' metaphors" (2004: 9). Later he no longer made this distinction. Instead he referred to the "life cycle of metaphors" (Drulák 2006: 506), which suggests metaphorically that metaphors age and die. Yet he also claimed that "many seemingly literal statements are actually hidden metaphors (Drulák 2006: 504). This is a significant metaphorical shift, suggesting that a metaphor ages and fades from view, but does not die. More abstractly, some of the observable properties of a metaphor change over time without adversely affecting their function in social construction. Indeed metaphors may function better as constituents in the process of concept formation because they are hidden.

That metaphors go from being novel to familiar to hidden results in "three stages of sedimentation" (Drulák 2006: 507). Linking stages and sedimentation results in a mixed metaphor. The metaphorical thrust of the term *sedimentation* derives from what is certainly a primary metaphor (UP IS NEW), while the term *stages* derives a different yet also primary metaphor (CHANGE IS FORWARD MOTION). Drulák has given Ole Wæver credit for the term *sedimentation*. In Drulák's summary (2006: 502), "social and discursive structures can be seen as layered. The different layers of sedimentation are the result of historical practices, while at the same time they impact on actual practices."[4]

Using the term *sedimentation* for the conventionalization of metaphors seems to be Drulák's innovation. This is a strikingly metaphorical way of talking about a cumulative but periodically discontinuous process. Indicatively, the earlier version of Drulák s piece titles a section "The Conventionalization of Metaphors" (2004: 11), which the later piece changes to "The Sedimentation of Metaphors" (Drulák 2006: 506). The three stages of sedimentation give us "a useful system for classifying metaphors. Metaphors can be categorized as sedimented, conventional, or unconventional" (Drulák 2006: 507). "Sedimented metaphors are taken for granted and, thus, uncontested," and they are "ubiquitous" (third stage); "conventional metaphors are frequent and contested" (second stage); "unconventional metaphors are rare but contested" (first stage) (Drulák 2006: 508).

Why the classificatory scheme reverses the order of the stages is unclear and somewhat confusing. Why contestation is one of the scheme's two discriminating properties (the other is frequency) is not explained. I would think that some few novel metaphors work well (for rhetorical purposes) because they seem incontestably right, and they are added to the stock of familiar metaphors because they are not generally contested. Those novel metaphors that do not work well and thus do not achieve rapid acceptance will simply die from neglect.

---

4   Drulák cites Wæver (1998: 106–12)—a text that I have not read. But see Wæver (2003: 23–47), for what appears to be similar exposition.

Instead of calling a metaphor no longer recognizable as a metaphor *sedimented*, I would call it naturalized and, in many cases, normativized. Often used by post-modern writers, the term *naturalization* suggests that the metaphor in question seems natural to its users—given by nature, rather than by human artifice. As with most of nature so-called, such a metaphor is subject to change, however gradual and causally complex. More than this, naturalized metaphors are active concepts, constantly put to use and infinitely subject to novel applications and alterations. Shifting metaphors, they are subject to metaphorical rehabilitation. The term *sedimented* suggests that once a metaphor is buried under layers of unconventional and conventional metaphors, "the harder it is to change it" (Drulák 2006: 502). In metaphorical terms, the accumulation of dead metaphors turns into rock.

Wæver addressed this issue: "the deeper structures [of discourse] are more solidly sedimented and more difficult to politicise and change, but change is always in principle possible since all of these structures are socially constituted" (2003: 32). Discursive structure consists of extended arrays of related metaphors, some of which are normativized. Such massively complex metaphors disrupt layers and afford opportunities for change, for example, through the circulation of novel metaphors. Because Drulák was dealing with discrete metaphors, sedimentation packs them together like specks of sand—they have no structure, metaphorically speaking.

Drulák associated *sedimentation* with *internalization*, the latter term referring to individuals, the former to "speech communities" (about which, see Drulák 2006: 505–6). We might better associate sedimentation with *socialization*—a term that points to external conditions (institutions, social-material factors) in the process of sedimentation. Drulák introduced internalization by reference to Wendt's "two levels of structure: micro-structure and macro-structure" (Drulák 2006: 501, citing Wendt 1999: 147–53). In my view, specific institutional contexts shape processes of internalization and socialization, not abstract structures as observers' metaphorical contrivances (unless, of course, those contrivances have become sedimented features of institutional arrangements; see further Chapter 6).

Metaphors in the discourse about European integration

Europe's novel institutional arrangements have prompted the metaphorical extension of familiar concepts (sedimented metaphors) to previously unnamed phenomena. Many of these metaphors have rapidly sedimented. *Spillover*, *engrenage*, *acquis* and *supranational* are obvious examples. Even the extension of the term *integration* to economic relations dates only from the 1940s. Some extensions of sedimented metaphors to European arrangements have been contested—for example, *federation*—on grounds of dissimilarity.

Drulák applied the "framework" he has so carefully constructed to the European Union as a case study. He claimed that this framework "relies on discourse analysis," but that it is "structure-oriented" (Drulák 2006: 511). Even if Wæver talked about discursive structures, Drulák has not. The sedimented metaphor *structure* adds a layer of concepts (additional sedimented metaphors) that would unduly complicate the framework if they were actually developed.

Because "there is a close connection between IR theories [that is, theories in the field of International Relations] and theories of European integration," Drulák identified "the EU as a type of international structure" (2006: 511) and proceeds to classify theories of European integration as either *intergovernmental* or *supranational* (2006: 509). Too much is going on here with too little clarification. Any claim that theories of international relations and theories of European integration are structurally similar is contestable. While intergovernmental theories do resemble theories of international relations in their emphasis on the relations between governments, supranational theories are anomalous at best in the field of International Relations, just as the prefix *supra-* implies. The frequent recourse to novel metaphors in supranational theories suggests that sedimented metaphors in International Relations do not fit the European situation.

Drulák 2006: 510) said that the "conceptual metaphors used by EU leaders" are the "actual subject" of his research. This claim is misleading. His paper has two actual subjects (in addition to itself). One subject is the conceptual metaphors constituting scholarly discourse, metaphorically identified as theory. The second subject is the conceptual metaphors leaders use in public, metaphorically identified as practice. The point of Drulák's study is to use each discourse to look at the other. If we call theories of European integration *discursive institutions* (discourse set apart as a relatively stable complex arrangement of metaphors), we avoid disadvantages of using structural metaphors and downplay the unhelpful comparison with theories of international relations. By doing so, we take European Union studies and the European Union's institutional arrangements to be discursive fields, each with at least some discursive conventions of its own, others that are shared between them, and yet others that are more widely shared.

Drulák limited his research to three years of official debate over a Constitution for the European Union. This framing of the subject effectively removed institutional arrangements from consideration, thereby leaving a nominally homogenous "speech community," and relieved him from complicating his exposition with talk of "micro-structure." The other subject— theories of European integration—he classified by reference to structure (in effect, different institutional features). Then he associated these theories with familiar metaphors: "while intergovernmental approaches see the EU as an EQUILIBRIUM OF CONTAINERS, supranational approaches imagine the EU as a CONTAINER" (Drulák 2006: 511).

Container metaphors are much favored in metaphor studies. In the field of International Relations, STATE AS CONTAINER is understandably treated as a constitutive metaphor. Insofar as intergovernmental theories start and end with states as units of analysis (as do most theories as discursive institutions in the field), the container metaphors will be found in abundance. With such an obvious finding, it is hard to see what is gained by subjecting these theories to a metaphorical assessment. If, however, we switch from International Relations to Political Theory or Constitutional Law as fields of study, we might expect to find metaphors about bodies and persons: THE BODY IS (NOT JUST) A CONTAINER, SOCIAL BODIES ARE PERSONS, LEADERS ARE HEADS, THE STATE IS A POLITICAL BODY, etc. Alternatively we might follow Weber and say the STATE IS A CHAIN OF COMMAND, and go on to say NATION IS BODY or NATION IS FAMILY.

In an *ad hoc* alteration of the initial classificatory scheme (side-by-side containers), Drulák took neo-functionalism out from under the supranational "umbrella" and designated it a container like the other two because "the central neofunctionalist metaphor sees the EU as a MOTION" (2006: 511). This claim seems wrong on the face of it. The central metaphors for neo-functionalism are FUNCTION IS NEED ADDRESSED and FUNCTION IS TASK PERFORMED. If this metaphorical complex is not obvious, then we should surmise that it is so sedimented in bureaucratic discourse (that is, institutionalized) that public officials and scholarly observers take it for granted. Motion is metaphorically highly visible because the future of the EU is much contested.

Drulák's texts have very little (two paragraphs) to say about the remaining contents of the supranational container. Yet federalism and constitutionalism (closely related as discursive institutions) offers sedimented metaphors as pervasive as they are unseen. Perhaps the best examples have to do with levels: LEVELS ARE PLATFORMS, LEVELS ARE LAYERS. Federalism is one important part of an exceptionally old and dense discursive institution which, as a whole, is no longer in view. This institution is called republicanism; as glossed by scholars, it is republican theory. Republicanism consists of a great many sedimented metaphors that no longer seem to be related in the way they once were.[5]

Drulák held that federalism and constitutionalism are among the most influential examples of "CONTAINER thinking" (2006: 512). I find this claim unconvincing. It rests on a tendency (hardly Drulák's alone) to extend the metaphor CATEGORY IS CONTAINER to social phenomena where relations are paramount. Even with respect to categories, we often prefer to employ the metaphor CATEGORY IS FAMILY, as in Aristotle's *species* and *genera*, and Wittgenstein's *family resemblance*.

Once we say, following Aristotle, that an association, as a whole, is a voluntary relation of like and that like associations form wholes by voluntarily associating, and so on (also see Chapter 10), we begin to visualize the relations within associations horizontally and between associations vertically (even if Aristotle

---

5   To illustrate the point, Hooghe and Marks (2003) discussed the concept of multi-level governance, as developed in several fields of study (European Union Studies, International Relations, Federalism, Local Government, and Public Policy), with no reference whatsoever to the republican tradition.

did not). Here we discover the metaphorical value of the metaphor LINES ARE BORDERS—in this case, horizontal lines. This metaphorical complex is at the heart of republican theory as a body of claims, for which Aristotle is the canonical source, about institutional arrangements for the common good. This metaphorical complex does not insist that LINES ARE BARRIERS (lines mark layers but do not make them impermeable). On the contrary, Aristotle took for granted that parts and wholes are always related, and Renaissance and early modern revival of republican theory developed *representation* as a metaphorical complex to show just how relations between levels worked in principle (and see Chapter 11).

Functional theory postulates a variety of human needs, a division of labor in meeting those human needs, and increased task specialization over time. Functionalists draw vertical lines between sectors differentiated by task. If we combine federal and functional theory (with Aristotle's figurative blessing and republican theory as discursive institution), we can visualize institutional arrangements as a *lattice* (Onuf 1998b: 271–2). Insofar as a lattice suggests straight lines both in parallel and at right angles, and thus an ordered arrangement of self-contained boxes (CONTAINERS ARE BOXES) or cells, then this metaphor may create the impression that stable relations across both vertical and horizontal lines are seriously hampered. Furthermore, when this metaphor is applied to European institutional arrangements, it is immediately clear that lines are irregularly spaced and cells vary considerably in size (hence *variable geometry* as an associated metaphor).

An alternative metaphor, well-known to students of the United States as a federal republic, is the layer cake (with local, state, federal layers). We can visualize this cake as a disk, and thus cut in different-sized wedges (separation of powers as constitutional doctrine, functional bureaux). If this metaphor is too tidy for descriptive purposes, then metaphor of a *marble cake*, which Morton Grodzins popularized (President's Commission on National Goals 1960: 265) may be too messy. Despite the sedimented status of the marble cake metaphor, it leaves no way to discriminate between association visualized by place or space, and function as activity fixed not by place but by needs, skills and tools.

Down and up

If every concept started off as a metaphor and most concepts have buried histories, then most of the metaphors deployed in a public debate go uncounted and their importance in discursive institutional change goes unrecognized. In other words, the deeper layers of meaning and significance do not register when the observer has "metaphoricity" in mind and chooses metaphors accordingly (Drulák 2006: 509). One could start with the claim that buried meanings are basic (PRIMARY IS BASIC). One could then proceed by digging through sedimented layers (LEARNING IS DIGGING) for metaphors that reveal what has later disappeared from view.

There is a methodological problem: How does the investigator identify an exemplary text, or metaphorical complex, from the accumulated rubble making up deeply sedimented layers? Must it protrude into higher layers, have "ripple effects" in its own layer, seem to be typical for its time and place, display exceptional craftsmanship? Many scholars will be relatively untroubled by these subjective considerations on the assumption that scholarship is cumulatively self-correcting (MORE IS UP). Those scholars (such as myself) who do not find this assumption persuasive will claim instead that the past is what we make it today, for reasons (REASONS ARE SUBJECTIVE CONSIDERATIONS) that some future scholar may wish to investigate.

PART II

The metaphysics of world-making

Time was when metaphysics was entitled the Queen of all the sciences; and if the will be taken for the deed, the preeminent importance of her accepted tasks gives her every right to this title of honour. Now, however, the changed fashion of the time brings her only scorn …

(Immanuel Kant, *Critique of Pure Reason*, Preface to First Edition 1781)

4

READING ARISTOTLE

(2006/2009)

I read Aristotle's major works on metaphysics, rhetoric, ethics and political society as an extensive yet incomplete inventory of propositions about the human condition. Taken as a whole, these propositions function as presuppositions for the more specific condition we call modernity. Whether we accept, contest or reformulate these propositions, we tend to do so serially or episodically. Yet for Aristotle they all fit together as a working whole.

Few scholars today work with the Aristotelian system as a whole. In this essay, I read Aristotle to have advanced a coherent set of propositions (a working whole that is no less a part of the larger whole) about the mind and its working. I do so as a constructivist—in philosophical terms, a Kantian constructivist. Kant's *Critique of Pure Reason* (1781, 1787) holds that we know reality, the world itself, only as our minds have constructed it. Of course, there is more to Kant than this one sentence expresses, and more to constructivism than one can glean from Kant, as I endeavor to show in Chapter 6. In the circumstance, I might better describe my position as post-Kantian.

However named, it is a radical position—too radical for most scholars, because it contradicts the commonsense view that our senses put us directly in touch with reality. Nevertheless, the kind of constructivism I favor does have other exponents, even if they do not always acknowledge their debt to Kant. For example, Hilary Putnam's "internal realism" is forthrightly Kantian (1981: 49–64). To give another example, the "embodied realism" that George Lakoff and Mark Johnson developed at great length in *Philosophy in the Flesh* (1999) is deeply Kantian without their having said so: "there are no objects-with-descriptions-and-categorizations existing in themselves" (p. 93).

Whether it is useful to retain the term *realism* in these cases is an open question. There is, however, no question that philosophers conventionally take

Aristotle to have been an unqualified empirical realist. Better to say, "he aimed to improve our understanding of the world as we ordinarily see it, and know it to be: not by refuting 'naïve realism,' but by simplifying it" (Atran 1990: 122). On my reading, Aristotle's claims about the mind and its workings do indeed make him the empirical realist that we see most clearly in his descriptive work on living things. They presuppose a world to which our minds have some sort of reasonably reliable access. We are realists by virtue of our being human. Yet Aristotle's realism is open to qualification; it is the *kind* of realism that Kant needed to formulate his constructivist position.

Scott Atran has convincingly argued that Aristotle translated the common-sense kinds of Greek "folkbiology" into a functionally ordered system of parts and wholes (Atran 1990: Part I). Lakoff and Johnson devote an illuminating chapter of their book to Aristotle, but only after they introduce several "folk theories" that constitute Greek metaphysics even before Socrates.

1   Every thing has a nature of its own;
2   At the same time, every thing is a kind of thing;
3   Kinds come in kinds;
4   Being is the most inclusive kind of thing.

(Lakoff and Johnson 1999: 347–50)

The world makes sense to us because we have sensory and cognitive powers to identify things by their nature, sort them by the kinds of natures they have, and "see" how all things are related in nature. Thanks to our powers, the sense of the world and the sense we make of it more or less correspond and, through the sustained application of our powers, can be made to correspond ever more closely.

These folk theories are grounded in metaphors that seem utterly natural to us, if not necessarily to people with other cultural histories. Aristotle spelled them out and put them together. By doing so he gave Western metaphysics its foundations, and these are the foundations that we pretty much take for granted in the world of scholarship. Aristotle held, and realism decrees, that the world, our senses, our minds, and speech all work the same way.

"Knowledge and sensation are divided," in Aristotle's formulation, "to correspond with the realities" (*On the Soul* III, 431b24; Barnes 1984: 686). If Aristotle's realism here seems unqualified, reviewing my inventory of his propositions about the mind and its working suggests otherwise.

Predication

All living beings have powers or faculties enabling them to function in their worlds. Only human beings have, as Aristotle said, "the gift of speech" (*Politics* I, 1253a10; Barnes 1984: 1988), which (we say) is indistinguishable from the ability to engage in reason. The primary meaning of the proto-Indo-European root *leg- is to collect. Its derivative meaning is to speak, as in putting words together. From this root comes the Greek verb legein, to gather, to speak, and its derivative logos, a gathering, speech, and the Latin verb legere, to gather, choose, read (American Heritage Dictionary, Appendix I: Indo-European Roots).

When Aristotle used the term logos, he generally meant an account or formula but also "reason that aims at some goal [or end: telos]" (Nicomachean Ethics VI, 1139a33; Aristotle 1999: 150). While we may speak and make no sense, we cannot think logically, as we say, without thinking in a language. Furthermore, the etymology of the term logos strongly implies that thinking is a social activity in the first instance, and not just a property of the human mind. Gathered together, we formulate goals and aim to persuade others that our goals should be theirs. We are, as Aristotle said, social animals unlike any other (Politics I, 1253a7–18; Barnes 1984: 1988).

Aristotle's conception of language as a distinctively human, necessarily social activity lends itself to a constructivist interpretation. As a species, we are peculiarly empowered to use language to make a world for ourselves, and not just to adapt to the world as we find it. Aristotle's conception does not prefigure or support the Saussurean distinction between langue and parole, language rules and language use: rules shape use, which has the general effect of reaffirming the rules in use. In every language, we form sentences variously connected to other sentences when we speak. Each sentence conveys at least one thought in an unfolding, often occluded exchange of thoughts, a vast, disjointed conversation. Every sentence has a topic: whatever it is about the world that the speaker has in mind.

In English, for example, we may start a sentence and especially the first sentence in a series by indicating the topic. "As a species" and "in every language" are phrases that provide context and set the stage for what remains to be said. Because English is a language that has rules giving priority to the "subject-predicate relation," we are free to leave the topic implicit on the assumption that listeners already know what the sentence is about. Or we may insert the topic elsewhere in the sentence for emphasis. If I say, "There's something about Fritz," the subject there comes first—a "dummy subject" shifting attention to Fritz as the topic of conversation (Li and Thompson 1976: 467–8).

As it happens, the English language belongs to a large family of languages for which the topic is discretionary and the "topic-comment relation" peripheral in any given sentence. These are the Indo-European languages, including, for example, modern Portuguese, Russian, Persian and Bengali, and the older languages Latin, Greek and Sanskrit. There is some evidence that proto-Indo-European may once have been a topic-prominent language. By the time Greek and Sanskrit appeared, the subject, and not the topic, signals its importance by coming first in most sentences (Lehmann 1976; Schmalstieg 1980: 166–9). Instead the topic, not the subject, marks and perhaps constitutes a series of sentences as the functional whole, or "statement." Every language has rules for making sentences and, less obviously, making statements in turn making up "discursive formations" (Foucault 1972: 106–17).

By contrast, Mandarin provides an example of a modern language that makes the subject a less important element in any given sentence. What in English we think of as dummy subjects and double subjects abound in Mandarin sentences. These constructions make more sense if we think of them as freely assembled in a commentary (Li and Thompson 1976: 477–83). It hardly seems a coincidence that pictographs free the written language from a mandated sequence of sentence parts.

Japanese works somewhat differently by using particles to mark topic and subject in a sentence. Thus marked, they may be arranged as speakers see fit. It is tempting to suggest that a topic-prominent language such as Japanese dampens the development of a sense of one's self apart from the world, at least when in comparison with languages that give the subject priority. While it is plausible, even persuasive, to construe the history of Western metaphysics as a quest for a search for the self (Taylor 1989), it is hardly plausible to do so in the instance of Chinese or Japanese metaphysics. There is, however, another property of Japanese sentences that points in the opposite direction. As with topic-prominent languages in general, Japanese sentences typically end with a verb (Li and Thompson 1976: 470). German is similar; the verb completes the sentence, just as the sentence completes the thought.

In any language, no sentence is complete without a verb. Its function is to say what is going on within the sentence. *Predication* is saying what something is, has or does. Thus the verb or verb phrase (any verb and its auxiliaries, associated adjectives and adverbs, nouns serving as direct and indirect objects) is the predicate. The *something* that predication is about is the sentence's subject. Predicates situate the subject of the sentence in a world that is here and now, but has a there before, a there next and a there after that.

Speech is predication in the first instance; on examination every sentence yields a predicate. Consider, for example, the sentence "Empires fall." The intransitive verb, *fall*, is the predicate telling us what happens to *empires* as the subject. Since imperial decline is the topic of the sentence, the predicate and the sentence as a whole are *about* the same condition. Most verbs are transitive or used transitively. They link objects and properties to the subject, thereby completing the sentence and the thought. "Empires foster excess." "Empires become corrupt."

The term *category* derives from the Greek word for predication. According to Aristotle, there are ten kinds of predication (*genêtôn katêgoriôn*). Each is a kind, or category, because none of them can be reduced to any of the others. Yet Aristotle gave us no way to be sure that his list is exhaustive. Substance (*ousia, ti esti*) comes first, followed by quantity (*poson*), quality (*poion*), relation (*pros ti*), place (*pou*), time (*pote*), position (*keisthai*), having (*echein*), doing (*poiein*), being done to (*paschein*) (*Categories*, 1b25–2a4, and *Topics* I, 103b20–23; Barnes 1984: 4, 172).

The term *substance* derives from the Latin word *substantia*, suggesting a relation between some thing and what stands beneath it. Indicatively, for Aristotle, subject and substratum are the same word: *hupokeimenon*. What lies beneath is some*thing* primary (*prôton*)—"that of which other things are predicated, while it is itself not predicated of anything else" (*Metaphysics* VII, 1028b36–37; Barnes 1984: 1624; also 1029a8–9, p. 1625). The ultimate subject is some *thing* uniquely in and of the world: that Fritz of whom I speak, the rabbit I see just now outside my window. There is in the term *subject*, as used here, no hint of subjectivity (Critchley 1996: 13–14).

Obviously Aristotle did not and could not use the term *hupokeimenon*, meaning subject, to specify the first and most important category of predication. When Aristotle enumerated the ten kinds of predication in *Categories*, the first kind is *ousia* (*being, entity*). Substance is some *thing* about which we can say other things or to which we can assign properties. In *Topics*, however, Aristotle used the phrase *ti esti* (literally, *what is*), and not *ousia* for the first category on his list of ten.

Latin writers invented the word *essentia* (*is-ness*), or *essence*, when compelled to translate the awkward expression *ti esti*. In doing so, they made it seem as if Aristotle viewed predication in the first instance as having to do with the fundamental properties of the world, and not with the many individual things in the world. Using the term *essence* also creates the impression, quite inappropriately, that Aristotle adopted Plato's cosmology. According to Plato, we use our minds to enter the world of forms (*eide*, s. *eidos*, also *idea*) that lies behind the world we experience and makes things what they are.

In the context of predication, Aristotle's recourse to the phrase *ti esti* leaves me with an altogether different impression. *What is* can only be what we say it is. Behind *what is* is not the world as sensed but the world as we all have made it with our talk. The words we choose, the thoughts we have, make things what they are by giving form to what we (think) our senses tells us about the world.

What lies behind *that* world is what we say about it to each other. Like chickens and eggs, worlds and words make each other what they are in an infinite regress. *This* is what I, as a constructivist, presuppose about the world I know. In that world, every proposition requires a speaker, has something about the world as its topic, indicates or implies a subject, demands a predicate, forms a thought and has the potential to make the world different, depending on the way listeners respond to whatever speakers propose.

Whatever the phrase *ti esti* may have meant to Aristotle (and it is most certainly *not* what I have just proposed), he insisted that substance is neither interchangeable with nor reducible to matter (*hulô*). By making a statue from bronze, a sculptor gives *that* matter a form or shape (*eidos, morphe*) it neither had previously nor indeed would otherwise ever have. (On the many difficulties in Aristotle's discussion of substance, matter and form, see Gill 1989.) To make a bronze sphere, for example, is "to produce this form in something else." Indeed everything—bronze, sphere, the art of sculpture—is made from something else. As Aristotle observed, "processes of making will regress to infinity" (*Metaphysics* VII, 1033a31–b1, b4–5; Barnes 1984: 1631).

All things are formed matter; both "the art of sculpture and the bronze are causes of the statue," but only together as parts; things thus formed become wholes and as such "sources of change or of rest" in themselves (*Metaphysics* V, 1013b6–7, b24; Barnes 1984: 1600, emphasis deleted). The sculptor forms the bronze as she does to achieve an end, and this end is related to the ends that other things also serve in ever larger wholes. What regresses to infinity must also proceed to infinity. This is, of course, Aristotle's familiar doctrine of the senses in which we speak of cause: material cause, formal cause, efficient cause, and final cause (see generally *Physics* II, 194b17–195a27, and *Metaphysics* V, 1013a24–1014a25; Barnes 1984: 332–3, 1600–1).

According to Aristotle, nature in the strict sense refers to those things that are in themselves "sources of movement" and therefore efficient causes (*Metaphysics* V, 1015a14–15; Barnes 1984: 1603; also see *Physics* II, 193a28–29; Barnes 1984: 330). Obviously, such causes are independent sources of change only in a proximate and provisional sense. Natural and social phenomena differ not in kind but in complexity. As things become more complex, the harder it is to locate the sources of whatever changes they undergo. Aristotle himself saw causal chains inevitably implicated in the relations of parts and wholes (*Metaphysics* V, 1013b20–24, in Barnes 1984: 1600); on relations between parts and wholes, see *Metaphysics* V, 1023b12–36; Onuf 1998a: 209–12, and below).

In nature, things are and have causes. Yet when we speak of things, "we say they have not their nature yet, unless they have their form or shape" (*Metaphysics* V, 1015a4–5; Barnes 1984: 1602; and see *Physics* II, 193a30–31; Barnes 1984: 330). Whether molten or solid, bronze exhibits its nature. The sensible things of the world—whatever we sense—we can sense only because they have form. They may appear to us in what we take to be their natural form, or we may give them a form that accords with their nature.

As with Aristotle's system of ideas, a constructivist framework resists the proposition that nature and society are separate domains that we are obliged to think about differently. Everything that we call natural we have made social, and not just by calling it natural. We make the natural resources that we use to make other things. This we do, as indeed we say, by nature. Formless matter is inconceivable; matter never comes first. Adding form is what we do, and the matter to which we do it must already be formed—as matter.

Aristotle never claimed that the world of the senses exists for us only insofar as we give form to its contents. As with Greek folk theory, individual things are the primary constituents of the world. In this respect, his realism is empirical and unqualified. Individual things always have form; in Aristotle's way of talking, these forms are real. If Aristotle was wrong—if his empirical realism is at odds with the whole, or at least the thrust, of his metaphysical claims—then the mind must give things their form. Once we give form to things, their form persists in the artifacts we make and the sentences that we form when we speak (see Chapter 6 for additional discussion of form).

Here is what Aristotle did say: Having form, the things of the world produce other things by giving form to them. From our point of view, natural products just happen because something other than ourselves gives them form. We also make things for our own ends, whether by art (*technê*), capacity (*dunamis*) or thought (*dianoia*) (*Metaphysics* VII, 1032a26–32; Barnes 1984: 1630). The process of producing or making things (*poiêsis*) is what we do by nature and thus what nature does.

In Chapter 8, I consider art or, more precisely, skill or craft. How thought by itself makes things Aristotle never made clear. If it is applied knowledge, then it is indistinguishable from skilled work. If not, then I would not hesitate to call him a constructivist of a Kantian sort, and not a realist at all. What Aristotle does make clear is that skill and working knowledge both depend on capacity.

The term *capacity* lacks the dynamism of the Greek *dunamis*. *Potentiality* is a better, more potent term. In defining potentiality, Aristotle said it was "a source of movement or change" either within some thing or applied to it (*Metaphysics* V, 1019a15; Barnes 1984: 1609; recall Aristotle's conception of an efficient cause). Healing is a potentiality within the person who comes to be healed, and the sculptor's craft gives a mass of bronze its potential to take form as sculpture. When we identify the potential in things, we use modal auxiliaries to modify the verbs we use to say what things are, have or do: Fritz may come; the emperor should put some clothes on, bronze can be sculpted, rain could stop tonight. When we perceive nothing potentially to interfere with something potential becoming actual, we speak accordingly: we must watch out for imperial excess; we must have some water to drink or we will die. Necessity, too, has its "source" either in itself or some other thing (*Metaphysics* V, 1015b10–11; Barnes 1984: 1602).

Actuality, potentiality and necessity coexist potentially in every act of predication. All things have a potential deriving from their nature; all things are related through their potential to affect other things; potentiality makes things whole. Living things have capacities, faculties or powers (these terms are effectively interchangeable) enabling them to fulfill their potential actively: to do, and not just to be or to happen. As I remarked earlier, human beings have faculties uniquely our own. What we sense about the world, speech and reason allow us formulate, put in perspective, transform and otherwise act upon with an inventiveness we take for granted. We are not alone in making things. We alone make worlds.

Distinctions

In the *Critique of Pure Reason*, Kant sought to reconstruct "general logic" to show how the ten categories of predication resolve into four categories of what he called the pure concepts of understanding (categories of quality, quantity, relation and modality, each possessing three "moments") (Kant 1965: 106–19). We must, however, give Aristotle's logic its due, if only because it has been the central feature of Western metaphysics ever since Aristotle's work became available to medieval scholars. According to Aristotle, true statements about things in the world—objects identified as such in speech—must honor laws of identity, non-contradiction and the excluded middle. Using the terms *A* and *B* to represent different things (they are distinguishable substances), then to say that "*A* belongs to no *B*," is no different from saying "*B* belongs to no *A*" (Aristotle, *Prior Analytics* I, 25a14–15; Barnes 1984: 40). If *A* is not *B*, which is therefore not *A*, then *A* and *B*, or *A* and not-*A*, stand as contradictories (*apophaseis*), and there can be no middle term *C* combining or sharing nonsubstantial properties of *A* and *B* (Aristotle, *De Interpretatione*, 17b17–26; Barnes 1984: 27).

When, however, the terms *A* and *B* have some stated nonsubstantial property in common, usually expressed with an adjective, then they can be represented by terms *D*, *E* and so on, reflecting the shared property, as we say, in degree. In such cases, terms *A* and *B* are contraries (*enantia*). As such, they are qualified in principle even if the shared property is barely detectable at one limit and overwhelmingly evident at the other. "Qualifications admit of a more and a less" (Aristotle, *Categories*, 10b26b; Barnes 1984: 17).

If two things differ in degree, we recognize them by comparing nonsubtantial properties. When these properties differ only in small degree, we no longer think of those things as contraries. We say they are *like* each other.

> Things are like if, not being absolutely the same, nor without difference in their compound substance, [e. g. bronze,] they are the same in form, e.g. the larger square is like the smaller … Other things are like if, having the same form, and being things in which difference of degree is possible, they have no difference of degree. Other things, if they have a quality [the Greek text does without this term] that is in form one and the same—e.g. whiteness—in a greater or less degree, are called like because their form is white. [See below on whiteness as a formal property] Other things are called like if the qualities they have in common are more numerous than those in which they differ.
>
> (Aristotle, *Metaphysics* X, 1054b4–13; Barnes 1984: 1665)

Like distinctions apply to the terms *unlike* and *other*. While as an individual you are "other than your neighbor" (Aristotle, *Metaphysics* X, 1054b17; Barnes 1984: 1666), people are like each other in many distinguishable properties. In a general sort of way, people are also alike in form, a *species* consisting of many sensibly real individuals.

If some thing *B* is the same as or identical to *A* in form, then *B* is *A*'s predicate, and *A* is *B*'s name. The same holds for *A* as *B*'s predicate: we call them the same thing. If *A* has nonsubstantial property *D* and *B* has property *E*, the more nearly *D* and *E* are alike, the more likely we are to think the properties have the same form and give them the same name. Conversely, when properties *D* and *E* are so unlike that we consider them contradictories, we give them different names. Aristotle observed that "there are no names for some qualities" (*Categories*, 10a31; Barnes 1984: 16). More precisely, turning contraries into contradictories excludes the middle and denies any third term a name.

Here is one of Aristotle's examples: "the man who exceeds in his desires is called ambitious, the man who falls short is unambitious, while the intermediate person has no name." Praise and blame, anger and not being angry, honor and dishonor offer other examples—for Aristotle, related examples—of contraries between which there are no named middle terms. For Aristotle, there is only one middle term of interest: the mean, or very middle. As I demonstrate below, the very middle term is one to which Aristotle attached a great deal of normative significance (*Nicomachean Ethics* II, 1107b27–1108a9; Barnes, 1984: 1749, quoting 1107b28–30; also see 1125b1–31, p. 1776).

Turning contrary properties into contradictory forms comes from naming them; this act of predication objectifies them. Aristotle himself gave an example, though inadvertently. "Since things which differ may differ from one another more or less, there is also a greatest difference, and this I call contrariety [contradictory, *enantia*]' (*Metaphysics* X, 1055a3–4; Barnes 1984: 1666). Aristotle explained why we tend to treat contraries as contradictory things, rather than as end points on a continuum, but got the process backwards: "the extremes seem to be opposed because the mean has not received a name" (*Nicomachean Ethics* IV, 1125b25–6; Barnes 1984: 1776). I would say, the mean has no name because we put things in opposition. We do this by objectifying the *relation* between two extremes—we name this relation an *opposition*. And we do this because we value one extreme extremely, and disvalue the other commensurately. (Assigning valence is a propensity I discuss below as the source of normativity.)

When we turn extreme properties into things and put them in a value-laden opposition, we neglect to consider the distribution of properties for example, quantity, position) by magnitude, in the first instance by naming what we see. Aristotle saw that many properties of interest to him form a normal distribution, and so, often enough, do we today. As language users, we are disposed to put contraries in opposition for obvious reasons. Qualitative extremes are themselves obvious; objectifying them as opposites makes them even more obvious; assigning them valence gives them weight as contradictories. Institutional logic functions as formal logic.

The opposition of justice and injustice illustrates this process all too well. Aristotle took justness to be a quality that people possess in degree. Confusingly, he launched his discussion by asking "what sort of mean justice is, and between what extremes the just act is intermediate," proceeded to equate justness with moderation and unjustness with greed or graspingness, thereby turning justness and unjustness into contraries, before concluding that "justice is, as a certain kind of state without qualification, excellence" (Aristotle, *Nicomachean Ethics* V, 1129a2–1130a14; Barnes 1984: 1781–3, quoting1129a4–5, 1130a13). Closely related to moderation, Aristotle's conception of justice as fairness also becomes an unqualified condition (*Nicomachean Ethics* V, 1130a14–1131b2; Barnes 1984: 1783–6).

Justice and injustice stand in contradiction because this is the way we speak of them. When, as adjectives, just and unjust are attached to a noun such as war, wars can only be just or unjust. In the process of objectification, the third term can never be named because we have excluded it. We cannot say just war-moderate war-unjust war and make sense; no wonder Aristotle felt compelled to make moderation an extreme. We must find another adjective, a close relation that still functions as a qualification, one that describes some object or condition by degrees. In this case, we often use the term justified—we can say that going to war is somewhat justified and proceed to argue the relative merits of this claim against any number of counter-claims.

For Aristotle, distinctions arise when we name things. Thus, the term *just* (*dikaion*) derives from the act of cutting something in half (*dicha*); fairness implies the two parts are equal (*Nicomachean Ethics* V, 1132a24–32; Barnes 1984: 1787). Justice, it seems, is a metaphorical term, which is itself a metaphor constructed from the verb *pherein* (to carry) and the suffix *meta-* (across). According to Aristotle, *metaphor* is a "transference": "Metaphor consists in giving the thing [any thing] a name that belongs to something else …" (*Poetics*, 1457b7–8; Barnes 1984: 2332). Aristotle held that metaphor was but one of several kinds of nouns, including ordinary words, foreign words, ornamental words, novel words and altered words. Of course, foreign words may be metaphorical in their own language (as metaphor is); novel words may be wholly made up, perhaps for ornamental effect, and then become ordinary words "in general use" (Aristotle, *Poetics* 1457b4; Barnes 1984: 2332); altered words are novel without appearing to be arbitrary inventions. Over time, Aristotle's several overlapping categories have collapsed into an opposition. There are ordinary words (those that are literal in meaning) and ornamental words (those that are figurative), among which metaphors are the most prominent.

Yet there is nothing in Aristotle's definition of metaphor that suggests this outcome. Instead, Aristotle should be seen as having offered an opposition between words that are strictly arbitrary inventions and words whose names convey an association with other words. Except perhaps for basic vocabulary in any *ur*-language (words with no discernible history), most words are borrowed or adapted from other words—they have names "that belong to something else," and these names end up "in general use." Whatever their origin, words cease to be figurative the more, the longer, we use them. To mark this transition, we call them "literal" (*littera*, Latin for letter of the alphabet, or document, is a metaphor for fixed content). Many of us end up thinking them "literally true" in the sense of corresponding to things and relations in the world.

Even as language use undermines Aristotle's implicit opposition between new and used terms, we constantly replenish the supply of new terms by giving less familiar things and relations the names of more familiar things and relations. Like *bricolage*, predication invites us to rummage about, borrow names and substitute them to see what works in our efforts to communicate with others. Not all metaphors do work. To improve the odds, Aristotle offered some well-known guidance": "Metaphors … must be fitting, which means they must fairly correspond to the thing signified …"; they should help us "get hold of something fresh"; they "must not be far-fetched, or they will be difficult to grasp, nor obvious, or they will have no effect" (*Rhetoric* III, 1405a10–12, 1410b13, 1410b32–33; Barnes 1984: 2240, 2250, 2251).

Obviously these predicated properties of a good metaphor are situationally contingent. An easily grasped metaphor gets repeated, becomes stale and loses its (metaphorical) effect. Finally it is absorbed into a community's working vocabulary. As I have already suggested, the metaphor is conventionalized and naturalized, its career as a metaphor ended. This process is much discussed today, and some scholars (for example, Gentner and Bowdle 2008) use the metaphorical construction "career of metaphor" in explicating it.

Aristotle observed that metaphors "must fairly correspond to the thing signified" (quoted above). If they were to correspond exactly, it could only be as a formal identity, in which case there is no thing with properties to compare. Claiming that "metaphors are similes" (*Rhetoric* III, 1413a14; Barnes 1984: 2255), Aristotle clearly understood the implications of his position. Saying "metaphors are similes" is like saying "metaphors are *like* similes"; "the difference is slight" (*Rhetoric* III, 1406b20; Barnes 1984: 2243) precisely because the two things named can never be exactly alike (see Chapter 3 for a closely related discussion of metaphor).

To say that things are like in some degree is to subject them to comparison. To say repeatedly that they are almost alike is to make them alike, just as saying they are extremely unalike makes them contraries and finally contradictories. The conventions of comparison operate on what we say things are, by convention making them what they are. In a world of similes, we are empirical realists insofar as we "see" and therefore know things that have "always" had names. Everything else we know by association and comparison with what (we think) we know.

Aristotle held that "an acute mind will perceive resemblances even in things far apart" (*Rhetoric* III, 1412a11–12; Barnes 1984: 2253). This process now has the name *abduction* (see below), and it is fittingly associated with our imaginative or creative faculties. One of the defining features of the Renaissance was its penchant for similes, its preoccupation with resemblances (Foucault 1971: 17–42; Chapter 12). Even if convention holds that Renaissance humanism is Scholastic Aristotelianism's contrary, humanists recovered not just Aristotle's interest in persuasive language but his conceptual premises. Predication produces similes—presumptive similarities in the world of things—in turn producing the chains of associations by which we make sense of the world. Never adequately named, these premises once again slipped from view (unnamed, unseen: in this context, hardly a mixed metaphor).

In ordinary language, similes and metaphors are often called analogies; as in the formula, *A* is to *B* as *C* is to *D*, analogies would seem to resemble similes. We could just as well say *A* is *like B*, *C* is *like D*, the relation of *A* to *B* is *like* the relation of *C* to *D*. Thus an analogy is just a second-order simile—a position entirely compatible with Aristotle's conception of similes. Yet Aristotle's formula is slightly different: "as *A* is in *B* or to *B*, *C* is in *D* or to *D*" (*Metaphysics* IX, 1048a36–b; Barnes 1984: 1655; also *Metaphysics* XII, 1071a4–7; p. 1692). The preposition *in* indicates a relation between what is actual (*A*, *C*) and what is potential (*B*, *D*). Such relations are functional (informed by purpose, parts working together make a whole informed by purpose in some larger whole: see below), and the point of the analogy is to draw attention to functional relations by identifying the patterns of similarities they produce. Understood as an asserted resemblance between complex wholes, analogy is an indicative feature of liberal thinking—and this despite modern hostility toward Aristotle's teleological system (here see Onuf and Onuf 2006: 111–18).

Classification

Aristotle was not especially given to classificatory schemes. Of course, he distinguished between living kinds of things and other kinds of things (and notably called human beings animals), and he struggled mightily to impose order on Greek folk biology. Otherwise those classificatory schemes for which he is famous seem to consist of empirical generalizations placed one after the other. Thus we have kinds of nouns; rhetorical strategies based on the speaker's character and reputation, appeals to emotion, and appeals to reason; rule by many, few or one. By contrast Kant, a cosmologist turned philosopher, was an ardent classifier. Indeed the "Classical age" that came to a close with Kant's death was the time of tables, of systems for classifying human knowledge of every sort (Foucault 1971: 71–6, 125–65).

In Aristotle's case, recall that his empirical realism starts with uniquely individual things: Fritz (as I remember him), the rabbit (that I just saw), Alexander's empire, this sentence. The more we subject things to predication, the more the accretion of particulars attests to their individual being. The pursuit of predicates defeats the very possibility of classifying them. The world is full of different things.

Nevertheless, Aristotle gave us some tools, or formulas, by which to order the world's contents or, I would say, to put our thoughts in order and make sense of the world. As I have already intimated, he did this by suggesting that predication works in two different ways. Indeed, we might say that the ten categories fall into two categories. However defined, substance is one kind of predicate, expressed by use of nouns, pronouns, noun phrases, and infinitives and gerunds acting as nouns and noun phrases. The remaining nine predicates form a second category signaled by the use of adjectives, adverbs and prepositional phrases.

By saying some thing *is* a substance, we attribute to that thing the form of some*thing* else (rabbit, empire). By saying that some thing *has* this or that quality, scale, time, place and so on (furry, small; large, ancient), we specify all those properties and relations making the thing what it uniquely is. While these predicates may assist us in identifying the form of some thing (this thing is too large to be a rabbit, too small to be an empire, but just about the right size for a house), they do not of themselves give the thing its form.

In Aristotle's words, some things "are *said of* a subject but are not *in* any subject." Conversely, some things cannot be said of a subject because they are present in the subject, and not just as a "part"—parts are wholes that can always stand alone (*Categories*, 1a20–24; Barnes 1984: 3, emphasis in text). There is, I think, something not quite right about this formulation. Whatever is in the subject must also be said of it. Predication is not just *saying* what we think things are (or are like) but also saying what we think *about* things.

Nevertheless, the distinction between what (we say) things are, or seem to us, and the properties (we say) they have itself seems to be a fundamental one. Once we speak of things as subjects, we can proceed to say how they are different from other things, or how they are alike. We do this by specifying some predicated property for any collection of things and inspecting them all for the presence or absence of that property. For example, having hair is a property of some things, but not others.

Once we assemble a collection of hairy things, we say of them, these are all things of the same *kind*: they all have hair. "Whenever one thing is predicated of another as a subject," Aristotle said, "all things said of what is predicated will be said of the subject also" (*Categories*, 1b10–11; Barnes 1984: 4). Deciding what (to say) things are means putting them together with other things that have the same properties, and only those things. For example, all things that have (what we call) hair are the same thing; let us call those things mammals. The result is a concept, in this case, the concept of mammal.

There are many such properties, all of which need to be sorted out, and the result will be a multiplicity of concepts. If Aristotle was a mammal but not a rabbit or an emperor, we need to agree on what makes rabbits, human beings and emperors what they are. For the most part, we do so by talking to each other. As a collective enterprise, we consider properties more generally shared by things that we say are different in other respects.

The process of concept formation (giving things recognizable forms) is simultaneously a process of generalization and differentiation (identifying which properties some things have in common and which properties they do not). As we form qualitatively differentiated things into sets by naming them, we form those sets, as things, into sets of sets, forms of forms. "For example, man is predicated of the individual man, so animal is predicated of the individual man also—for the individual man is both a man and an animal" (Aristotle, *Categories*, 1b11–15; Barnes 1984: 4).

For Aristotle, human beings constitute a species (*eidos*, form) or, as we say today, a life form. Other kinds of animals, appropriately differentiated, also constitute species. These life forms are, for any empirical realist (which is to say, every cognitively competent human being), obviously discernible as natural kinds, given common names and otherwise subject to predication. They are "basic" not because they dominate our experiential world—empirical realism gives us a world of individual rabbits, rainbows and sentences—but because we have evolved sensory and kinesthetic equipment to identify and interact with "overall shapes" for "object utilization" (Gibbs 2005: 81–90, quoting pp. 82, 87).

In this context, the term *basic* suggests that things presuppose kinds, which we recognize because they have familiar forms and functions. Against empirical realism, such a view holds the world to consist entirely of natural kinds, and comparison is the means by which to isolate the distinguishing properties of actual things. Identifying species, as natural kinds, might involve singling out and naming an exemplary instance or individual for every kind (prototypes representing an observed or presumed norm). Or it might depend on specifying the properties that instances or individuals of any kind must possess. In my view, both are cognitive processes linked to sensory-kinesthetic dispositions. They depend on predication and operate in tandem, if not always to good effect. Natural kinds are naturalized social kinds.

A discernible and therefore predicable set of species is, on Aristotle's account, not just a higher-order species but a *genos*. For Aristotle as a zoologist (see *Generation of Animals*; Barnes 1984: 1111–218), nature uses a fixed ensemble of materials—the way a sculptor forms bronze—to (re)produce the species we already know to exist. "However, there is nothing to prevent genera subordinate one to the other from having the same differentiae [differentiating properties]. For the higher are predicated of the genera below them, so that all differentiae of the predicated genus will be differentiae of the subject [species, individual] also" (Aristotle, *Categories*, 1b21–24; Barnes 1984: 4; also see *Topics* I, 102a31–102b2; Barnes 1984: 170). While genera may themselves consist of sets of genera, the process of generating genera differs in form from the process of generating species. If the latter has nature acting on the world directly, the predication of forms by references to the properties of other forms distances the former from an empirically real world of flesh and bones, copper and tin.

The Greek term *genos* (kin, offspring, descendants, generation, race, kind) suggests that Greek folk biology gave Aristotle's logic, and related processes of generalization and differentiation, a metaphorical warrant (see Atran 1990: 292n3, for discussion). Aristotle need not have thought that genera spawn species in any direct way to have grasped the rhetorical advantage of treating kinds like families of (generations) of prototypical individuals. Today we favor the same rhetorical strategy when, following Wittgenstein, we form and group concepts by identifying "family resemblances"—by itemizing multiple properties of prototypical things (see Davis 2005: 31–42, for a lucid exposition). Such a procedure centers on Aristotle's last sense of likeness ("things are called like if the qualities they have in common are more numerous than those in which they differ") and rejects the move from contrary qualities to contradictory things whose very names place them in opposition.

When, however, we fix concepts by naming them and locating them by reference to other concepts (they are called *like* in Aristotle's first sense:

"they are the same in form"), we are choosing a different view of concept formation supported by a different rhetorical strategy. Metaphorically speaking, concepts are containers, not families. Containers are relatively well-formed, families relatively formless. As contraries, containers invite formalization as contradictories. Families do not.

Containers have contents: these names have a common source (the Latin verb *continere*, to hold together). The contents of many containers are themselves containers (Lakoff and Johnson 1999: 19–20). In other words, we sort individual things into more abstractly designated things (species, kinds as containers), and those things into even more abstract things (families, kinds of kinds). Aristotle was a philosopher, all philosophers are human beings, all human beings are mammals, all mammals are animals, all animals are living things and so on.

Aristotle recognized that differentiation and generalization are basic tools for putting things in order. We call these activities modes of reasoning. In Aristotle's terms, deductive reasoning (*sullogismos*) proceeds from universals to particulars, and inductive reasoning (*epagôgê*) in the other direction (*Posterior Analytics* I, 71a5–9; Barnes 1984: 114). Deduction proceeds downward, from larger containers to the smaller containers therein, while induction goes upward searching for the larger container within which the smaller belongs. Sideways movement—from one kind of thing (container, concept) to a different kind—others have called abductive reasoning (also see Onuf 1989: 97–110).

In Aristotle's way of talking, individuals are parts of wholes, and wholes are parts of yet larger wholes. An individual human being (or rabbit, or empire) is one of a kind, its parts also kinds. If the most inclusive whole is nature itself, every lesser whole is a natural kind. Deductive reasoning starts with a stipulated universal (*katholou*, of a whole—some one thing taken as a whole). It ends with discrete individuals—the smallest things, or parts, that we can speak of. Induction starts from a given universe of individuals known by their particular properties. It finds the whole that these things are parts of and continues from parts to wholes, as parts, to the last conceivable whole. Abduction starts and ends with wholes that are never parts of each other.

Whether we conceptualize (imagine, speak metaphorically of) concepts as (individual) families of (individual) families (of individuals), containers within containers, or whole parts of wholes, we turn a particular kind of relation among kinds of concepts into a set of tools for making things. We make things by taking other things apart, putting things together or jumping from one thing to another. In the process, we make order among things—all of the things we form with the cognitive tools I just described. It is not easy to make sense of the order we make; the whole is an abstraction that we have learned to talk about in metaphorical terms.

While Aristotle seems never to have resorted to the metaphorical language of containers and levels, we do so routinely. We say and therefore see that concepts are containers and that levels are a stacked set of platforms, or large containers. Located on each level are the many things (concepts) that (we say) are alike in most predicable respects, or at least in what we take to be the most important respects. Each level (as a thing itself) has different properties because the kinds of properties and relations that things exhibit differ from level to level (see further Onuf 1998a: 214–19). We could just as well say something like this about families sorted by generations.

Thus formed, levels tend not to change very much. Furthermore, things tend not to move between levels unless they are formed into things (by being taken apart or put together) that exhibit properties locating them at the next level up or down. Only if there is massive movement of things between levels, will the relations among levels be susceptible to change. A world of levels assigns all things a place in what philosophers once extolled as a great chain of being. Levels correspond to links in the chain of being; evidently what separates things into levels also binds them together.

We can render these generalizations in a more modern and familiar form. Efficient causes operate within levels. Between levels, we tend not to speak of cause. Thus we say that atoms have an effect on each other, but not generally on the molecules containing them. Or we say that societal changes do not affect the cognitive faculties of human beings that make society possible. When we do want to talk about causal effects across levels, we resort to concepts such as *emergence* and *supervenience*—metaphors that many scholars find to be vague and unsatisfactory.

By talking about efficient causes and not about the relations of things at different levels, scholars construct a world of levels and locate themselves accordingly. In the process they limit the possibility or, as they see it, the need to take into account what (other scholars say) goes on at other levels. Over several centuries, sorting everything we think we know into levels has made the modern world what we think it is. This proposition is of course overstated for rhetorical purposes. Yet it suggests another way of talking, one that substitutes the imagery of parts and wholes for the imagery of causes and levels.

In Aristotelian terms, parts make things whole by *doing* something indispensable for the whole. They do work; they put things to use; they perform tasks, jobs, functions; they act and they are acted on. When we focus on the relations of parts, we have set aside the imagery of levels and causes. Instead we speak of *systems*—systems of relations. Parts are systems of relations within wholes that are also systems of relations.

Parts are things, things apart, only insofar as we see them severed from the system of relations in which they operate—as a system of relations. When we situate systems in levels, we have already turned them into things. When we claim to have discovered a causal relation, we have picked out one relation at the expense of the many others making up the system. If, instead, we consider relations as a whole, we say that systems of relations have form (and this is what enables us to say that systems are things). Yet we do not identify such forms through an inventory of properties; we identify form with function. The system is what it does in and for the system of which it is a part.

We also talk metaphorically about the forces affecting a system of relations, indeed about the relations of forces. The metaphor is physical and direct: with force comes movement (Lakoff and Johnson 1999: 184–7). When we act, we exert force (physically, directly) for a purpose or to an end. Form and force go together in the performance of a function.

The metaphor gets its force, if I may say, not just from our inability to sense whatever it is that we call force directly—the same goes, after all, for cause. The force of the metaphor stems from the sense of mystery its use so often conveys. Does force have a form even if we can never observe it directly? Does function give force its form, or does form give force to function?

When we do talk about forces as if they were things with uniform, identifiable properties subject to generalization, we identify them with efficient causes, theory construction and what we often call scientific explanation. When we talk about force, form and function as whole, we end up with a looser conception of what it means to theorize about things and their relations. We speak of generation, growth, decay. We sound like Aristotle, even if we find his language alien or at least unduly metaphorical. To claim, as Aristotle did, that all things, animate or otherwise, have their own aims or principles of action, or that every whole serves a purpose in a larger whole, or that nature does nothing in vain, seems very much like attributing human powers to the contents of the world.

Are levels real, causes efficient? Does nature think the way we like to think we do? Does the order implicit in what we say about the world correspond to the order of things in the world, an order beyond what we say? I am skeptical about all such propositions and, of course, the presuppositions behind them. Nevertheless, I believe that Aristotle's ten categories of predicates do resolve into a classificatory scheme with three, not two, categories of predication—a whole in three parts.

Predicates that say what things *are* constitute one category; nouns typically do the job. Predicates telling us what properties things *have* constitute a second category; adjectives and adverbs take over. Predicates telling us what things *do* in relation to other things constitute a third category. Doing (*poiein*), being done to (*paschein*) are the last two categories on Aristotle's list; the present participle of a limited number of transitive verbs do the job.

Making, doing, acting, working, using are the kind of predicates that make the world more than its sensible or imagined contents. As I have said, we make the world what it is. We do this not just by saying what the things (relations, forces) of the world are and what properties these things (relations, forces) have. We also say what they do to each other and for each other: this is the third category of predication, the one that makes the world whole.

Kant said that Aristotle's ten categories of predication were "the result of a haphazard search" (1965: 114). I suggest that Aristotle developed a classificatory scheme without realizing that he had done so. The ten categories of predication fall into three classes (containers) roughly corresponding to the functions that parts of speech perform in syntactically sound sentences. Aristotle's discussion of "what a name is and what a verb is" does not tell us what nouns and verbs do (*De Interpretatione*, 16a19–b26; Barnes 1984: 25–6; also see *Rhetoric* III, 1404b21, p. 2249; *Poetics*, 1456b20–22, p. 2331). While his treatment of matter in relation to substance, for example, conveys a subtle appreciation of bronze as noun (matter, metal in some form) and as adjective (metal as nonsubstantial property; see Gill 1989: 101–2, 122–6), he did not, to my knowledge, talk about adjectives as such, much less about their function in speech. We, however, routinely discuss nouns, verbs, adjectives, adverbs and so on in functional terms.

The functions that the parts of speech perform in making a sentence a whole reflect the way we make the world, part by part, into wholes within wholes. This is a presupposition on my part: we can never be sure whether these functional units actually reflect the way the world works, and therefore we can never be sure that this is how our minds work. Kant was sure he knew how the mind makes sense of the world, but he turned to a different feature of Aristotle's metaphysics to show how it does so. The use of logic in the process of concept formation gives Aristotle's ten categories an order that he did not recognize himself.

Valence

As I suggested earlier, Aristotle held that what we know if what we say about the world is true or not only by the application of his logical rules to the properties and relations of things we know the world to consist of. "For if it is true to say" that some thing is white or not, "it is necessary for it to be white or not white" (*De Interpretatione*, 18a38–b1; Barnes 1984: 29). Yet we cannot start here. Is being white or not a matter of degree, white being at one end of a continuum and not being white at the other end? Or is being white a condition or state of affairs excluding any other condition involving a property such as whiteness? If the property of being white shades into not quite white, then white and not-white are contraries. If white can only be white or it is not white at all, then white and not-white are contradictories. In the latter case, shades of white are logically excluded (*De Interpretatione*, 17b17–26; Barnes 1984: 27).

By making white a thing, we have given whiteness a form and all white things the same form. Thus formed, white things cannot be less than white. We might say, however, that various and sundry white things have additional properties detracting from their (formal) whiteness. (Recall that I quoted Aristotle on what makes things like other things to say just this.) Or we might identify some part as the white thing actually in question. Even if logic applies only to the forms and not the properties of things, any property can be formalized and said what it is: a thing itself that, by logic, cannot be something else, except of course as a kind of thing.

Some writers refer to Aristotle's logic as bivalent (see *Prior Analytics* for a detailed exposition; Barnes 1984: 39–113). As I suggested earlier about this kind of logic (there now being other kinds), propositions are true or not because things in the world obey so-called logical laws of identity, non-contradiction and the excluded middle. Identity and contradiction are contradictory states, a relation of opposition. Two things said to stand together in opposition also stand in opposition to an imagined third thing called the middle; pairs of contraries and pairs of contradictories are opposed things. Pairings of things by the logic of opposition—forming things into a binary relation—is one of the most pervasive, characteristic features of human experience, a faculty that all cognitively competent human beings possess. Reasoning processes presuppose its use; the result is classification by kinds of kinds. Valence is a property of the world, whether reproduced in the mind or produced by the mind.

As used in a variety of disciplines, the term *valence* points to the position of some thing in a binary relation, but not just this. The Latin adjective *valens* means strong, robust or healthy. The noun *valentia* suggests good health. *Valens* is the past participle of the verb *valēre*, to be strong or worthy), which is the root of the terms *valor* and *value*.

As human beings with bodies, minds and various powers, we think of ourselves as strong or weak, healthy or not. These properties are contraries. We consider them as continuous variables—the included middle—when we make comparisons (her will is stronger than his is). Yet we also oppose them as things in a binary relation (people are either healthy or sick, strong willed or weak willed), and we tend to classify people accordingly (men are strong, children and emperors are willful, women are caring and resourceful).

Yet this is not all we do. We often say, being robust or healthy is good; it is better to be stronger; strength and health are good things, as opposed to being weak and sick, which are bad things. We talk about growth and decay the same way. Strong and healthy bodies (minds, powers) are good, and what is good is to be encouraged. Weakness is bad and to be discouraged.

We see here an equation taking us from an empirical generalization (the sick and the weak die before the healthy and the strong do) to a normative judgment (living is good, health is good, strength is good). Underlying this equation is a presupposition (nature intends that we live to the fullest) that the Greeks unequivocally accepted, and so do we most of the time. Insofar as we think that nature intends the same for all living things, the same presupposition grounds modern biology and evolutionary theory.

Aristotle had much to say about good and bad, both as contraries and as contradictories (see especially *De Interpretatione*, 23a27–24b9; Barnes 1984: 37–8). In *Nicomachean Ethics*, he linked good and bad to pleasure and pain as the kinds of feelings or emotions that we all have. "By feelings I mean appetite, anger, fear, confidence, envy, joy, love, hate, longing, jealousy, pity, in general whatever implies pleasure and pain" (*Nicomachean Ethics* II, 1105b23–25). I am using the Irwin translation here (Aristotle 1999: 23), which translates *pathos* as *feeling*; the Barnes edition uses the term *passion* instead (1984: 1746). *Pathos* derives from *paschein* (to be affected, undergo, or, as I said above, to be done to; also see Terence Irwin's glossary entry for *pathos*, Aristotle 1999: 400–1).

As we experience the world, we feel pleasure and pain. Our feelings are positive or negative, and so is our response. This is the sense of *valence* as the term is used in contemporary social psychology (see Ortony *et al.* 1988; Chapter 5). Each of the feelings on Aristotle's list relates to pleasure and pain as a primary relation of contraries. Judged by the pleasure or pain they induce, fear and confidence, love and hate are opposite extremes. Other terms imply their opposites: appetite and loss of appetite, sympathy and envy. Whether we feel pleasure or pain, we pass judgment on what we feel, and we act accordingly.

Aristotle claimed that "feelings, capacities and states" are "three conditions arising in the soul" (*Nicomachean Ethics* II, 1105b20–21; Aristotle 1999: 41). We have already seen what Aristotle meant by feelings. "By capacities I mean what we have when we are said to be capable of these feelings—capable of being angry, for instance, or of being afraid, or of feeling pity. By states I mean what we have when we are well or badly off in relation to feelings" (*Nicomachean Ethics* II, 1105b25–28; Aristotle 1999: 41).

We have feelings only insofar as we experience them as happening to us. We have capacities in a stronger sense—we use them to make things happen in the world, even to control our feelings. Feelings and capacities would seem to correspond to being done to and doing as categories of predication. We also have states of mind, but not in the usual sense. How indeed can a process even be a state (*hexis*, literally *having*)?

The ambiguity in Aristotle's formula opens the possibility that *state*, as defined in the passage just quoted, is a "condition" that lies between being acted on and acting as contraries. Thus it has at least some of the properties of a capacity, but we experience it the way we experience feelings. More precisely, we have the capacity to know what good and bad is beyond the experience of pleasurable and painful feelings. Furthermore, we have the capacity to choose good states—to feel good by doing good things.

Given Aristotle's empirical realism, we might also see him as a moral realist for whom good and bad are objective conditions. As an alternative, I suggest that Aristotle saw our moral sense as the product of distinctively human cognitive processes. Our minds take us from feelings (a passive condition) to the exercises of our capacities (an active condition) to the constitution of normative states (the condition of being good or bad). This is how our bodies work and our minds work together, and this is what language registers when we move from *is* to *ought*. Constructivists do not deny the distinction between is and ought; they presume that we know how to move from one state to the other with striking facility.

Since we are capable of evaluating the effects of our choices on ourselves (on our health, for example), we can also choose whether to have good or bad effects on the world (*Nicomachean Ethics* II, 1104b4–23; Aristotle 1999: 37–8). When we do what is good, we make the world better, and when we do bad we make it worse. When we do what is good, we are good—a good thing in and for the world. Doing bad is a bad thing; it makes us bad. Given valence, going from feelings and capacities to states and finally to the constitution of social arrangements (for example, good and bad forms of rule): this is how we make our way in the world, this is how the world works.

The state of being good is a virtue (excellence, *aretê*); there are as many such states as there are feelings that we choose to actualize. Taken together these choices constitute character (*êthos*). If we take them separately, how do we know when we have achieved a good state? The contradictory of good and bad assumes we already know what makes them different: the effect of choosing one or the other on ourselves (our strength, health) and the world (its well-being). The standard for choosing what we should and should not do (as contradictories) would be the threshold between good and bad that all of us are capable of identifying and acting on.

If this standard seems obvious, it was not so for Aristotle. Instead, he recommended that we strive for the mean (*mesotês*) in every instance. While we think about our feelings in bivalent terms, as contradictories, we experience them as contraries. In Aristotle's view, too much or too little of any feeling is always possible. Even here, the equation ends up bivalent, as all things normative must. Between the contraries *excess* and *deficiency* lies the *mean* as a good; excess and deficiency stand together as the mean's contradictory and thus a bad thing in itself (*Nicomachean Ethics* II, 1104a12–27, 1108b12–1109a19; Aristotle 1999: 36, 49–51). As I argued earlier, Aristotle's conception of justice as fairness, expressed metaphorically as splitting any difference in two, also takes an extreme and turns it into an unqualified condition.

The rationale for Aristotle's standard is hardly obvious. Sometimes moderate behavior will bring us long, full lives, sometimes not. Sometimes pursuing excellence in one thing warrants a deficiency in some other; perhaps the mean should apply to an aggregate of states. Choosing the mean between any pair of extreme feelings has the effect of making normal conduct normative. As our feelings flow over us, we should navigate between the extremes in order to optimize the potential for good.

Operationally, the question is knowing how to act as we experience the world. The obvious answer is to see what most people actually do most of the time, and then act as they do. Wherever human beings are in a position to monitor and emulate each other's acts, there are rules. Every rule must form at least one sentence with its verb modified to indicate an act that should or must be performed or not; every rule offers a standard for conduct. We all know how to make sentences with these properties, and we all know what they mean. As an empirical matter, rules are everywhere. Yet Aristotle held that character is everything.

This is not altogether the contradiction it seems. Character is an aggregate of traits exemplified by the exercise of our faculties to their fullest potential. Exercising our faculties produces rules reflecting not just the mean for those feelings that we act on, but the mean for a great many practices that work for us in general. When these rules do work for us (for example, by moderating the way we act on our feelings), we see the benefit in following them if other people do. When the rules do not work the way we think they should, we will consider not following the rule or even acting to change it.

As the rules change, so does normal conduct and the criteria for deciding on what constitutes good character. Rules are things, as such, good or not. In Aristotle's view, we know the rules will be good if we are good ourselves. We are more inclined to say today that rules are good if they conform to more general standards by which to evaluate the goodness of rules. We ask, for example, if they are fair or just. Once generalized to the greatest possible whole, we dignify these systems of rules for judging rules by calling them moral (see further Onuf, 1998b).

5

PARSING PERSONAL IDENTITY

(2003)

Identity is one of the most fashionable concepts now in use in the field of International Relations. It is also one of the murkiest—so difficult to fathom that, as a scholar in this field, I have been reluctant to use it. Scholars who do use it start with easy assumptions and put them together with little attention to conceptual consistency. Quite a few post-modern and post-colonial scholars see identity as a collective delusion, an unstable symptom of alienation that comes from insisting on the otherness of others. We are nothing but the difference. These scholars have achieved conceptual coherence by making identity a process of reciprocal differentiation and not a fixed condition for any of us. Yet the process itself presupposes participants already aware of themselves. If subjectivity comes first, then *self* becomes an unexamined primitive term.

Alternatively, constructivist scholars argue that identity is a process of social construction involving agents' choices for themselves. Here we find two assumptions. Constructivists also tend to treat *self* as an unproblematic primitive term, but in their case it is an objective condition. As individual human beings mature in any society, they come to possess an active, coherent sense of self, or identity. Constructivists further assume that having a sense of self does not imply alienation in any radical sense: any socially connected set of human individuals will come to have some sense of themselves together, or collective identity.

Post-modern and post-colonial scholars are skeptical about an objectivist account that puts agents and their intentions in the foreground. Constructivists are skeptical of any account that leaves agents and their intentions out of the picture. Selves act, in the first instance, for themselves; any self-identified collective is capable of acting for itself. By contrast, most positivist scholars in the field seem to think that they can dispense with assumptions about identity and then go on to treat agency as an unproblematic primitive term.

Nevertheless, the self remains as an unexamined primitive: agents must have some sense of self in order to be able to act on their preferences or interests—they act for themselves. Nor do these theorists very often examine the assumption that agents with common preferences are capable of forming self-identified collectives, any one of which is capable of acting for itself. Taking these assumptions for granted, some positivist scholars concede that preferences or interests are socially constructed, but not identities. Other positivists suggest that agents impute identities to individual or collective others as a way of simplifying their choices, and still others argue that agents form identities, individually or collectively, as an unintended consequence of what other agents do or say about them. In every instance, agents already have selves in order to acquire identities altering their sense of self.

To make sense of claims about identity, agency and collectives (and thus social arrangements of any kind), I will subject the notion of *personal identity* to a more detailed examination than is customary in the field of International Relations. John Locke may have been the first writer to refer specifically to personal identity. Locke was a physician, and his time saw great advances in the study of human anatomy. Tempting though it is to think of *dissecting* personal identity, I use quite a different metaphor to convey my analytical intentions. *Parsing* personal identity, at least figuratively, is acknowledgment that language makes us who we are.

As I shall argue below, language matters in several ways. One is by reminding us that even our analytical undertakings take form as stories about the world. When I parse personal identity, I also tell a story about the *modern* world and how it came to be what it is. My story starts with the René Descartes and the self-conscious self. This is, after all, the only self each of us can experience directly. More precisely, I start with a strictly subjective yet discursive point of view. In the first instance *I* must be grasped indexically: I am myself here and now, and perhaps only here and now. By extension, knowing myself necessarily in this way gives the contingent world, as I know it, the organizing properties of space and form, time and causality.

I then proceed to show how the indexical self becomes an agent. From Locke onward, personal identity depends on a relation between self and body—specifically, the human body. Becoming aware of my body as an extension of myself—the other side of myself—and, by extension, filling the world with all kinds of bodies permits me (the indexical I) to see my own and other embodied selves acting on my behalf (by seeing, for example, or speaking). In different ways, Adam Smith, who prefigured Sigmund Freud and many of his followers, and David Hume add to the normative and social content of the Lockean scheme. Introducing limited though well-known aspects of their work allows me to conclude the essay with a too brief discussion of the problem of collective identity and collective agency.

My story of the self is simultaneously a story about *me*, as I see myself, and a story about the world that I inhabit, a world of many such selves, and finally a story formed into episodes, with highly styled characters (myself, Descartes, Locke and others) and a fairly conventional plot. Here is the plot: Descartes created the conscious self by strictly separating consciousness from the world of experience. Descartes's self is incomplete yet indispensable. Locke's conception of personal identity complements the Cartesian story without completing it. Other characters (among them Jacques Lacan, Louis Althusser, G.H. Mead, Paul Ricoeur, John Searle, Melanie Klein and D.W. Winnicott) suggest ways of rounding out the self in relation to the world and its contents.

By retelling the story, I make it mine. If I leave myself out of the story, others will see through the passive voice and find me anyway. If I leave Descartes out of the story, others will tell me that he is in it whatever I say. Indeed, I am obliged to tell the story as a story about a world (my world, *the* world) that Descartes irrevocably changed, *or* launched, by discovering *or* inventing a self conscious of itself as a conscious self (these are all different versions of the same story).

Yet I cannot pretend to have told the whole story. Missing from it is any consideration of moral personality and thus such early modern writers as Hugo Grotius and Samuel Pufendorf. Moral persons are not to be confused with individual human beings. Thomas Hobbes developed the conceptual implications of this way of thinking in *Leviathan* (Book I, Chapter xvi):

> a *Person*, is the same as an *Actor* is, both on the Stage and in common Conversation; and to *Personate*, is to *Act*, or *Represent* himselfe, or another; and he that acteth another, is said to beare his Person, or act in his name.
>
> (Hobbes 1991: 112)

The Hobbesian person is an agent whose task it is to act on some*body*'s behalf.

In Hobbes's highly original analysis, the relation between agent and body is, in his terms, a civil relation. Hobbes emphasized one relation over all others: the sovereign person acting on behalf of all, and objective subjects owing obedience to the sovereign. Locke took that same subject and emphasized freedom over subjection. Immanuel Kant and then G.W.F. Hegel sent the Cartesian self in a different direction by emphasizing the subjectivity of consciousness. Granting that these diverging emphases are central to the story of modernity as a collective exercise in identity construction, I nevertheless leave them largely unexplored. Indeed I tax the reader's patience quite enough in an already complicated effort to show how our conscious, embodied, normatively oriented and actively social selves function as agents, for ourselves and others, in a world made social by collective agency.

First person: self and other

Writing autobiographically, Roland Barthes affirmed the principle that "*the subject is merely an effect of language*" (1977: 79).[1] This subject is not just a syntactical unit,

---

1   Quoted in Eakin (1999: 139). Paul John Eakin's constructivist account of autobiographical practices helped me enormously in clarifying and organizing my thoughts for this section of the essay.

the subject in a sentence. Barthes's subject is a substantive unity, the one who speaks or writes sentences, including those sentences whose subject is *I*. As one such subject, I affirm the same principle. I also affirm a complementary principle, implicit in the first. Language is social activity that depends on speaking subjects (and, in the absence of language, no activity is fully *social*).

Together these principles suggest that subjectivity and sociality are conditions, or states of affairs, each of which is necessary for the other to exist. In effect, they constitute each other in an ongoing process for which there is neither beginning nor end. Subjectively speaking (this the only way I *can* speak), I may not come first, but I do have practical priority: without me, there is, at least for me, nothing. In other words, the only place to start is from a strictly subjective point of view which nevertheless makes me "an implicate of language."[2] This is, I believe, the very place that Barthes started. It is, indeed, the place that Descartes taught us all to start—even if it is the place from which to extend, qualify or (attempt to) repudiate Descartes's claim, "I think, therefore I am."

Descartes derived subjectivity from the act, and incontrovertible experience, of thinking for oneself. Such a view would seem to presuppose consciousness, and not just the primary consciousness, or general awareness, that we may impute to a wide range of sentient beings. Cats and whales are conscious in this sense. Descartes's higher-order consciousness requires an awareness of oneself apart from the world of experience, including the very experience of thinking for oneself.[3]

Let me put the conventional Cartesian formula somewhat differently. I am conscious here and now. This is primary consciousness; so are cats and whales conscious here and now. I am further conscious of being here, now. This consciousness is of a higher order than cats and whales possess, it constitutes the (conscious) self from an awareness of here and now, and it is only possible for a linguistically competent being to achieve such an awareness. I must know what it means to say *here* and *now*. I am conscious of being here, now; therefore I am.[4]

I do not wish to suggest that I had utterly no sense of self before I knew what it meant to say I, or here and now. From a very early age, infants actively exhibit an awareness of their surroundings (Stern 1985: 37–68). To do so, it seems

---

2 "One of the enduring myths of modern thought may be that the self is a prelinguistic datum, an 'I' that is the source and monitor of consciousness rather than an implicate of language. If, however, we regard the self as a neurological arrangement whose defining expression is language, then the self as a subject of thought and action must be produced in language" (Frohock 1999: 104–5).

3 Here I follow Edelman (1992: 117–23, 131–6) and more generally subscribe to Edelman's account of the neural basis for consciousness; Searle (1992: 82–100).

4 Descartes himself came to a similar conclusion, at least as I see it: "the proposition *I am, I exist*, is true of necessity every time I state it or conceive of it in my mind" (*Meditations*, 2, in Descartes 1960: 108, emphasis in translation). This essay leaves aside the problem of Descartes's dualism, which depends on a conception of the mind as a "thinking thing" (1960: 110–11), or "interiorized mental substance" (Schrag 1997: 4), and not a description of what the brain does.

likely that they need to be able to integrate their experiences in some fashion and degree, just as cats and whales seem to be able to. Perhaps this process constitutes some sort of self that can express itself (I am reluctant even to use this turn of phrase) obliquely in a social context. Nevertheless, in my infancy, my experiences were, for me, substantially independent of each other. They were here and now events in their own time and place. Having no means to connect these events, and therefore no way to experience the world continuously, I have no memories myself of those events—no memory at all (Nelson 1996: 56–9; Eakin 1999: 106–10). Before I could speak, I had no sense of being *myself*.

Here and *now* are indexical terms. When I use them, they identify me as a subject and locate me in the world. If I am here, I cannot be there; here is the place I am now; now is not then. Bertrand Russell suggested that such terms are necessarily "relative to the speaker" (1940: 108). *This*, for example, has a constant meaning but not a constant referent. *This* can only refer to *I-now* (Russell 1940: 108–15), and, according to Colin McGinn, the indexical pronoun *I* denotes "the self made up of a sequence of I-now stages" (1983: 16n18).[5]

Thinking with indexicals means that I can always place here against there, now against then. I can also relate me—the *I* who I am, here and now—to the *I* who I had been, there and then, by making myself a continuous presence in what is, for me, an ever-changing here and now. This self, through which I am conscious of the world, I call the *indexical self*. It is mine alone, indubitably experienced here and now, imperfectly remembered as there and then in any future here and now that I consciously experience.

Earlier I suggested that I am, as subject, not just a syntactical unit. Nor am I merely a syntactical relation to an ever changing here and now. Writing these words (here and now), I feel the need to respond to Jacques Lacan's indictment (as I take it) that I am an illusion, my conscious self a fiction. Lacan would say that such feelings come from within; the need speaks to an absence of wholeness that the apparent wholeness of others can only remind me of. In responding this need, I produced myself, by thinking, or speaking, of myself as *I*.

When I stop speaking, then and there my self disappears into a void, which, for Lacan at least, is populated by unconscious desires and a profound sense of lacking. When others speak of themselves, the term *I* reappears as an artifact of language; so it is when I speak again. As an indexical term, *I* "belongs to no

---

5   The term *indexical* is due to C.S. Peirce. I draw on McGinn (1983: 15–22); Mühlhäusler and Harré (1990: 87–167); Ricoeur (1992: 44–55); Harré and Gillett (1994: 103–10); and Harré (1998: 56–64), for my understanding of indexical expressions and their importance for a subjective point of view. My exposition of indexical thinking centers on the English pronouns *I* and *you*, both because English is the language that I think in and because English is exceptionally impoverished in its use of pronouns. While this property of English makes the analysis simpler to conduct, the results would be no different for any other language, no matter how rich its pronoun system and various the indexical expressions that it makes available to do the work of pronouns. Also see Mühlhäusler and Harré (1990: 63, Table 4.1); Harré and Gillett (1994: 104–6).

one," as Fred Alford (1991: 39) has aptly observed. I am an invention of the moment (Lacan 1977: 81–8; see Alford 1991: 38–41, for a helpful recapitulation of Lacan's elliptically presented position).

To respond to Lacan, I (need to) ask (him, myself: figuratively) how I learned to produce myself. For Lacan it is all a matter of mirrors, or, should I say, smoke and mirrors. As infants, we respond to what we see when we look in the mirror (Lacan 1977: 1–7). I am skeptical about this argument, both on empirical grounds (many infants never see their own images) and on theoretical grounds (in the absence of outside help in constituting the primordial *I*, it is hard to see what would do the job).

If indeed there need be no actual mirror (cf. Alford 1991: 36), then we might ask what infants do see all the time at this interval in their lives. D.W. Winnicott claimed, against Lacan (1971: 111), that infants see the faces of their caregivers, normally reassuring, sometimes worried or withholding. In those faces, they see themselves as they are seen. Thus has begun "a significant exchange with the world, a two-way process in which self-enrichment alternates with the discovery of meaning in the world of seen things" (Winnicott 1971: 112).

Winnicott saw this process as one in which the self internalizes itself as a whole being. Lacan saw it as a process of incomplete internalization and failed comparison. Failing to see ourselves whole—as whole as others seem to us—we experience emptiness and rage (Alford 1991: 176). Either way, mirror models of the self (as Alford 1991, calls them) are incomplete, basically because they rely too much on ocular metaphors. These models have us relying entirely on our powers of observation and discrimination, and thus they have us learning what we are by ourselves. I learn that I am myself *alone*.

Yet this is not all that has happened. Even if my indexical self is mine alone, I did not acquire it on my own. As John Shotter has suggested, "when small children are addressed as 'you', rather than having information reported to them upon which to base (or not) their individual actions, they are being 'in-structed' in how *to be*" (1989: 145, his emphasis). On Paul John Eakin's reading (1999: 63), this process is *interpellation*. I exist for myself by having been "interpellated"— hailed into existence—by others.

The now familiar concept of *interpellation* is Louis Althusser's: "*all ideology hails or interpellates concrete individuals as concrete subjects*, by the functioning of the category of the subject" (1971: 173, emphasis in translation). Althusser's formulation seems to ignore the hailing voice because of his concern for ideology—voice instrumentally dissociated from particular voices for discursive effect (Butler 1997: 32). Yet, for Althusser, the process of interpellation depends on particular voices. If a policeman says "'Hey, you there!'," the "hailed individual" turns around and, in doing so, "becomes a *subject*" (Althusser 1971: 174, emphasis in translation).

For Shotter, the same process is at work. Hailing voices belong to actual speakers in the infant's world. At some point, the infant responds to a voice saying "Hey, *you*, there," by thinking—by becoming conscious that—"you, there, means I, here: I am here, now." The indexical pronoun *you* brings the indexical self into being.

The self thus constituted—hailed into being—is not Althusser's concrete individual. Interpellating voices implicate the infant's body incidentally and irregularly, and the infant has yet to correlate tactile and visual experiences with voiced messages in any systematic way. At some point, however, the indexical self comes to experience its body as *my* body and thus to recognize itself as a *person*. In this act of *recognition* (an important concept for Althusser 1971: 172–3; also see Benjamin 1995: 27–48), the self hails *you*—the self's body, to which others constantly, indiscriminately apply the term *you*—into an enduring existential relation with *me*. We are life partners in the project of being a person. Eventually the indexical self comes to recognize that it does not, and cannot, exist except as an *embodied self*.[6]

In ordinary language, a person is a human individual who is conscious of being just that. To be conscious is to know oneself as a singular and continuous presence in the world, just as Descartes intimated. This view of the person got its most striking and still influential formulation from Locke, not long after Descartes. Locke's formulation is to be found in a chapter of *An Essay concerning Human Understanding* (1691) entitled "Of Identity and Diversity" (Book II, Chapter xxvii; Locke 1975: 328–48). However contemporary such a title may seem, the chapter opens with a discussion, not of consciousness or selves, but of ideas and substances. Drawn from distinctly pre-modern sources, this was Descartes's frame of reference as well as Locke's.

> §2. We have *Ideas* but of three sorts of Substances; 1. God. 2. Finite Intelligences. 3. *Bodies*. First, God is without beginning, eternal inalterable, and every where; and therefore concerning his Identity, there can be no doubt. Secondly, Finite Spirits having had each its determinate time and place of beginning to exist, the relation to that time and place will always determine to each of them its Identity as long as it exists.
>
> Thirdly, the same will hold for every Particle of Matter, to which no Addition or Subtraction of Matter being made, it is the same.
> (Book II, Chapter xxvii; Locke 1975: 329, his emphasis)

For any substance to have an identity, we must have a clear idea, or concept, of what it is. Inert objects gain their identity because we can perceive the regular conditions of their existence. The same is true for machines and animals, both being the sort of objects that consist of "a fit Organization, or Constructions of Parts, to a certain end, which, when a sufficient force is added to it, it is capable to attain" (Book II, Chapter xxvii, §6; Locke 1975: 331). Finally, the same is true for human minds because the bodies containing them provide the conditions

---

6   For more on the "embodied self," see Schrag (1997: 44–58); Eakin (1999: 26–42). Compare Lakoff and Johnson (1999), on the "embodied mind."

for their existence. Thus the identity of a human being consists "in nothing but a participation of the same continued Life, by constantly fleeting Particles of Matter, in succession vitally united to the same organized Body" (§6; 329–30).

The identity of a human being depends, as a necessary condition, on having a body of one's own. Self-consciousness is another requirement. On Locke's account,

> to find wherein *personal Identity* consists, we must consider what *Person* stands for; which I think, is a thinking, intelligent being, that has reason and reflection, and can consider it self as it self, the same thinking thing in different times and places; which it does by that consciousness, which is inseparable from thinking, and as it seems to me essential to it.
>
> (Book II, Chapter xxvii, §9; Locke 1975: 335, his emphasis)

Here is Descartes's "thinking thing," not just here and now, but "in different times and places."

To engage in thinking in different times and places, one must occupy the same body all the time and everywhere. Thus embodied, consciousness is singular and continuous. This is

> *personal Identity, i.e.* the sameness of rational being: And as far as this consciousness can be extended backwards to any present Action or Thought, so far reaches the Identity of that *Person*; it is the same *self* now it was then.
>
> (Book II, Chapter xxvii, §9; Locke 1975: 335, his emphasis)

As a singular, continuous self, a person experiences the world through perception. "*Self* is that conscious thinking thing, … which is sensible, or conscious of Pleasure and Pain, capable of Happiness or Misery, as far as that consciousness extends" (§17; Locke 1975: 341). Consciousness such as this extends only as far as the body does. If severed from the body, the "little Finger" (Locke 1975: 341) ceases to play a part in a person's conscious life.

The integral relation of mind and body, and not the operations of mind (such as memory), accounts for the self as a singular and continuous consciousness (Rovane 1998: 14). Reconciling the indexical self and the embodied self is an arduous task. Children experience a great deal of frustration as they master motor skills and assemble them into smooth routines. Physical coordination and proprioception take time to develop, as does the process of correlating feelings and desires with distinguishable body states and sensations.

Interpellation is ongoing; the embodied self is a work in progress; the partnered selves never fully merge.[7] The indexical self is always conscious of

---

7   It may, of course, be a cultural prejudice of mine to think that we never fully effectuate this merger. The point of the many Asian arts of self-discipline is to erase

the body—*my* body—as its symbiotic *other*. I find myself perpetually hailing, interrogating, castigating, complimenting and, of course, seeking to control my body—as myself. Nor is this simply a conscious operation, as the many symptoms of emptiness and alienation attest.

Second person: other as agent

The model I present here posits a radically subjective, indexical self that is prior to, dependent on, and more or less at ease with the body. As does Paul Ricoeur's masterful inquiry into "the question of selfhood" (Ricoeur 1992: 1–23), it proceeds from "the subject of utterance" to utterance as action (44–52), and thence to the agent (88–112)—a step that I take below. Ricoeur went on to discuss "personal identity and narrative identity" (1992: 113–39), and so will I. Ricoeur's inquiry emphasized "the dialectical tie between selfhood and otherness" (1992: 317). I do the same by claiming that the body is the *you*, the other, the object, which the indexical self inhabits.

Ricoeur drew on Edmund Husserl's phenomenological conception of "the intrinsically first other" (Ricoeur 1992: 323) to develop his version of self and other dialectics. Husserl is notoriously identified with a subjective point of view so radical that the self has no escape from itself; solipsism ensues. On Ricoeur's account (1967: 123–37; 1992: 319–34), Husserl struggled to devise an escape in three stages. First, we come to recognize our bodies as our own. Then, by analogy, we extend that recognition to other bodies. Finally, and again by analogy, we come to appreciate that other bodies are selves like ourselves. In this context, "analogy is a very general process of prereflective, antepredicative experience" (Ricoeur 1967: 126). Evidently children possess this faculty before they even begin to participate in the world of talk.

Ricoeur doubted that this escape was consistent with the requirements of Husserl's system. Even Husserl entertained these doubts (Ricoeur 1967: 130, 136–7, 142). My doubts are of a different order. Subjectivist from beginning to the end, the Husserlian dialectic of self and other makes the body an abstraction, a necessary term in a series of analogies. Building on Husserl, Ricoeur's inquiry into selfhood moves dialectically from consciousness and subjectivity, to analytic philosophy, the properties of speech and agency, and finally back to subjectivity in confronting the problem of the other. If the body's appearance in Husserl's dialectic is only nominal, it fares no better in Ricoeur's Husserlian turn. There are no bodies in the end because there is only consciousness and thus no way of being—at least no way of being anything other than conscious.

The problem with the subjectivist dialectic of self and other is the disappearance of an objective world, a world of objects including bodies. Leaving philosophical issues aside, one might think the best way to get bodies back into the dialectic

---

the gap between mind and body, "between the will and the act," by getting rid, as the Japanese say, of the "interfering self" (Benedict 1946: 235–6).

is by adopting an objectivist stance. Husserl's contemporary, G.H. Mead, did just this in considering "mind, self, and society from the standpoint of a social behaviorist" (1934; this is the book's full title). Decades later, Mead's discussion of self and other, *I* in relation to *me*, continues to shape scholarly discourse (see, for example, Mühlhäusler and Harré 1990: 90–1; Habermas 1992: 149–204; Gergen 1999: 123–4; Wendt 1999: 327–34; Elliott 2001: 24–31).

"There is," as Mead quite properly claimed, "neither 'I' nor 'me', in the conversation of gestures; … " (1934: 175). The infant experiences conversation in a world of words. "The 'I' is the response of the organism to the attitudes of the others; the 'me' is the organized set of attitudes of others which one himself assumes. The attitudes of the others constitute the organized 'me,' and then one reacts toward that as an 'I'" (Mead 1934: 175, footnote deleted).

The attitudes of others are revealed in speech. As I have said, others hail the indexical self into being. Whether Mead might have accepted this process as a stage in the emergence of the self is not clear from what he did say (but see Habermas 1992: 162, 175–7). Nevertheless, Mead did *not* say, and should not be construed as implying, that the "attitudes of others" constitute *me* as a body. Against Mead, I would say that *I* embody myself. Thus the *I* that others have hailed into being experiences the body as the *you* that *I* come to identify as *mine*—an object belonging to me—and thus as *me*. By contrast, others hail Mead's self into an "organized" yet bodiless existence as *me*, and *I*, reacting to this process, become the self's even more spectral other.

My model of the self, like Husserl's, proceeds in stages. Once hailed into being, *I*, as subject and with the help of others, come to recognize my body as my own and make it my permanent other. By contrast, Mead's model identifies "the 'I' and 'me' as phases of the self" (1934: section title, 192, footnote deleted), the latter dependent on "the recognition of others" and the former on "the recognition of ourselves in the others" (194). We cannot distinguish Mead's *me* from others and their attitudes. Nor can *I*. Not only is Mead's self disembodied. Child or adult, it disappears into whatever society, or "generalized other", in which it happens to be conversationally situated and whose "organized social attitudes" it helplessly absorbs (1934: 152–6).

Neither Husserl's subjective self nor Mead's objective self has a body. Either way, nobody is out there. No wonder many recent scholars of the self start on the other side of the Cartesian equation. The body comes first, and it comes with primary consciousness. According to Eakin (1999: 30, glossing Sacks 1994), primary consciousness is "the organism's unreflexive awareness of its bodily experience" or "body image." There is something fishy about this claim. Consider cats as conscious beings. On the one hand, cats would seem to be unreflexively aware of other bodies as a matter of perceptual differentiation and experience. On the other hand, cats seem to have no image of their own bodies except perhaps as just another body reflected, for example, in a mirror.

As Searle observed, "it is just a fact of biology that organisms that have consciousness have, in general, much greater powers of discrimination than those that do not" (1992: 108). Human beings have remarkable powers when it comes to recognizing human faces and reading emotional states in them. Cats almost certainly do not. Primates may in some degree.

Cats do have perceptual faculties—the five senses, sense of balance, proprioception—that are together far more sensitive than ours. As a property of general awareness, cats no doubt share with human infants the capacity to integrate sensory stimuli into a unified field of experience, a rolling present, at which they are, for all practical purposes, always at the center (see Searle 1992: 128–30; Searle 1998: 80–3). In the circumstance, we should expect cats to have a highly developed capacity to discriminate bodies by identifying particular features to which they respond, as we say, without thinking. If these parts include faces, cats do not naturally respond to them as infants do. These faces are no interface; cats do not think about faces.

More to the point, cats do not think *about* bodies. They never need to, and they never learn to. Nor do very young infants think about bodies. As they become generally aware of the bodies around them—family members, household pets, playthings—and of their own bodies, they become conscious of bodies *as* bodies. They learn to think about bodies, but only by first acquiring their indexical selves: they are conscious, not just here and now in some rolling present, but of *being* here, now.

This sort of consciousness is of a higher order than cats can ever achieve, and it gives us a relation to the world that analytic philosophers call *intentional*. According to Searle, intentionality "is the general term for all the various forms by which the mind can be directed at, or be about, or of, objects and states of affairs in the world" (1998: 85). Searle left two words out of this perhaps too concise definition: "the mind can be directed at, or *think* about, or be *conscious* of objects and states of affairs ..." Oddly, Searle considered the possibility of unconscious intentional states (they are possible only because the "notion of an unconscious mental state implies accessibility to consciousness" (1992: 152, emphasis deleted), but not the possibility of intentional states accompanying primary consciousness such as cats and infants possess.

Nevertheless, it seems clear, at least to me, that such states are *not* possible (but see Nussbaum 2001: 89–138, for a contrary view in the case of at least some animals). Cats and infants do not act intentionally; they do not have goals and they do not make plans for their achievement. Directing the mind to, thinking about, or being conscious of something depends on an indexical self that others have (intentionally) hailed into being. As Searle has pointed out, we for whom intentionality is indistinguishable from consciousness are prone to impute intentionality to objects and states of affairs that we think about. This he has called *as-if* intentionality (1992: 78–82).

We commonly impute intentionality to cats, as if they had indexical selves. In return, cats may mimic intentional states, thereby reinforcing the satisfying fiction that they are conscious of themselves. We do the same with infants. In the process we hail their indexical selves into being and make our imputations of intentionality a self-fulfilling prophecy. As infants grow, they become aware that they need their bodies to be able to act on their own intentions. Having learned to associate bodies with intentional states, they begin to impute intentionality rather indiscriminately to people, pets and playthings. In time, they become more discriminating. They also become more skilled in the practice of assigning consciousness and ascribing intentions to other bodies.

Speaking is indispensable to this process. Only as an embodied self can I speak for my indexical self. Just as others speak for me, my body does the speaking for me. As mind and body working in tandem, I speak for others. Speaking *to* always implies speaking *for*; any speech act must tacitly begin, "Speaking for myself, I hereby say to you that …," unless it is otherwise prefaced.

By speaking for somebody, and by extension acting by any means on somebody's behalf, the speaker, or actor, has become an agent. We do not confine these acts to singular, material bodies. Starting as children, we become exceedingly adept at taking some set of objects and relating them (how this happens is a question for the next section) *as if* they constituted an ensemble with self-organizing properties, a notional body containing a mind for which we presume to speak. We notice others speaking for notional bodies, including some that they construe as including ourselves. As-if intentionality takes the self's relation to one's own body and immediate others, and extends it to a much larger world of bodies, as-if mind-containers, all to be spoken for even as they speak, at least figuratively, for others.

Being a person requires some sort of body, but not necessarily a human body. It does require an agent. Persons exist because other persons, as agents, act to make them so—as Hobbes suggested, some person must personate them. What persons do—*all* that they do—is act on behalf of others, chiefly by speaking for them. Selves are connected to persons through voices that speak, hands that shake other hands or push buttons or throw rocks or hold infants to the breast, living bodies that feel pain and joy. When we speak for ourselves, we are, in Hobbesian language, civil persons, embodied as such, speaking for our conscious, indexical selves.[8]

Third person: object relations

Models of self-other relations—at least those that I have considered so far—posit selves that are equipped to *see* and to respond to what they see. Here Mead's "conversation of gestures" is indicative, as is Lacan's mirror stage in human development. Language enters the picture as an adjunct to sensory experience. An ensemble of "sensible signs" or signifiers, language represents the world in our minds (Locke's *Essay*, Book III, Chapter i–iii; Locke 1975: 361–76), whether

---

8   Notice, as Jessica Benjamin (1998: 7) has, that the German term *Mundigkeit*, normally understood to mean that a person has come of age, literally refers to speaking for oneself, and that Kant described that Enlightenment project as *Unmundigkeit*, or freedom from tutelage.

Locke's conscious world of ideas, Mead's semi-conscious world of attitudes, or Lacan's unconscious world of desires. Signs stand in for objects and relations; as second-order objects, they do not by themselves constitute the object relations upon which intentionality and agency are necessarily predicated.

Fortunately, post-Freudian psychoanalytic theorists such as Winnicott, to whom I return presently, and Klein have directed a good deal of attention to object relations, albeit with less attention to the function of language than one might have hoped. Klein's pioneering work makes it clear that infants start off life with an enveloping physical relation to other bodies—a relation dominated by desire (Klein 1937: 58–62, and Riviere 1937: 6–11; see Alford 1989 for a careful discussion of Klein's work and its implications for social theory). Lacan took desires to be objectless, at least until they are embodied in words.[9] Klein's infants make their mothers objects of desire. Infants have desires about objects in the world; from desires such as these intentions are born.

"The baby's first object of love and hate—his mother—is both desired and hated with all the intensity and strength that is characteristic of the early urges of the baby" (Klein 1937: 58). Love stems from being fed and stimulated; when the infant's desires are thwarted, "he becomes dominated by impulses to destroy the very person who is the object of all his desires and who in his mind is linked up with everything he experiences—good and bad alike." There are some obvious things to say about this pithy formulation. Caregivers are not always mothers, or even women; having destructive impulses is one thing, intending to destroy a person is something else.[10] Less obvious perhaps is the confusion that comes from characterizing the infant's experiences in terms that are ambiguously affective *and* normative.

Klein may have had something quite simple in mind. Experiencing love and hate, infants already know good from bad. Klein's well-known juxtaposition of the "good breast" and the "bad breast" (Klein 1937: 59–62) suggests an infant's, and not a mother's point of view. If so, infants already have the higher-order consciousness that makes a point of view even possible. Klein has taken for granted precisely what I should think is open to challenge. Yet Klein may just as well have intended these terms to function as an arresting metaphor for the concrete and immediate character of object relations in infancy: mothers and

---

9   According to Lacan (1977: 87), "language is not immaterial. It is a subtle body, but body it is. Words are trapped in all the corporeal images that captivate the subject." One might object, however, that objects are not to be confused with images, mirror models notwithstanding.

10   Klein clearly held the latter view: "the baby feels that what he desires in his phantasies has really taken place; that is to say he feels that he *has really destroyed* the object of his destructive impulses, and is going on destroying it ..." (Klein 1937: 61, her emphasis). Mention of "death-wishes" in this context suggests that Freud's theoretical legacy yields an excessive and unsupportable claim. Winnicott (1971: 86–94) also made *destruction* a significant feature of his analysis of object relations in infancy, but with an important qualification: "The word 'destruction' is needed, not because of the baby's impulse to destroy, but because of the subject's liability not to survive, which also means to suffer change in quality, in attitude" (p. 93).

infants share feelings as one. At least for the infant, shared feelings are free of normative content, and so we should construe the terms that Klein used to described them.

It seems likely that Klein had something theoretically richer in mind. She might have meant to say that the infant *feels* good or bad. She also might have meant to say that caregivers, not to mention observers such as herself, have ideas about what *is* good and bad for infants, and that, in keeping with these ideas, people *should* try to make infants feel good. If so, then the problem is not so much confusion as conflation. Given the very intensity of infant desires, people are unlikely to think it always practical or desirable to give infants what they want or even to agree among themselves on what might be desirable in principle. To complicate matters even further, caretakers often feel bad for making infants feel bad, even if they have good reasons for doing so.

In consideration of these ambiguities, it is surely good policy to avoid the terms *good* and *bad* in discussing what goes on in the minds of infants (or cats, for that matter). When I find Klein's colleague Joan Riviere (1937: 46) asserting that the "'desire for goodness' originally (in our babyhood) stirred greed and aggression as well as love and tenderness in us," I first notice the ambiguity introduced by the scare marks. Then the two affective categories—Klein's *love* and *hate*—marking an infant's emotional makeup catch my attention. Finally I am struck by the utter implausibility of the claimed causal relation between good on the one hand and love and hate on the other.

Yet the two categories do seem right, perhaps for all beings possessing primary consciousness (cats for example), even if the right labels for these categories is a problem. As Andrew Ortony and his colleagues (1988: 6–7) have emphasized, the "emotion words" by which we appraise our feelings are always *valenced* (also see Chapter 4). Since there seem to be "two kinds of affective reactions (positive and negative)," and just those two, we should think of them as "the most undifferentiated forms of emotions" (Ortony *et al.* 1988: 29). What makes them affective is that they involve our bodies, or at least our embodied selves. Nevertheless, even the simplest emotions are not just bodily responses to physical stimuli.

Emotions are affective reactions subject to cognitive operations that infants begin to perform at a very early age. As such, emotions always implicate us, as objects, in a world of objects: "all emotions involve some sort of negative or positive reaction to something or other. When additional factor are brought into consideration, increasingly differentiated emotional states may result" (Ortony *et al.* 1988: 29). Infants learn to differentiate objects of both valences into three classes—events as "things that happen," objects as things occupying space, and agents as things "causing or contributing to events" (p. 18). "The distinction between reactions to events, agents, and objects gives rise to three basic classes of emotions: being *pleased* vs. *displeased* (reaction to events), *approving* vs. *disapproving* (reaction to agents), and *liking* vs. *disliking* (reaction to objects)" (p. 33, their emphases).

Whether this elegant scheme works as comprehensive framework for assessing "the cognitive structure of emotions" (Ortony *et al*. 1988: book title), is not my concern here—although I think it does, or at least can be made to. Clearly its authors chose terms indicating that all of these additional cognitive operations involve *appraisal* (Ortony *et al*. 1988: 34–58; also see Nussbaum 2001: 19–56) while trying to avoid such misleading terms as *good* and *bad* (and note Nussbaum's careless claim (2001: 107), that their scheme uses "the good-bad distinction"). Inevitably appraisals have normative implications. As Adam Smith suggested long ago, human passions take form as *sentiments*, and sentiments always have moral properties.

Although Ortony and his colleagues seem not to have been aware how closely Smith's theory of moral sentiments prefigures their framework, we can readily see that each category of appraisal has an implicit normative content above and beyond its positive and negative valences. The least normative appraisals describe reactions to events (pleasure), the most normative describe reactions to agents (approval), and the appraisals of reactions to objects (attraction) fall in the middle. Infants undoubtedly learn the necessary cognitive operations by stages, making more discriminating appraisals as they go along. They become progressively more aware of normative implications. For Smith, human beings desire praise and dread blame—they want to be loved—and this makes admiration and approval the sentiment most central to moral awareness, or sense of duty that all of us possess (*The Theory of Moral Sentiments*, Part III; 1976: 109–78).

Learning to speak makes all of this possible. Infants learn that transitive verbs bring subjects to bear on objects. They say, I want that, and caregivers respond. Infants learn the power of imperatives. They say, give me, and caregivers give. Infants learn that they can cause events by repetition—they say, give me, again and again. As Hume realized, we learn from repetition to make causal inferences. (I say more about this in the following section.) Infants have learned this when they say to caregivers, you *can* give that to me again.

Eventually infants learn that deontic speech ("the language of obligation and permission," Forrester 1989: 1) is an effective, seemingly impersonal, even disinterested—in short, a *good* way—to get others to respond. They say, you *should* give that to me. Infants learn that deontic speech allows them to make judgments by imagining counterfactual situations (Forrester 1989: 35–46). They say, you should always give me that; I should never do this; doing that is right, doing this is wrong. Deontic speech gives children (for they are no longer infants) the power to stand apart from events, objects and relations. As I became skilled in praising or blaming others, or myself, for whatever happens, accepting or rejecting them, or myself, for what we are, approving or condemning them, or myself, for what we choose to do, I acquire a *deontic self*.

Children learn deontic lessons by listening to others and echoing them (this is the auditory equivalent of mirroring). In the process, they internalize a large number of rules, or general deontic propositions, to follow more or less unreflectively. They also act out a variety of object relations, with help from others or their own, by making use of the objects around them. Wraps and blankets, clothes, household items, stuffed animals, toys and pets all serve this function. Winnicott called them "transitional objects"—transitional because these objects occupy an "intermediate zone" or "potential space" between what children have already come to experience as inner and outer realities (Winnicott 1971: 104–10).[11]

In this space, children develop a "third way of living" (Winnicott 1971: 107) where they engage in play, find that "doing things takes time" (p. 41, emphasis deleted), learn self-confidence, and ready themselves for life in the culture of their caregivers. Underlying these developments is a paradox: "the baby creates the object, but the object was there waiting to be created" (Winnicott 1971: 89); discovery and invention cannot be extricated. I suggest that this is not a paradox but a cognitive operation associated with the developing capacity for speech. Children substitute transitional objects for themselves and others, thereby creating new object relations, but only provisionally. Switching back and forth, they explore these relations safely, *as if* they are real for the moment. By speaking for and to their playthings, they master the implications of as-if intentionality (as I observed in the preceding section).

Yet children do more than substitute transitional objects for themselves and others when playing by themselves. Winnicott pointed to it with another of his seeming paradoxes: "the child is alone only in the presence of someone" (1971: 96). Absorbed in play, children shut out the external world, fill space with agents substituting for themselves and others, and watch object relations ensue as if the agents had minds of their own. They are spectators in worlds of their own making. Standing at a distance, they meddle nonetheless by questioning agents' intentions, counseling them on their choices, commending their successes and blaming them for their failures. Children speak to their surrogates in the same deontic terms that they hear themselves and others spoken to.

In short, the intermediate zone is a place of moral sentiments. Smith recognized the importance of the engaged spectator in any such world. In his opinion, "the spectator must, first of all, endeavour, as much as he can, to put himself in the situation of the other …" (*The Theory of Moral Sentiments*, Part I, Section I, Chapter iv, §6; Smith 1976: 21). Nevertheless, the spectator should endeavor to be impartial, and to be impartial one must keep one's distance (III, iii, §41; Smith 1976: 154). More than observer, Smith's spectator passes judgment, not just on the actions of others, but on one's own actions. Within

---

11 "From the beginning the baby has maximally intense experiences *in the potential space between the subjective object and the object objectively perceived*, between me-extensions and not-me. This potential space is at the interplay between there being nothing but me and there being objects and phenomena outside omnipotent control" (Winnicott 1971: 100, his emphasis). I might add body parts and wastes (for example, fingers, feces) to the objects in this space, although Winnicott seems not to have had them in mind (p. 9).

each of us resides an impartial spectator, "the great inmate of the breast" (*The Theory of Moral Sentiments*, III, iii, §1; Smith 1976: 134), who always speaks in deontic terms.

In Smith's famous characterization, the impartial observer who resides within is *conscience*. Discovered, or invented, as an object that can only function by standing apart, the conscience resists complete internalization. Instead we take the child's world of transitional objects with us into adulthood, where it shelters the deontic self. To the extent that the deontic self functions as a third party arrangement, we should see a reflective stance toward rules and a disposition to appraise the actions of all persons impartially. Not least are those persons whom we identify as ourselves.

It seems likely that cultural variations in childcare, and especially in the provision of transitional objects, time alone and opportunities for play, will have a significant effect on the development of the deontic self. The striking resemblance between Smith's impartial spectator and Freud's super-ego (Freud 1960: 22–36; 1961: 83–96) suggests a particular cultural variation emphasizing solitude, distance and impartiality at the expense of "fellow feeling" (*The Theory of Moral Sentiments*, I, i, i, §5; 1976: 10; and see Roland 1988). The voice of conscience need not depend on, or eventuate in, Cartesian consciousness or Kantian autonomy. Nor does it warrant Smith's preoccupation with "self-command" as "self-denial" (*The Theory of Moral Sentiments*, V, ii, §§8–9; 1976: 204–7) or Freud's with "unconscious guilt" (Freud 1960: 50–4; Klein 1937: 62–6).

Deontic speech grants us many ways in which to express our moral sentiments. We talk to ourselves (better: our selves); we echo the sentiments of others. As Winnicott's work so clearly implies (and Benjamin's confirms, 1995: 6), these are not mutually exclusive processes of moral development. They should never be construed as such.

Person plural: being with others

Psychoanalytic theorists have much to say about *relational selves*.[12] So, too, have constructivist scholars of the self (Eakin 1999: 43–98; Gergen 1999: 115–41). What the latter fail to say is that the relation of self to others (one's own body, other embodied selves) proceeds beyond the infant's world of family intimates on two dimensions. One is spatial, the other temporal.

The *spatial* extension of the infant's world depends on an imaginative capacity to discover (and thus to invent) bodies that speak to and for each other, both by mimicry and play. The constructivist treatment of relational selves ignores this

---

12 "In recent years analysts from diverse psychoanalytic schools have converged in the effort to formulate relational theories of the self. What these approaches share is the belief that the human mind is interactive rather than monadic, that the psychoanalytic process should be understood as occurring between subjects rather than within the individual" (Benjamin 1995: 27–8, citations deleted).

process. Instead, it makes the self's extension a *temporal* process. The self comes to apprehend that its relation to others is continuous over time, and that the experience of continuity applies to oneself. Such a process turns on memory (in both senses of the phrase).

Memory is, of course, a conspicuous property of higher-order consciousness. Not least does it allow us to escape the rolling present to which our sensory faculties would otherwise condemn us. Locke had little to say about memory. Were it the key to self-consciousness, Locke could not have said, with no qualification or explanation, that "a Man Drunk and Sober" is "the same person," as such responsible for acts that he cannot remember (*Essay*, Book II, Chapter xxvii, §22; 1975: 343).

Yet most interpretations of Locke make personal identity dependent on the "memory relation" (Rovane 1998: 14; see Perry 1975: 12–15; Kerby 1991: 24–7, for conspicuous examples). Hume, not Locke, deserves credit for insisting on the importance of memory for personal identity. For Hume, memory is the key because it gives meaning to the many disconnected perceptions that our senses shower upon us.

> As memory alone acquaints us with the continuance and extent of this succession of perceptions, 'tis to be consider'd, upon that account chiefly, as the source of personal identity. Had we no memory, we never shou'd have any notion of causation, nor consequently of that chain of causes and effects, which constitute our self or person. But having once acquir'd this notion of causation from the memory, we can extend the same chain of causes, and consequently the identity of our persons beyond our memory, and can comprehend times, and circumstances, and actions, which we have entirely forgot, but suppose in general to have existed.
>
> (*A Treatise of Human Nature*, Book I, Part iv, Section vi, "Of personal identity"; Hume 1978: 261–2)

The meaning that memory confers on perception Hume took to be one sort of relation—the relation of cause and effect—by which the mind gives order to the world (*Treatise*, I, I, v, "Of relations"; Hume 1978: 15). Memory alone cannot account for our sense of singular and continuous consciousness because all of us, and not just Locke's drunkard, forget or misremember. By supplementing and correcting memory with causal inference, we can fill the gaps. Furthermore, this is a collective activity. We fill the gaps by sharing memories and by drawing inferences from our shared habits, or customs (*Treatise*, I, III, xvi, "Of the reason of animals"; Hume 1978: 176–9). Hume's self-conscious beings are creatures like none other: they are creatures of convention.

Hume's masterful analysis takes memory beyond the recall of events and the exchange of reports. Memory is inextricable from the construction of a coherent past and the projection of a plausible future. Such acts are characteristically social (indeed they take their most characteristic form in the stories we tell) and yet they eventuate in personal identity—a strictly personal identity at that. This is because each self can vouch for its very own existence in the past and project itself into the future. While any*one* can perform these operations at any given moment of consciousness, with coaching from others as needed, *one* must do so within *one*'s own body.

Following Hume, though perhaps unawares, constructivists hold that there is more to memory than recall; "memories share the constructed nature of all brain events" (Eakin 1999: 18, 106, drawing on Rosenfield 1988: 81–9). The construction of memory proceeds within minds but, even more, it is a social process. Every time we speak of the past, the very act of speaking alters the past as we remember it. From an early age, children hear others speak of their memories; as speaking subjects, children share their memories with others. What we share with others—the play, the give and take, of speech—alters all the more.

Our memories tend to be fragmentary, inconsistent with what others claim to remember, distorted by so much else that we think and feel. To make sense of the past, we are likely to fit our jumbled memories into a conventional format. No format is more conventional, more commonly deployed, than the story. We order our memories about ourselves and others from beginning to end. The serial arrangement of memories we take to correspond to the continuous unfolding of time it*self*.

Telling stories about ourselves complements the spatial process of populating the world with bodies. Everybody has a story; the embodied self is the story's one indispensable *character*. The characters in any story experience the world as a series of encounters, reflect on it as a sequence of *events*. Telling a story brings order to this experience by forming encounters into *episodes*, and the sequence of events into a *plot*—a sequence of relations. Characters occupy bodies; bodies have beginnings, continuous histories, foreseeable ends. Bodies acquire minds, bodies lose minds, minds come to an end of some sort when bodies do.[13]

There is more. We tell stories to others, and we listen to others tell their stories. Already social, memory turns collective as we go on telling our stories. The joint record of overlapping experiences excuses forgetting and compels remembering; it functions as a standard. Always the other in others' stories that duly become our stories, we substantiate what it means to be *we*—a body of others (of which I am one) who are embodied selves (just like me). The speaking self is a fully social self only as a *storied self*.[14]

---

13 Even Descartes, believing that "we are essentially composite beings consisting of body and mind" (Schneewind 1998, 190), told such a story: "I am, I exist, that is certain. But for how long? For as long as I think. If I ceased to think, I might very well cease to be, or to exist, at that moment" (*Meditations*, 2; Descartes 1960: 110).

14 I had settled on the term *storied self* before reading Eakin's engrossing discussion (1999: 99–141), in which it occupies a central place. Also see Nelson (1996: 183–219) on "the emergence of the 'storied mind.'" *Narrative* is the term favored in the literature. See, for example, MacIntyre (1984: 118, "narrative selfhood"); Polkinghorne (1988: 105, "self-narrative," and 148, "narrative and the self"); Kerby (1991, "narrative and

After Locke, the discussion of personal identity took the individual human being for granted as its unit of analysis. If the "we-experience," as Calvin Schrag has said, consists of "being-with-others" (1997: 77–80), being—*being* in a double sense—sets the terms of reference. After Hume, no one could safely disregard the social content of personal identity (although its social construction is another matter). Singular human beings share memories, tell stories, synchronize their habits, preferences and expectations, and otherwise engage each other in an amazing variety of social practices. Their identities are shaped accordingly.

Collective identity is another matter. Insofar as *being* constitutes our frame of reference, the concept of collective identity is hard to specify, its use for the most part metaphorical. Yet the concept is everywhere. "Someone's 'identity', in much contemporary writing, is not their singularity as a unique person, but the group, class or type to which they belong" (Harré 1998: 6).

Humean conventionalism allows for the possibility of collective identity, but only in a weak sense. Memories shared, embellished, rationalized, and imaginatively deployed constitute a collective, yet ephemeral state of affairs. Not only is such an identity radically disembodied, the collective, such as it is, lacks consciousness. Lacking a body, there is no one to act. Lacking consciousness, there is no one at all.

Even in the absence of collective consciousness, it is still possible to make a stronger case for collective identity. Consider Carol Rovane's "normative analysis of personal identity" (1998: 160–9). Rovane compared two situations: some collection of human beings (*group person*), and a single human being who seems to have two or more personalities (*multiple person*). In the latter case, these personalities may be co-conscious. Yet this does not help us to locate personal identity.

In both cases, each person(ality) must be capable of long-term planning and coordinated activity, allowing them to "deliberate and act together—that is, as one person with a rational point of view" (Rovane 1998: 173). Implied by these claims is a larger one that I touched on earlier: possessed as we are of higher-order consciousness, we are beings with "goals and projects" (a phrase that Nussbaum, 2001, for example, used repeatedly). We make plans to achieve our goals; long-term plans turn goals into projects. Long-term planning is Rovane's key to personal identity.

By planning, we formulate our current intentions for future action in such a way that we will remember then what we wanted to accomplish later and, later having become then, act accordingly.[15] There is nothing about long-term

---

self"); Alford (1991: 14, "the narrative self"); Ricoeur (1992: 140–68, "the self and narrative identity"); Neisser and Fivush (1994: subtitle, "self-narrative"); Schrag (1997: 26, "narrating self"); Benhabib (1998: 341–8, "the narrative model of identity constitution"); Frohock (1999: 76–113, "narrative persons").

15 See Rovane (1997: 149–50) for a full and formal treatment of what is involved for a person to engage in long-term planning, and see Chapter 7, below, on the relation of intentions, plans and policies in strategic contexts.

planning that restricts it to individual human beings. Shared memory and accessible records make collective planning feasible. After, shared memories and joint plans are both schematic representations of states of affairs, one imposed on the past, the other projected on the future.

Having planned together, any one (or more) of us whose plans these are can act on them. Nevertheless, these acts do not constitute a group person, or collective identity, in any stronger sense than Hume's, until a further condition is met. We need to know on whose behalf individual human beings are acting when they act on a joint plan. In making clear *who* acts, Rovane failed to specify for *whom* such acts are taken.

Rovane held that we are *agents* when we execute joint plans. In her words, "the sort of agency that individual persons exercise in long-term activities does not differ in any essential way from the sort of joint agency that persons exercise together" (Rovane 1998: 150). I propose that we are agents only insofar as we act for some *person*. When we act individually, in hopes that others' acts fit together with our own acts, according to plan, we act for ourselves.

In the process of acting for ourselves, we substantiate our personal identities as individual human beings. We may also act as agents for others individually, with the same effect on ourselves and perhaps on those others. When we act, as agents, for a group of others (which may include ourselves), we act for the others *as if* they, or we, are a single *body*, known to us all as such. Again, we substantiate our personal identities through such acts, and perhaps we do the same for the identities of that body's other members.

Joint plans may designate agents. Or agency may be taken for granted as a background condition. Either way, individually conscious human beings are the body's agents. As agents, they are the bearers of personal identity. Indeed they are the bearers of identity whether they are agents for themselves (as persons), or for other conscious human beings (as persons), or for bodies of individually conscious human beings with whom they identify and on whose behalf they act (as persons). There is more than one sort of person in the world.

6

STRUCTURE? WHAT STRUCTURE?

(2009)

Kenneth Waltz's name is irrevocably associated with the term *structure*. Waltz's theory of international politics, as expounded in the 1970s, is a systemic theory and, for that reason, a structural theory (1975: 45; 1979: 40). His systemic perspective quickly came to be known as *structural realism*, and Waltz (2000) has himself adopted this label. In an act of sublime flattery, one of Waltz's most strident critics, Alexander Wendt, went so far as to describe constructivism in the field of International Relations "as a kind of 'structural idealism'" (1999: 1; also see p. xiii). In this essay, I suggest that Waltz's theory also bears describing as a kind of structural idealism, though hardly the kind that Wendt has espoused. Appropriately developed, Waltz's conception of structure suits, even supports, a strong version of constructivist social theory.

More precisely, I take Waltz's theory to be grounded in a philosophical position closer to Immanuel Kant's than to the philosophical realism that Wendt has promoted. *Philosophical realism* and its variants *scientific realism* and *critical realism* (not be confused with *political realism*) start with the claim that "the world is independent of the mind and language of individual observers" (Wendt 1999: 1; see below for Wendt's full definition). According to Michael Devitt (a realist himself), modern philosophical constructivism draws on two ideas from Kant and a third one that does not.

> *Constructivism* The only independent reality is beyond the reach of our knowledge and language. A known world is partly constructed by the imposition of concepts. These concepts differ from (linguistic, social, scientific, etc.) group to group, and hence the worlds of groups differ. Each such world differs only relative to an imposition of concepts.
>
> (Devitt 1997: 235)

Constructivism is typically, if unhelpfully, described as philosophically idealist. The updated, post-Kantian constructivism defended in these pages, and with it the constructivist social theory that I prefer, draws on Aristotle to avoid the idealist-materialist binary suggested in Wendt's characterization of constructivism.

In developing a structural theory, Waltz devoted almost no attention to philosophical matters. He simply declared that testing a theory should meet "philosophy-of-science standards" and assumed that positivist philosophy does the job (1975: 2; 1979: 1).[1] Indeed his stringently expressed positivism and tidy theory encouraged a later generation of scholars, confronted with Continental social theory and philosophy, to pose post-positivist philosophical challenges that Waltz found bewildering (Waltz 1986: 337). Nevertheless, his treatment of structure brings a central philosophical issue to the fore: are structures *real*— really "out there" in the world—even if they cannot be observed? Philosophical realists set themselves against strong positivists *and* post-Kantian constructivists on this question. The former answer yes, the latter no.

For all the importance of Waltz's conception of structure, it is not, in my opinion, well-understood. Scholars have subjected it to intermittent, sometimes acute commentary, but they have never made its most consequential features the center of attention. After Waltz presented his structural theory in the 1970s, he has not given his critics a concerted response to their interpretations. Nor has he systematically restated his position. I attempt to do so, however presumptuously, because I believe Waltz's philosophical stance is sounder than most of his critics claim, most recently, from a realist point of view.

Philosophical realism is now in fashion among International Relations theorists (Wendt 1999: Chapter 2; C. Wight 2006; Kurki 2008: Chapters 5–6). That Waltz's stringently expressed positivism and a post-Kantian constructivism turn out to be philosophical allies against philosophical realism, many scholars will find an odd and uncongenial claim. Waltz may find it so. As we shall see, there are many places where he seems to undercut his declared position on theory by imputing objective properties to system structure. In some instances, he may simply have been careless. Cumulatively, they raise the possibility that he is an unreflective philosophical realist after all.

In substantiating these several claims, I divide this essay into six sections. The first section traces Waltz's view of political structure in his early work. The next section recapitulates Waltz's conceptualization of structure and its philosophical grounding. The third section addresses the question of his (or any) theory's relation to "reality." Waltz has drawn a line between theory and reality, only to subvert in it in a way that any philosophical realist would applaud. The fourth section further illustrates Waltz's difficulty with structural theory and

---

1   For a checklist of these standards, see Waltz (1975: 12; 1979: 13). Waltz could plausibly assume that his readers would be familiar with the *deductive-nomological* or *covering law* model of scientific explanation favored by positivist philosophers. See Hempel (1965).

institutional reality. The fifth section summons the ghost of Milton Friedman to confront two of Waltz's critics.

The last section considers the vexing question of any theory's fit to a world already talked into existence. It shows how close Waltz has been to a stance, grounded in post-Kantian constructivism, that solves his problem with theory's relation to reality and specifies the conditions under which any social theory can make sense or use of the term *structure*. The essay concludes on a speculative note. Had Waltz come to appreciate philosophical differences among positivists, realists and constructivists, he might better have guarded against the realist tendency to find causal structures in the world. Had he seen the value in situating his structural theory of international politics in an updated constructivism, our field might look very different today.

Political structure

Waltz's first book, *Man, The State and War*, makes occasional use of the term *structure* in discussing the three "images" or coherent sets of ideas commonly invoked to explain the incidence of war. Thus the chapter spelling out the second image is subtitled "International Conflict and the Internal Structure of States" (1959: 80). We soon learn, however, that, "the internal organization of states is the key to understanding war and peace." *Structure* and *organization* are synonyms.

Waltz described the third image as an absence of "social structure"— "institutionalized restraints and institutionalized methods of altering and adjusting interests"—and, as such, a condition that is conducive to war. While states have "political structure" and "military organization," the absence of institutional arrangements among states is itself "a general structure that permits them to exist and wreak their disasters." We see here an early version of Waltz's famous claim (1959: 81, 124, 159, 184–5, 231) that "international anarchy" has structure even if it has no discernible institutional features giving it a social character. How we would know what this structure is in the absence of institutional clues he did not yet say.

A few years later, Waltz offered a clue. Here defined as "the pattern according to which power is distributed," structure reveals itself in the "global balance of power" (1967a: 229n18, 228). Treated by states' leaders as a "game" with its own rules, the balance of power would seem to qualify as an institution, though an institution (unlike those constituting the internal structure of states) conducive to at least limited war (1967a: 218). Had Waltz construed the balance of power as an institution, he would have found congenial company.[2] That did

---

2   The Treaty of Utrecht gave the balance of power formal notice in 1713. "Thenceforward, for two hundred years, the balance of power was generally spoken of as if it were the constituent principle of international society, and legal writers described it as an indispensable condition of international law" (M. Wight 1968a: 153, footnote deleted).

not spare him the need to consider other patterned features of international politics in institutional terms: international law, diplomacy, great power concert and war itself (Bull 1977: 74; also see Chapter 10). Instead he distanced himself from states' relations, where social content expresses itself with kaleidoscopic complexity, and took the balance of power to be a "model"—whether his own model stipulating the presence of at least two states, or the "old" model based on three or more states (Waltz 1967a: 218).

Waltz's second book, *Foreign Policy and Democratic Politics*, is a straightforward consideration of the question: "Do the institutions and processes of democracy make excellence in foreign policy difficult to achieve?" (1967b: 8) To answer this question, with its second image resonances, Waltz compared "various characteristics of the British and American political systems" to see how "political structures differ and, in their differences, affect the processes and policies of governments (1967b: 17). Systems have structure; political systems, or states, have political structures, political arrangements, governmental structures or, more simply, governments. Waltz used these terms more or less interchangeably to characterize institutions of a familiar kind (1967b: 36). They do not signal a theoretical stance about the way Waltz's three images might be related, and they carry no conceptual freight beyond the standard concerns of political science at the time that Waltz wrote the book.

When Waltz turned directly to theory-building in the following decade, we see a continuing interest in "political structure." Waltz's definitive exposition of his structural theory, *Theory of International Politics*, contains a comparative discussion of "political institutions" (also called "governmental systems") in Britain and the United States (1979: 82–8) that could have been taken directly from *Foreign Policy and Democratic Politics*. Preceding this discussion, however, is a newly developed conceptualization of structure.

> A domestic political structure is thus defined, first, according to the principle by which it is ordered; second, by specification of the functions of formally differentiated units; and third, by the distribution of capabilities across those units ... The three-part definition of structure includes only what is needed to show how the units are positioned or arranged. Everything else is omitted.

Thanks to a readily identified ordering principle, "[s]tructure is not a collection of political institutions but rather the arrangement of them." For the political structure of the state, this principle is hierarchy. "The units—institutions and agencies—stand vis-à-vis each other in relations of super- and subordination." Thus organized, "governmental institutions and offices" engage in functionally specified activities as the "concrete counterparts" of functionally differentiated structures (Waltz 1979: 82, 88).

By contrast, international politics constitute a system consisting of functionally undifferentiated units, or states, over which there is no political structure or, concretely, subordinating institutions. Anarchy is the organizing principle, not hierarchy (Waltz 1979: 93–7). In a preliminary version of Waltz's structural theory, he was more concise. "Domestic systems are centralized and hierarchic. International systems are decentralized and anarchic" (1975: 46).

Models, theories, science

In his 1967 essay, Waltz made passing reference to the balance of power as a model. In the 1970s, he specified his conception of *model* to anchor his definition of *theory* and illustrate a theory's relation to *reality*. Although Waltz's views on theory are well-known, I want to emphasize—as few other scholars have—the importance that Waltz attached to models in linking theories to "the real world."[3]

> A theory, while related to the world about which explanations are wanted, always remains distinct from that world. Theories are not descriptions of the real world; they are instruments that we design in order to apprehend some part of it. "Reality" will therefore be congruent neither with a theory nor with a model that may represent it.
>
> (1975: 8)[4]

The referent for the pronoun "it" concluding this passage is not reality but theory. Waltz held that the term *model* has two senses: "a model represents a theory" or "a model pictures reality while simplifying it, say, through omission or reduction in scale" (1975: 8–9; 1979: 7). Precisely what Waltz meant by the term *represent* in this context is not at all clear. I suggest that every theory *is*, or must take the form of, a model, that theories *represent* one kind of model (theoretical models), and that all models are simplifications, as indeed are all representations. Thus a model airplane represents reality ("A model airplane should look like a real airplane"), but this kind of model cannot, by itself, explain how airplanes manage to stay airborne. By contrast, a theoretical model might explain why airplanes fly but would not look like an airplane. "Explanatory power is gained by moving away from 'reality'" (1975: 9; 1979: 7).

---

3   This omission is particularly telling in Goddard and Nexon (2005). Rather than taking advantage of Waltz's discussion of models, they introduced the concept of analytical systems. Such systems "are not *real* in an ontological sense—for the most part there is no real distinction between personalities, culture and social systems, and in reality all will affect action and order" (p. 17, their emphasis). As I hope to make clear, analytical systems are models, and conversely all models are analytical in this sense. Yet Waltz quite properly reserved the term *analysis* and its cognates for the procedure of "reducing the entity to its discrete parts and examining their properties and connections" (1975: 44; 1979: 39). Systemic models are *not* reductive, or analytical, in Waltz's sense.

4   Waltz (1979) omits the second sentence in this passage and slightly alters the first sentence of the remainder (pp. 6–7).

Waltz was not saying that models are not real in themselves. "Theories do construct *a* reality, but no one can say it ever is *the* reality" (1979: 9, his emphasis). Maps are models too. They provisionally substitute one reality for another, in the process becoming an integral feature of the world they are said to represent. A theoretical model is a map representing/simplifying "some part" of the world—"a picture, mentally formed, of a bounded realm or domain of activity" (1979: 10)—on which the theorist has marked a sequence of events that will necessarily take place. Necessity arises not from the world as such, but from the choices the theorist has made in representing the world. A model airplane may fly if the plans for it (map) provide for all the right components—motor, wings, controls, etc.—connected in the right order.

Drawing maps, making choices on what events to connect, putting things in the right order are imaginative acts, involving guesswork but harnessed to experience. Does the theorist's model work—does it seem to explain events in the real world that it purports to? Can it be made to work better? These questions follow from the familiar model of modern science, itself institutionalized through general acceptance of the procedural rules (the scientific method) for checking theoretical models (models stipulating necessary relations) against evidence taken to represent some feature of "the real world" and refining those models accordingly.

Thirty years ago, Waltz endorsed this model of science. I see no reason to think he would repudiate it now. He acknowledged the importance it assigns to imagination (in his words, creativity and intuition): "To form a theory requires envisioning a pattern where none is visible to the naked eye" (1979: 10)—or, for that matter, to any of the senses no matter how much instrumental assistance we give them.[5] By implication, there are many patterns visible as such, if not to all observers, then to those observers with some idea where to look.

For most observers, rules, institutions, and agents variously constitute visible patterns (*constitute* in both passive and active senses). The invisible patterns that models propose are structures, and structures are theoretically relevant if they function either as causes or as limits on causal processes (Waltz 1979: 73, where Waltz considered "structures as causes"). Different models assign causal significance to different structures and direct observers to look for visible patterns (including especially frequent if not constant conjunctions). Rather contentiously, Waltz's theory (1979: 99–101) invokes a restrictive conception of structure—so restrictive it eliminates most visible patterns from consideration (Kaplan 1979: 36–48).

Waltz's restrictive conception of structure discounts the visible presence of institutions plausibly enabling Waltz's structure of international politics to function as the model requires. Other scholars propose models defining structure

---

5   It should be clear that, for Waltz, the familiar expression "naked eye" is not to be taken literally, as if we do *not* subject perceptions to cognitive processing when we *are* not specifically forming a theory. As will become clear below, Waltz's position is quite the converse: we are envisioning patterns whatever we do.

less restrictively and, like Waltz, ask how they comport with some part of the world (see James 2002: 44–9, for a good summary). In the pursuit of reliable knowledge about the world, scholars oriented to science tack between their theoretical models and the best evidence they can muster. Doing so reconciles the rationalist and empiricist strands in Western philosophy and eventuates in demonstrable progress in explaining and predicting the course of events. Lack of progress means weak theory, bad science, an absence of cumulative findings and an incentive to devise better (logically sound, empirically testable) theories (James 2002: 66–116).

Behind Waltz's affirmative view of science is the Humean presumption that we can never conclusively know the causes of the world's many apparent regularities. Where Hume's constant conjunctions remain constant, we can construe them as *laws*. "Each descriptive term in a law is directly tied to observational or laboratory procedures, and laws are established only if they pass observational or experimental tests." Concepts such as "force, and absolute space and time" Waltz called "theoretical notions"; his conception of a law in science is another such theoretical notion (1975: 3; 1979: 5). Waltz's conviction that the world consists of observable phenomena and theoretical notions, neither reducing to the other, makes him a strong positivist.

"Of purported laws," Waltz would have us ask, "are they true?" (1975: 4; 1979: 6). But this is not quite right. We ask instead, can we trust them? Insofar as any given theory seems to explain the constancy of an empirical generalization, that theory increases our confidence in the generalization it explains, just as factual constancy increases confidence in a given theory. Yet this virtuous circle never produces truth beyond the causal links stipulated to be true by a given theory's very terms. If a theory is true, it is true only of, or to, itself, and not true of the world to which it claims to refer.

Formal causes, institutional effects

As Waltz has said, to form a theory, we must sense a pattern. It is possible that Waltz has always subscribed to a Platonic doctrine of forms. Behind the many patterns that our senses make real to us, and their sole cause, is a truly real world, consisting entirely of perfect forms only dimly available to the senses. Early modern natural law thinkers advanced a similar metaphysical doctrine. By exercise of reason, we can find the underlying order of the world in what we see. Even now, quite a few scientists reflexively hold this view. Constant conjunctions are no accident, laws capture truths, theories order laws, science finds the larger truth informing laws we know to be true.

On the evidence presented in the preceding section, I doubt that Waltz is, or has ever been, a Platonist or, in Kant's terms, a dogmatic philosopher. Waltz would seem to be closer to Aristotle than to Plato or the dogmatic rationalists. Aristotle rejected Plato's doctrine of forms: "things cannot come from the Form in any of the usual senses of 'from'" (*Metaphysics* I, 987a29–992a23, quoting

991a20–1; Barnes 1984: 1561–8, quoting p. 1566). Nevertheless, forms matter, but not as matter. Consider the second of Aristotle's four senses of the term *cause*—material, formal, efficient and final. A *formal cause* is the "form [*eidos*] or pattern [*paradeigma*], i.e., the formula [*logos*] of the essence [*ti esti*, what is, rendered by medieval Platonists as *essentia*, is-ness]" (*Metaphysics* V, 1013a26; Barnes 1984: 1600); see Chapter 4 on Aristotle's metaphysical "system").

Aristotle used the production of a bronze sphere to illustrate formal causality. We see spheres in the world consisting of various materials (for example, water droplets, soap bubbles), just as we see disks (the sun, moon). Any given sphere is made "by art [*technê*] or by nature [*phusis*, the whole to which all causes ultimately lead] or by some capacity [*dunamis*, developmental potential, where form is an emergent property]" (Aristotle, *Metaphysics* VII, 1033b8; Barnes 1984: 1632). Forms have many sources in a world already laden with forms. Forms must be realized materially; they give the formless stuff of the world recognizable properties. Mindless empiricism and pure materialism are no more plausible than Platonic idealism.

Aristotle's use of the term *poieô* (to make or produce) does favor art over nature in telling us where forms "come from."[6] "But that there is a *bronze sphere*, this we make. For we make it out of the bronze and the sphere; we bring the form into this particular matter, and the result is a bronze sphere" (Aristotle, *Metaphysics* VII, 1033b8–10; Barnes 1984: 1632; emphasis in translation). Given this example (Aristotle's only one), it would seem that form—in this case a spherical form—is a property that an artisan gives to a formless medium such as bronze (which is then a *material cause*). In such a case, the artisan must have this form in mind, as a goal, and use it as a model or pattern (thereby serving as the *efficient* cause).

Aristotle's conception of formal cause is ambiguous. It does seem to imply the prior existence of a model (map, formula). If not a Platonic essence, then the model must "come from" a human mind and be given to the stuff of the world. Produced as an imaginative act, the model generalizes and idealizes the human experience with relevant forms. What then does anyone using the model produce? It can only be a model: a sphere that happens to be made of brass, or an object unlike any other that testifies to the imaginative power of the mind responsible for it, or an airplane that, as a working model or prototype, invites the production of any number of airplanes of the same model.

Every model assigns formal properties to its contents. If the model stipulates a formal causal relation between some set of elements making it up, then *that* relation is internal to the model. As a theorist, Waltz has formed a model of international politics in which a formally specified structure functions as a formal cause. That cause has effects that are no less formal—they are entailed

---

6   Aristotle's discussion of "why some things are produced spontaneously as well as by art" is tautological: in some instances matter "can move itself" while in other instances it "is incapable of this"; form drops out of the discussion (*Metaphysics* VII, 1034a9–21; Barnes 1984: 1632–3).

by the model, as a closed system of relations, and they can only take place within the model.

"A systems approach is successful only if structural effects are clearly defined and displayed" (Waltz 1979: 58). Given Waltz's Aristotelian model of models, this demanding standard must be honored. He issued it in a critique of Morton Kaplan's several models of international systems (Waltz 1975: 56–54; 1979: 50–9). In turn, Kaplan criticized Waltz for denying that Kaplan's models properly specified structural causes (1979: 42–8). In my opinion, *Theory of International Politics* warrants criticism because it fails to meet Waltz's own standard for specifying structural effects.

Two chapter titles reveal as much: "Structural Causes and Economic Effects" and "Structural Causes and Military Effects" (Chapters 7–8). Few of these effects are "structural" in the formal sense that Waltz's model requires. Thus Waltz opened the second of these chapters with a brief discussion of stability as a structural effect in balance of power systems. Indeed, states of (in)stability or (dis)equilibrium are standard concerns in systemic theorizing, and they are typically treated in functional terms. Passing over these concerns, Waltz's discussion quickly turned to the institutional dynamics of alliance formation and interaction.

Most observers would call these dynamics *real effects*, to be found in the world, not the model. I would call them *institutional effects*. When agents "see" a world of patterns and act on them, in the first instance by telling each other what they see, they have begun a process of transforming patterns into institutions (models whose formal properties are more or less fixed and publicly available as ensembles of rules). Both chapters detail what governments do: agents' choices take effect in and through institutions. In this process, agents have an effect on those institutions through their choices, if only to reinforce institutional rules.

Waltz has never denied the causal significance of agents and institutions (recall the first and second images). Indeed he has acknowledged that structures do no more than "condition behaviors and outcomes" (1986: 343). If agents are moved by unseen forces, their choices foreclosed by conditions they are not even aware of, then there is little point in calling them agents at all. If agents do make choices with consequences, then we need to ask, how do agents *know* which structures constrain them in what ways? To suggest that agents must have a relevant structural model in mind, or that institutional rules must somehow accord with such a model, calls for theories about structural effects as causes of institutional effects.

"Structures select"

Speaking metaphorically (metaphors are simple models), Waltz drew a clear line between theory and reality in *Theory of International Politics*, and proceeded to blur it. The most striking example of this tendency arises in his well-known defense of his structural theory of international anarchy "through analogy with microeconomic theory." Waltz advocated "reasoning by analogy" when "different domains are structurally similar" (Waltz 1979: 89–93, quoting p. 89; on Waltz and analogy, see C. Jones 1993: 178–99). In this context, the term *domain* is ambiguous insofar as it suggests a resemblance between different "parts" of the real world—in this case, firms and states, well-formed markets and international anarchy. Even if Waltz's discussion puts theory first, the analogy seems to operate on both sides of the theory-reality divide.

"Microeconomic theory describes how an order is spontaneously formed from the self-interested acts and interactions of individual units—in this case, persons and firms." Key to this formulation is the phrase *spontaneously formed*. Markets are "individualist in origin, spontaneously generated, and unintended." Not designed or produced on any model, a "market is not an institution or an agent in any palpable sense." And yet "[t]he market is a cause interposed between the economic actors and the results they produce" (Waltz 1979: 89, 90).

Waltz appears to have it both ways. Markets do not really exist, but they operate causally in producing real results. Appearances are deceiving. Either markets are institutions, which seem to be causally implicated in market behavior, or markets are structural causes producing structural effects, as stipulated in a theoretical model.

It is easy enough to show—devise a model showing—that markets are always institutions ("hedged about," as Waltz said himself), even if some markets form spontaneously (Waltz 1979: 91; also see C. Jones 1993: 195). It is almost as easy to show that people respond to institutions as models or by reference to other models already available to them. "Seeing" markets in action reinforces market behavior in turn validating markets as a model and reinforcing them as institutions.

As I have just remarked, additional theories offer a fuller picture. They also cast doubt on the notion that the spontaneous emergence of markets means that they need not really exist to have real effects. From the time of David Hume and Adam Ferguson, observers have grasped the institutional effects of agents' self-interested choices, even if agents do not (Chapter 10). As with markets, so with anarchy. Following John Ruggie's review of *Theory of International Politics* (1983), few scholars would venture to say that the Western state system emerged spontaneously, whole cloth out of whole cloth. There is a mountain of recent scholarship explicating the system's institutional moorings, as if any student of international law, at least since Vattel, could have doubted the extent and significance of the system's institutional features. And there is a sizeable literature on the social construction of sovereignty (see especially Biersteker and Weber 1996).

On Waltz's account, anarchy is a model of the international system. A theoretically enhanced account would construe anarchy as a model and, at the same time, an institution that system observers and states' agents have made together. States' agents are themselves system observers; models mediate whatever all observers (and not just states' agents) think they "see"; agents acting on what they see give rise to institutions; observers take these institutions into account in forming models and acting on their conclusions (whether reporting on them as observers or doing something about them as agents). In the process, models (structural models, constitutive models) and institutions "structured" by models (anarchy, sovereignty) lend each other credibility.[7]

Waltz seems to have been deeply, even hopelessly confused in explicating the analogy between microeconomic theory and his structural theory. Yet his concluding remarks redeem him (Waltz 1979: 92). "To say that 'the structure selects' means simply that those who conform to accepted and successful practices more often rise to the top and are likelier to stay there." To say that structure selects is to summarize the model's terms with a crisp metaphor made familiar by well-known evolutionary models. What Waltz called "selection according to behavior" is behavior that accords with the model but responds, in the first instance, to the institutional possibilities that agents "see" for themselves. Insofar as relevant models tell them what to see, their behavior may *also* respond to the constraints stipulated in those models.

Friedman's ghost

Waltz's careless tendency to move from the formal causes stipulated in his theoretical model to institutional effects has troubled his critics less than has his careful segregation of structural models and institutional reality. "[H]ow can something which does not really exist … 'shape and shove' anything"? (C. Wight 2006: 97, quoting Waltz 1986: 343). If one believes that structures really do exist even if they cannot be directly observed, then one never needs to ask this question, much less engage in conceptual contortions to answer it. And this is exactly what philosophical realists believe.

Wendt (1999: 51) has reduced scientific realism (a prominent species of philosophical realism) to three propositions:

1   the world is independent of the mind and language of individual observers;
2   mature scientific theories typically refer to this world,
3   even when it is not directly observable.

Practically speaking, most us are empirical realists most of the time; proposition 1 summarizes what we think as we get along in the world.[8] Positivists routinely accept proposition 2 along with proposition 1. They resist proposition 3 on methodological grounds, although they (have little choice but to) tolerate

---

7   I should be clear that I am endorsing the way Waltz's model can be enhanced, and not Waltz's model, whether enhanced or not. See Onuf (1989: Part II) and Chapter 1 for the structural model that I prefer.

8   Milja Kurki has suggested that positivists, being "at their core empiricists" (or phenomenalists: see below), believe that "reality consists literally of *our* observations" and therefore do not accept proposition 1 (personal communication). I would say instead that positivists, even Humean skeptics, are empirical realists: our observations represent reality insofar as they work for us.

proposed nonobservables if they have consistently observable implications (see, for example, King *et al.* 1994: 109–10). They would not criticize Waltz, as I have, for moving from structural causes to institutional effects, if he drew out observable implications with appropriate care. Yet they would join philosophical realists in rejecting Waltz's enterprise insofar as it does not comport with proposition 2.

Compare these remarks, one from a positivist willing to countenance unobservables with observable effects (Robert Keohane) and the other more recently from a philosophical realist (Milja Kurki):

> Although Waltz is content to make theoretical assumptions about units that deviate sharply from their known patterns of behavior, this is not, *pace* Milton Friedman (1953), a universally accepted practice in the natural or social sciences.
>
> (Keohane 1986: 12, two references deleted)

> While trying to avoid seeing the international system as logically 'necessitating' effects in the 'when A, then B' manner, Waltz finds it hard to resist deducing logical effects from the system. Arguably, this is because the microeconomic model his theory is based on works on the basis of a 'closed system' view of the social world.
>
> (Kurki 2008: 112)

Both comments direct attention to Waltz's reliance on microeconomic theory in developing his structural theory of international politics, and more especially to these claims of Waltz's:

> Economic units and economic markets are concepts, not descriptive realities or concrete entities. This must be emphasized since the early eighteenth century to the present, from the sociologist Auguste Comte to the psychologist George Katona, economic theory has been faulted because its assumptions fail to correspond to realities. Unrealistically, economic theorists conceive of an economy operating in isolation from its society and polity. Unrealistically, economists assume the economic world is the whole of the world.
>
> (1979: 89, two references deleted;
> Waltz probably meant nineteenth century)

Some microeconomists may regard the "economic world" a model of the whole world—Gary Becker (1976) comes to mind—but most are "content to make theoretical assumptions" (Keohane's words) that are based on, or result in, a more limited model. Waltz was clearly not troubled by microeconomic theory's unrealistic assumptions, or by his own analogous assumptions. For Keohane, erecting a model based on unrealistic assumptions runs against "accepted practice." For Waltz, doing so is an accepted practice—one, he might have said, that Milton Friedman (whose ghost Keohane, no doubt insincerely, sought to pacify) authoritatively sanctioned.

Friedman's position hardly seems inflammatory.

> More generally a hypothesis or theory consists of an assertion that certain forces are, and by implication others are not, important for a particular class of phenomena and a specification of the manner of action of the forces it asserts to be important. We can regard the hypothesis as consisting of two parts: first a conceptual world or abstract model simpler than the "real world" and containing only the forces that the hypothesis asserts to be important; second a set of rules defining a class of phenomena for which "the model" can be taken to be an adequate representation of the "real world" and specifying the correspondence between the variables or entities in the model and observable phenomena.
>
> (Friedman 1953: 24)

As I suggested earlier, Friedman was a strong positivist; only "observable phenomena" count for empirical purposes. He acknowledged the competing tendencies of rationalism and empiricism in Western philosophy by discriminating clearly between conceptual worlds and the real world. He implied that anyone schooled in science would be concerned about the correspondence between the model's elements and that part of the world to which it presumably refers. The only trouble then would seem to be the dissonance between Wendt's proposition 2—theories should refer to a real world available to the senses—and Friedman's view that "[a] theory or its 'assumptions' cannot possibly be thoroughly 'realistic' in the immediate descriptive sense so often assigned to this term" (1953: 32).

Indeed the trouble here is not the unreality of Friedman's and Waltz's models. The source of trouble is the notion of *correspondence* between the model and the world. At least for Friedman and Waltz, correspondence is a loose criterion for deciding on theoretical assumptions and building models. Furthermore, it does not tell you how to negotiate between theory and reality, such as it is. Waltz turned to figurative language in explaining this process. "You take the theory," he remarked in an interview, "and then you have to hook it up to the real world" (Halliday and Rosenberg 1998: 380). While his implicit model of the process would seem to require a great deal more than sensory experience, his language suggests that he has not fully considered what this might be.

By contrast, Keohane as an empirical realist and Kurki as a philosophical realist have assumed that we all have some kind of access to an independently real world. As informed observers, theorists know what is real because what they know reflects the consensus of many other informed observers. Waltz himself has adopted this position: "some part of the scientific community has to decide whether enough of an empirical warrant exists to give a theory credibility" (1986: 336). Once again Waltz has gotten into trouble—being realistic does not matter, and yet it does.

Post-Kantian constructivism

If some community of observers decides that a given theory is empirically credible, then, at least for them, the theory is realistic. Waltz's realism by default raises awkward questions. "What is the criterion," Friedman asked, "by which to judge whether a particular departure from realism is or is not acceptable?" (1953: 32). How can Waltz, or any realist, say the world even has parts? How does a realist know that Aristotle's *ti esti*—what is—is real? For Aristotle, at least, *what it is* is but the first, and presumably the most important, in a list of ten kinds of predication (*genêtôn kategoriôn*), or universal categories for talking about the world (*Topics* I, 103b20–23; Barnes 1984: 172).[9]

It is easy enough to read Aristotle as an empirical realist: the world out there is more or less as we sense it. Generalizing from what I said earlier about formal causes, we can also read him as a proto-constructivist: the world is what we say it is. In such a view, any realist's models of the world dovetails with other widely accepted models. Yet all such models are made up, just as Friedman and Waltz insisted. When we talk, we make our models (maps, formulae) available for others to use in making their own models. In this process (as modeled), there is no reality beyond what our models collectively say it is.

Insofar as we make models by imposing form (patterns, structure) on what we think we see, the mind's "eye" does most of the work, and not the senses. I take this point of view to be Kant's, as propounded in *The Critique of Pure Reason*. What Kant called an *appearance* ("the undetermined object of an empirical intuition") has two components. That which corresponds to sensation (appears as the stuff of the world) Kant termed *matter*. That which "so determines the manifold of appearance that it allows of being ordered in certain relations" (appears as a pattern), Kant termed "the *form* of appearance." For Kant, this "pure form of sensibility," which gives "extension and figure" to the world of appearances, "must be found in the mind *a priori*" (1965: 65–6).

In Kant's view, the sensing mind imposes order on the manifold of appearances. It does so, in the first instance, by situating appearances in space and time and then by putting them together (Kant called this operation *synthesis*; on space and time, see 1965: 67–91). And it does so with the help of "pure concepts of synthesis" that the mind "contains within itself *a priori*." Kant identified twelve such concepts. Following Aristotle, he called them categories but claimed, against Aristotle, that his twelve categories constitute an "exhaustive inventory." Among the twelve are three categories of relation: "inherence and subsistence," "causality and dependence," and "community (reciprocity between agent and patient)" (1965: 111–19).

Once the synthetic operations of the mind have conceptually reordered the manifold of appearances, we have in our minds a "manifold of representations." Thanks to the faculty of apperception, these representations are in turn subject to a final, unifying synthesis filling space and time with "the continuous and

---

9   In *Categories*, 1b25, Aristotle used the term *substance* (*ousia*, not be confused with matter, *hulê*) to lead off the list (Barnes 1984: 4). Also see Chapter 4.

uniform production" of "things in themselves (thinghood, reality)." Without this final operation of the sensing, synthesizing mind, consciousness—of things in themselves, of one's self, of the whole world as a thing in itself—would not be possible (Kant 1965: 133–8, 180–7, quoting pp. 134, 184). Kant's philosophical stance is radically constructivist. In giving form to the world, the mind makes the world real—*in our heads*. And yet the world *appears* to exist, more or less as we sense it, outside the mind.

Kant's constructivism is also radically incomplete. In Kant's model, we are solitary souls imprisoned in cells of our own construction. Indeed, there is no *we*. To escape our solitary confinement, *we* need an additional model—one that grants intersubjectivity, or sociality, to the Kantian subject. Our faculty for language would appear to do the job.

No longer is the question of fit between model (as something you and I "see" in our respective mind's eye) and world (as something independent of us both), but between your words (formulating a model in a public, standardized symbolic format) and my words (formulating a similar model in much the same format). Whether we *really* have escaped our solitary cells is impossible to say conclusively. As Nietzsche remarked, language is a prison-house. Reality resolves into a constant proliferation, and no less an infinite regression, of models seen and heard. Such is the world we have talked into existence. Some models converge, some conflict, some are superseded and some forgotten, some are only distantly related, some we all seem to be able to count on. Every proposition we utter performs an operation on some kind of model and thereby affects the world as we know it.

Jonathan Joseph has called this model of mine "models all the way down" to point up the relevance of enduring disputes between idealists and materialists and to indicate the difference between my model and Waltz's "phenomenalist' model," which (in Joseph's model) uses sensory evidence alone to explain what happens in the world.[10] What happens, in my model, is that agents make models with institutional effects by resorting to models with institutional effects. I fail to see why Waltz would not come to the same conclusion once he conceded the constructivist underpinning of his structural model. Waltz's model of models is surely not materialist in the usual sense attributed to political realists (only an empiricist deserves this charge), or even "rump materialist" in the sense that Wendt has advocated (1999: 109–113, 130–5). Instead Waltz's strong positivism ends up making him a structural idealist in a deeper, more consistent sense than Wendt is.

As positivists, Friedman and Waltz resisted the claim that theoretical notions such as form, cause, structure and agent, not to mention space and time, have a reality independent of the observer. Post-Kantian constructivism offers an alternative. Qualified along the lines I have just suggested, constructivism

---

10 Joseph coined this formula, and characterized Waltz's model as phenomenalist, in discussion of my presentation at Aberystwyth (I offered "models all the way back" as an alternative formula). I have also relied on a personal communication from him, and see Joseph 2010: 487–9).

escapes the solipsism implicit in Kant's stance. Observers can get into each other's minds, as agents, by using models to invent and exchange models; intersubjectivity ensues.

Friedman's defense of *as if* formulations—"firms can be treated *as if* they are perfect competitors" (1953: 37–8; also see p. 40)—is distinctly Kantian (see Onuf 1998a: 95–8). Kant himself defended empirical realism for most practical purposes: our world is more or less as we experience it (1965: 347). Indeed, Waltz called himself "a Kantian, not a positivist" (Halliday and Rosenberg 1998: 379), although the context is Kant's *Perpetual Peace*, not the *Critique of Pure Reason*. If Waltz had ever considered fully the philosophical implications of his Kantian affinities, he might indeed have acknowledged how close he is to an updated constructivism. Given Waltz's stature, we might wonder what his impact on the field would have been.

As it is, we take sides early on in our careers. We do so naively and unequivocally, more or less as an act of faith. On one side are scholars with largely unexamined realist commitments, positivist training and, in some cases, an irrational zeal for rational choice theory; on the other are scholars who dabble, too often indiscriminately, in post-positivist philosophy and Continental social theory. Had Waltz gone philosophical, the chasm would not have disappeared. On the contrary, the distance between the two sides might have widened as scholars made a sustained effort to defend their philosophical predilections.

If indeed the world is what we make it, post-Kantian constructivists are necessarily relativists (recall Devitt's characterization, quoted above). So are post-positivists in general. Realists always invoke the correspondence theory of truth in order to combat relativism with what they take to be common sense. "The theoretical statements of a science are true or false," as Rom Harré has put it, "by virtue of the way the world is" (1986: 38; on the "common-sense" of realism, see Devitt 1997: Chapter 5). Most positivists simply accept the common-sense view without further ado. Yet they need not repudiate relativism if they see truth in Humean terms: at any given moment, systematically supported, provisionally reliable inferences convey the truth as we know it.

Perhaps positivists would have ended up choosing sides. Perhaps the more thorough-going among them could have mediated between realists and constructivists in the pursuit of knowledge, not truth. Perhaps both sides would have tempered their contempt for the other. Perhaps not.

If Waltz had declared himself a thorough-going constructivist, other scholars might have followed suit. There would have ensued a substantial, necessarily inconclusive debate between realists and constructivists on the issues I have raised in this essay. Vacuous discussions of idealism and materialism might never have arisen. A post-Wall generation of liberal internationalists might not be calling themselves constructivists. Positivists and constructivists might have accepted their differences on philosophical issues and come together to develop and elaborate structural models of international politics, theories about institutions, agents and motives and, not least, theoretical frameworks linking theoretical models of structure and agency in larger social processes. Just perhaps.

PART III
The art of world-making

Many worlds have been botched and bungled, throughout an eternity, ere this system was struck out: Much labour lost: Many fruitless trials made: And a slow, but continued improvement carried on during infinite ages in the art of world-making.

(David Hume, *Dialogues concerning Natural Religion* (1779), Part V)

7

SPEAKING OF POLICY

(2001)

Few terms are more prominent in public discourse and political studies than *policy*. Few terms are used more freely, with less attention to conceptual implications and empirical referents. Discussions of foreign policy illustrate the point. Here it is almost impossible to find a sustained connection between the use of the term *policy* and claims about specific policies made by reference to their origins, contents, targets, uses and effects.

This essay is a conceptual investigation of a term as elusive as it is familiar. Underlying the investigation is a constructivist framework, which I have developed elsewhere for making sense of the world (Onuf 1989; Chapter 1). In representing the way things are and how they work in relation to each other, language makes things (including ourselves as agents) what they are by making the world (any world of social relations) what it is. Each of us uses language as an instrument (one of many instruments that language makes available to us) to carry out our individual intentions—ends that we hold for ourselves and take to be within our capacities to achieve. Yet it is never possible for us to carry out those intentions without the participation of others, because of the language that we use together, and the world—the manifold of ends and capacities—that we make for ourselves collectively.

Policies do not exist apart from the words that we, as agents, use to characterize them. In this respect it does not matter whether we are acting on our own behalf, or on behalf of others. Policies only exist when we put our intentions into words and frame courses of action, or plans, to achieve them. We can always form plans without communicating them to anyone else. In such cases, we can always change our plans as we see fit. While we may refer to our unspoken plans as "personal policies" (Bratman 1999), they are exceedingly unreliable as instruments for achieving our intentions.[1]

Speaking is an activity with normative consequences. When we speak, our words lead others to expect that we will act in a certain way—in accordance with our stated intention—and that we ought to do so. Our words matter to us. Simply by being spoken, our stated intentions and plans have some degree of normative force in their own right.[2]

If we do not wish (intend) to be held to our stated intentions, it is better not to state them at all. Even then, other agents are obliged to make inferences about *our* intentions in order to be able to act on *their* intentions. They put words into our mouths, and call them our policies. In this case too, it is better not to affirm, or even deny, what others have to say about our intentions and the plans that we adopt for achieving them, if indeed we wish not to be held to them.

Often enough, we do not want to hold other agents in the dark about our intentions. Instead, we want others to hold us to standards of conduct that we accept for ourselves by stating our intentions. We welcome the normative force of stated intentions, and we state those intentions in ways that reinforce their normative effects. We declare our intentions; we go so far as to make pledges about our intentions. Paradoxically these policy statements are so familiar that we tend to take them for granted when we detach ourselves sufficiently from any world of agents and intentions to observe it closely.

The first section of this essay starts with undisclosed or misrepresented intentions and considers them from the point of view of rational agents who are engaged in strategic interaction.[3] Strategically engaged agents must make inferences about the actual intentions of their counterparts in order to make choices best suited to achieving ends that they themselves are not disposed to reveal to others. The analysis of strategic interaction looks behind threats, lies, and promises to the commitments motivating such overt acts. Many threats and certainly most lies and promises are spoken. Analyzing their properties as speech acts tells us a good deal about agents' undisclosed intentions when they make strategic moves. Like policies, commitments exist only as inferences made by agents forced to anticipate what other agents who have obscured their intentions are going to do.

Strategic interaction often eventuates in agreements understood as acts of reciprocal commitment. The second section of this essay again examines the

---

1   As are commitments to one's self (see below) and private rules: William Kincade prompted me to consider the relation between plans and policies, but see Bratman (1999: 52–6) for a different conclusion.

2   Hereafter I use the term *normative force*, in preference to *binding force* (as in "the binding force of speech acts"; Johnson 1993: 81), to make it clear that normativity is a relative condition. By contrast, positivist legal theory and ordinary language both take the condition of being bound to be absolute. One is either bound, or not.

3   "A situation is strategic if an actor's ability to further its ends depends on the actions that others take" (Lake and Powell 1999: 8, footnote deleted; see pp. 6–20 for a helpful introduction to the study of strategic interaction).

properties of speech acts to show that many agreements do not depend on agents exchanging promises. Instead they are coordinated declarations of agents' intentions. Each such declaration is capable of standing alone. Individually and collectively they are policy statements, to which all agents accord great normative significance. They do the work of public standards, or rules.

The next section shows that declarations of intention are comparable to gifts and shows how both relate to pledges. While the ceremonial aspects of social life seem far removed from strategic interaction, speech acts are common to both spheres. Speech acts have the properties that they do only in relation to agents' intentions. The concluding section looks into the wide space between disguised intentions and declared intentions, between bluffs and pledges (a space warped by the occasional convergence of bluffs and pledges). There we find policies attributed to agents who, for their part, often have good reason not to agree with or even acknowledge what others say. It is no surprise, then, that when we look closely, alleged policies vanish from view.

Commitments

To illustrate my claim that policies vanish under the gaze of any close observer, let me turn to the most thorough discussion of the term *foreign policy* that I have come across (Meehan 1971). For Eugene Meehan, "a 'policy' is by definition the instrument needed to make a reasoned choice in a specific situation," with *reasoned choice* further defined as "all human actions based on deliberate comparison of alternative possible outcomes in terms of known standards or principles" (Meehan 1971: 268, 269). Standards enable agents to set priorities among competing goals and order preferences. Policies are "intellectual tools" reworked for each use but always according to available standards (Meehan 1971: 275).[4]

To say, then, that agents know what their policies are is to say that they know how to fashion tools and use them in various situations in order to make choices. Observers are able to make appropriate inferences about agents' policies by examining those choices, no doubt in conjunction with information about relevant standards that agents can be supposed to have used for guidance. Of course, agents often make statements about situations, standards, preferences and choices. To be sure, they have many reasons to be less than truthful about their policies. On Meehan's account, they rarely are. "Policy statements," as Meehan (1971: 286) called them, "are not very useful as sources of information about policy."

---

4   Students of public policy have made instruments a focus of attention, but they do so on the assumption that policies are set in place and ready to be carried out (Peters and van Nispen 1998). In these circumstances, agents devise regulatory, financial and informational instruments whose properties suit the mechanics of program administration and use them accordingly. Clearly this focus has little bearing on Meehan's conception of policies as tools.

Meehan's concern for the accuracy of policy statements misses the point of his own position. Policy statements should be "treated as *actions* rather than policies," because policies are instruments that result in action (Meehan 1971: 286). Situations change; standards point to previously unconsidered courses of action; preferences assume new orderings; choices bear little or no relation to each other; and the diverse reasons that people give for making unrelated choices cannot be reconciled. If policies do not seem fixed because, as tools, they have many uses, then statements about particular policies must seem vague, deceptive or fabricated when taken together. Agents may not intend this result, and observers are mistaken in assuming that ambiguity or deception must be intended or indeed that agents care what conclusions observers draw.

According to Meehan (1971: 287), "policy statements may contain lies, bluffing, and threatening information that can be highly beneficial to the actor, at least in the short run." Agents may indeed lie, bluff or threaten, as a matter of policy, to achieve goals or solve problems. Yet Meehan never said that these acts—typically spoken—are statements of policy in their own right. What kind of statement they might be is another matter. Meehan's rather offhand reference to threat offers a clue.

Rational agents make threats and promises as strategic moves in interactions with other agents. These interactions make pairs of agents into adversaries and/ or partners, always dependent on the others' choices in making choices of their own. Moves communicate information about agents' intentions, sometimes tacitly (for example, by aiming a weapon or dropping it) and often not reliably (because they are lying or bluffing about their intentions). Typically, agents do not know if statements or other indications of intention are credible. They can simply accept such statements at face value and act accordingly. Or they can respond with the sort of move that forces other agents to act on, qualify or repudiate their stated intentions.

No one has analyzed these interactions more effectively or accessibly than Thomas Schelling. *Policy* is not a term that figures in Schelling's game theoretic vocabulary. Nevertheless, statements of intentions, which may indeed contains lies, bluffs and threats, are policy statements, as Meehan conceived them. Schelling's term for what agents have in mind when they talk this way is *commitment*.

Never precisely defined, commitment is "a *strategic* move, a move that induces another player to choose in one's favor." It should be "interpreted broadly" to include a variety of "maneuvers." Yet it seems to exist independently of any particular move. Thus, a commitment "must lie behind" a threat (Schelling 1960: 122, 127, 124; his emphasis).

Located in the minds of agents, commitments are beliefs that these agents are prepared to act on, or convictions. The stronger these beliefs are, the greater their normative force. They are also instruments available for many uses. Agents can suit these instruments to circumstances by making them more or less firm or inclusive, or by expressing them with more or less clarity or intensity. It is difficult to imagine policies that agents are not committed to, at least in some measure.

In Schelling's way of thinking, moves are events. By giving voice to policies, moves serve agents' intentions and reflect their commitments. At the same time, moves are policies. Agents' intentions and commitments exist only as moves express them. Even those moves intended to rescind agents' commitments or hide their intentions express intentions and commitments that exist only for that move.

Other writers have responded to Schelling's ambiguous terminology by using a neologism, *precommitment*, that otherwise makes no sense.[5] Commitments are anticipatory by definition. This is so because they precede some state of affairs that agents intend to bring about through their actions. If commitments are simply acts that agents decide to take, then they anticipate other such events, including subsequent commitments. They cannot be *pre*-events.

If, however, commitment is something—a conviction—that agents possess, use, act on, in making commitments, then calling that thing a precommitment always distinguishes it from commitments-as-events. Thus, Nicholas Rowe (1989: 23) could say that an "agent who rationally follows a rule acts *as if* he had precommitted his actions," and make perfect sense. The agent treats the rule's content as a firmly held belief. Acting on a rule, or acting on one's convictions, is an event, a rationally chosen move. As an instrument, precommitment eliminates the need to make some other sort of move, or series of moves quite possibly including commitments, in situations covered by the rule. Precommitment also explains behavior that would otherwise seem to be irrational. To avoid the impression of granting causal efficacy to a disposition or mental state, Rowe covered himself by adding the "as if."

Awkward, self-conscious word choices tell us that strategic analysts are not comfortable speaking about commitments-as-beliefs and commitments-as-instruments. When they make events the subject of discussion, their word choices seem less forced. Schelling (1960: 35–52, 123–37) used familiar terms, *threat* and *promise*, in his discussion of commitments-as-events, and substantiated their meaning with a variety of vivid illustrations. Other writers have followed suit. Yet even here ambiguities arise. By turning to the properties of those acts—hereinafter, *speech acts*—through which agents convey threats and promises, we can see what these ambiguities are.[6]

Most moves consist of a bundle of acts, and many of those acts are likely to be speech acts. For example, agent A will make an assertion about agent B's last move: "Your country has been massing troops along the border—your actions

---

5   Jon Elster (1979: 37) seems to have coined the term, which he used, rather narrowly, to express the concept of "binding oneself" directly and not through strategic interaction; "*precommitment* is a generic technique lending credibility to threats and promises" (Elster 1989: 278, his emphasis, footnote directing attention to Schelling deleted) and therefore available for strategic use (pp.170–2).

6   James Johnson (1993: 80–2) has pointed out that speech acts have properties—specifically normative properties—that the analysis of strategic interaction should take into account. As far as I know, neither he nor anyone else has followed up on this suggestion.

speak for themselves." Agent A goes on to say, "On behalf of my country, I demand that you send your troops back to their barracks and desist from all other expressions of hostility." Finally, agent A says: "If you do not comply with these demands, we will take appropriate measures." Only when these three speech acts are taken together, in series, do they constitute agent A's move, which would seem to answer a threat with a threat.

The first statement is an assertive speech act. It presumes to match words (a proposition about some state of affairs) and the world (an actual state of affairs) by having agent B agree with the proposition as stated (making it an actual state of affairs for agents A and B). The second statement is a directive speech act. It seeks to (have agent B) change the world in conformity with that statement's propositional content. Finally, the third statement is another assertive speech act. It predicts a state of affairs that agent B will surely regret. Agent B may accept this assertion as credible or construe it as a bluff.

One might think that the third statement in A's move is not an assertion, but a commitment to effectuate the proposed state of affairs. Commissive speech acts specify states of affairs that agents intend to bring about. These agents propose to do so, not by using words to change the world (*you should* change it), but by speaking of a world that will have changed, thanks to their commitment (*we will* change it). As spoken, agents' words fit promised worlds.

Commissive speech acts constitute promises, however, only if other agents accept them. Rejected or ignored promises bear no consequences for the agents offering them, even if those agents remain committed (we might say, as a matter of policy) to goals that such acts were intended to achieve. Clearly, agent B is not likely to construe agent A's prediction ("we will take appropriate measures") as a promise which, if rejected or ignored, agent A will feel no need to fulfill. Quite the opposite: ignoring agent A's prediction may well inspire agent A to act as if a promise had been accepted.

There are only three fundamental categories of speech acts: assertive, directive, and commissive.[7] Speech acts help speakers to achieve goals through their effect on others: they are necessarily social. Speech acts belong to the categories that they do because of the ways that they work. Assertive speech acts ask for hearers to accept their propositional content; rejecting or ignoring assertions limits their effect on the state of the world. Directives would have hearers accept indicated tasks as theirs to perform; rejecting or ignoring directives thwarts speakers' efforts to change the world. Commissives call for hearers to accept speakers' intentions to change the world; rejecting or ignoring commissives does not thwart speakers so much as it relieves them of what would have been an obligation to change the world.

Obligation is clearest in the instance of a promise accepted. Obligation is implied when hearers accede to a directive: by their consent, they are obligated

---

7   I defend this claim in Onuf (1989: 82–94). It depends on, but departs from, John Searle's taxonomy of speech acts (Searle 1979: 1–29; Searle and Vanderveken 1985: 13–5, 51–62).

to change the world. Even the acceptance of an assertion suggests an obligation to affirm that assertion as opportunity arises. Obligation is the beginning of normativity, but only a beginning. When hearers refuse to accept speech acts, they deny obligation in any measure. Speakers will bundle speech acts to increase the likelihood that any one of them is accepted and obligation secured. One of the most familiar bundles is a directive supported by a *conditional* assertion—an assertion of probable consequences if the hearer does not accede to the directive.

The directive followed by a conditional assertion is the model for a legal rule in positivist legal theory. The rule is a general order (Hart 1961: 18–25), and not simply a speech act, or event. Invoking a rule is a move, normally in the form of a speech act, that puts the rule to use. In theory, this move is most likely to succeed, and the rule demonstrated to be effective, if it includes an assertion about consequences, or sanction. The sanction may well be a rule on its own—a general order directing any agent properly invoking the rule to bring specified consequences about—and all the more credible for being so. Obligation attaches to legal rules directly, and not just to the speech acts that agents use to invoke them.

Agents use rules the way that they use policies and commitments to affect other agents' conduct. For the most part, those other agents are deterred from conduct not consistent with the standards reflected in the rules. When rules do not work, agents bring sanctions to bear. Sanctions need not be negative from the point of view of the agents to whom they are directed. Positive sanctions, or inducements, may be available, and they may cost less than negative sanctions to use.[8]

Clearly, moves that feature negative sanctions threaten punishment. Should we say, then, that positive sanctions promise rewards? Schelling (1960: 133) remarked that the "definition of a promise—for example, in distinction to a threat—is not obvious. It might seem that a promise is a commitment (conditional or unconditional) that the second party welcomes," and thus a positive sanction. Jon Elster (1989: 40n40) was less tentative when he spoke of "promises to reward and threats to punish." Schelling waffled. "A better definition, perhaps, would make the promise a commitment that is controlled by the second party," in which case it is not a sanction at all (Schelling 1960: 134).

As we have already seen, Schelling was right the second time. As an alternative to issuing directives backed by assertions about consequences, agents can make unconditional promises which, if accepted, bring consequences of their own. Both moves change the world, but they do it differently, by obligating different sets of agents. For Schelling, unconditional promises rarely commend themselves in strategic situations. Thus Schelling's two examples (1960: 132–3) are both desperate measures. If moves include so many bluffs, lies and deceptive

---

8   "The sanction might consist in the manipulation of symbols (praise or censure), or in the redistribution of goods and services, or in the use of violence, or, generally, speaking, in reward or punishment by way of any value whatever. The sanction is *positive* when it enhances values for the actor to whom it is applied, *negative* when it deprives him of values" (Lasswell and Kaplan 1950: 48–9, their emphasis).

assertions that agents know better than to trust each other, we can only agree with him. In such circumstances, however, agents are unlikely to agree on very much of anything that they say to each other.

Agreements

Even if unconditional promises are strategically unpromising, agents nevertheless do come to agreement. Indeed, *agreement* is a familiar but undefined term in Schelling's work, as it is in most discussions of strategic interaction. As we shall soon see, there are three different ways that agents come to agreement. If one of them tells us a great deal about strategy, yet another tells us just as much about policy.

Schelling seems to have thought that agreement results from pairing conditional promises. Such promises are "bilateral (contractual) commitments given against a quid pro quo that is a promise in return."[9] If benefiting from others' promises depends on keeping promises made to those other agents, then both sets of agents have an incentive to abide by their promises. In the instance of "spot contracts" providing for the immediate discharge of obligations, cheating is least likely to be a problem (Kratochwil 1995: 76). To the contrary, successful spot contracts are events that agents have an incentive to repeat; success breeds success, and many successes breed trust; agents earn reputations that they have an incentive to protect (Rowe 1989: 36–59).

As Schelling himself demonstrated (1960: 89–113), conventions arise as agents succeed in coordinating moves. Conventions are not agreements; agents have no control over the obligations they create. Accepting an unconditional promise does not constitute an agreement in any but the weakest sense of the term. Even the reciprocal obligations of a spot contract falls short of constituting an agreement, insofar as the term suggests a lasting arrangement. Conventions are instruments, not events. So are agreements. Schelling made just this assumption, and so has everyone else writing on the subject.

The longer an agreement is intended to last, the less likely it is to specify all possible contingencies, and the more opportunities agents will have to cheat (Kratochwil 1995: 75–9). Schelling drew the obvious conclusion (1960: 131): "Enforceable promises cannot be taken for granted. Agreements must be in enforceable terms and involve enforceable types of behavior." Charles Lipson (1991: 508) put the matter in even stronger terms: "In international affairs, then, the term 'binding agreement' is misleading hyperbole. To enforce their bargains, states must act for themselves." Notice that this sort of claim parallels the legal positivist claim that laws, as general orders, depend on sanctions to back them up. Its rhetorical power derives precisely from the reader's recognition that enforcement is a property of legal orders.

---

9   To similar effect: "once an agreement has been concluded, the contracting parties will feel an obligation to fulfill their promises." In saying this, Jon Hovi (1998: 80) intended to cast doubt on the claim but not the terms in which he couched it.

If one believes that the anarchic world of states and their agents is largely lawless, then agreements cannot last, and the obligations that they create are bound to wither. If one believes that the international legal rule *pacta sunt servanda* (treaties must be observed) brings into play an impressive set of tools for agents of states to use in defense of their agreements, then all such agents have disincentives to cheat on the obligations that they have agreed to. Schelling's conclusion that everything depends on enforcement may seem obvious, but it is not the only one possible. Nor indeed is his conclusion that agreements are best thought of as jointly conditional promises, or contracts.

Two properties of lasting agreements (more generally, properties of speech) affect the likelihood that agents will perform their obligations: specificity and formality.[10] Schelling himself alluded to the property of specificity when he said that agreements must be rendered in enforceable terms. The more specific the terms of an agreement, the more difficult it is for agents to avoid doing what they have promised—or so it would seem. The problem comes in trying to make agreements so specific that their obligations are inescapable. The process itself becomes interminable as the specification of particular contingencies brings to light other, even more particular contingencies in need of specification. Specificity risks irrelevance; the complexity of so many interlocking terms invites confusion; the sheer density of a fully specified agreement deters agents from taking it seriously. Beyond some point, the quest for specificity is self-defeating.

As an alternative, agents can make their agreements formal. The more formal their agreements, the more difficult it is for them to claim that they did not intend to be obligated by their words. Formality is not a relevant property of promises as such; an informal promise is no less a promise than a formal promise is, however (in)formally either is accepted. The effect is always the same. Agents keep promises by changing the world, not with the words constituting their promises, but through other acts (which may include speech acts of high formality). If formal agreements are more likely to be honored than informal ones, then it would seem that these agreements are not, or not just, the reciprocal promises, or contracts, that Schelling took them to be.

Schelling has had good company. Early in the seventeenth century, Hugo Grotius held that treaties are analogous to contracts in civil law. Ever since, lawyers have affirmed that treaties work the same way that contracts do to create obligations (Lauterpacht 1927: 155–80; Onuma 1993). "International treaties are agreements, of a contractual character, between States or organisations of States creating legal rights and obligations between the Parties." Thus begins the chapter on treaties in the century's foremost English language treatise on international law (Oppenheim 1955: 877, footnotes deleted). By inference,

---

10   Elsewhere I have argued that these are also properties of rules (Onuf 1998b: 175–6). Compare Kratochwil (1995: 84–92), where explicitness, openness, and formality are the relevant properties of agreements. With Lipson (1991: 527–32), I believe that formality brings openness (see below).

then, any "international" instrument that reciprocally obligates must be a treaty. Joint declarations are not treaties, despite their formality, if "they are intended as formulating general statements of principle and policy rather than legal obligations" (Oppenheim 1955: 900). Conversely, treaties may take any number of forms; formality has no effect on obligations that arise from exchanging conditional promises.

The difficulty comes with unilateral declarations. In some instances, at least, these highly formal acts have been construed to create legal obligations. Yet they cannot do so as conditional promises because obligations arise only when such promises are reciprocated. More plausibly, they are unconditional promises, obligating their makers only insofar as other agents construe them as promises, accept them as such, and proceed to rely on them. In this case, however, they are not agreements at all, and they are classified as treaties only because lawyers think it makes even less sense to classify them as customary legal rules.[11]

If unilateral declarations are unconditional promises, then it seems rather odd for them to be rendered in declaratory form. Their formality suggests that it does not matter to the agents making such promises whether they are accepted by other agents. If agents intend their words as promises, they would couch them in such terms as to elicit acceptance. Formality calls for a response in kind—a counter-declaration that would turn the pair of declarations into an exchange of promises—or no response at all.

The most plausible way of all to look at unilateral declarations is as assertions, and not promises of any kind. The advantage of doing so is to shift focus from the intentions of agents in accepting promises, or not, to the intentions of agents when they make such declarations. According to John Searle (1979: 16–20, 26–7), declarations are neither assertives nor commissives, but a category of speech acts in their own right. They differ from all other speech acts because the act of declaring some state of affairs is complete and sufficient.

Declaring something makes it so. For example, to say, "I declare a state of emergency," brings such a state into existence, then and there. As Searle pointed out (1979: 18), it does so only if some "extra-linguistic institution" gives me the authority to issue such a declaration. Declarations differ from assertives for this reason alone.

What Searle failed to realize is that the credibility of any assertion depends, at least in measure, on the status of its speaker (also see Mühlhäusler and Harré 1990: 41–2). Status is an extra-linguistic institution. Declarations, then, are assertions for which there exists an extra-linguistic institution that makes them *formally* complete and self-fulfilling. Declarations of independence may constitute a special case insofar as they create the extra-linguistic institution giving them their force.

---

11 Not that unilateral declarations are irrelevant to the emergence of customary rules. In Schelling's terms (1960: 54–8), they can serve as "focal points" for the tacit coordination of strategic moves, with conventions resulting. Also see Kratochwil (1995: 91).

Acceptance is beside the point. When I declare a state of emergency, no one in particular needs to accept it (except, of course, subordinates who are obliged to consider my declaration a directive speech act). Even if the declaration does refer to particular agents, their acceptance is irrelevant. Take this example: "We declare war on you."

Such a declaration brings a state of war into existence at that moment, and not in the future as a consequence of promised hostile conduct. Agents to whom the declaration refers are perfectly free to ignore it. They are more likely to match it with their own declaration of war. Taken together, the two declarations resemble an agreement which both sides will treat *as if* it produces obligations that cannot be ignored.

Gifts

If indeed paired declarations produce obligations, they are obligations that agents have created for themselves, not each other. These obligations have the force they do both because of the formalities of agency and the formality with which agents assert states of affairs. Association with extra-linguistic institutions also contributes to the normative force that declarations unilaterally bring to bear, insofar as those institutions create obligations in their own right. In this respect, no institution seems more important than the gift.

Declarations resemble gifts in a number of respects. First, gifts need not have designated recipients, even if they often do. Second, there are always rules telling agents when, and to whom, they are free to give gifts, obliged to do so, or indeed sometimes obliged not to do so. Second, there are counterpart rules for accepting gifts. Third, there are rules, often quite elaborate, telling agents when they are obliged to exchange gifts (Mauss 1967: 37–43). The first two sets of rules parallel extra-linguistic institutions placing some agents in a position to issue declarations and others in a position to receive them. The third set of rules reflects the general norm of reciprocity that every society seems to have (but see Onuf 2010b for an extended discussion of giving *not* subject to reciprocity).

Such a norm does not require an exchange of gifts, or declarations, on every occasion for which giving a gift, or issuing a declaration, might be appropriate. When agents are formal equals, and when occasions are themselves formally marked, the rule of reciprocity is most likely to apply. Holidays call for reciprocity in giving gifts; declaring war calls for, not does not compel, a declaration of war in return. Reciprocity fosters a shared commitment to live by agreements taking the form of exchanged promises, and it fosters a shared appreciation of paired declarations as agreements of another kind.

Just what kind of agreement they are remains to be clarified. We often think of agreements as propositions that agents have actively accepted. Consent is one way to respond to directive speech acts, although we rarely think of such exchanges as agreements. Assenting to others' assertion—"I agree with you"—is a different matter. Yet agents often assent to propositions that no one in particular has asserted: "I agree that war is sometimes the best policy." To say, "I agree with you (when you say) that war is the best policy," does not signify an agreement between us to go to war. Our agreement is passive, and it reduces to its two constituents—what I say and what you say—with no loss of meaning.

Our passive agreement differs from a contract—for example, an agreement by each of us to go to war if the other does—in two respects. First, our agreement says nothing about our intentions, while the other agreement is centrally concerned with intentions. Second, our agreement consists of unconditional assertions, while the other consists of conditional promises. Now we can easily see a third possibility: agreement in the form of parallel unconditional assertions about our respective intentions. When we both assert, "I intend to go to war," we have jointly agreed to do so, without having actively accepted, or assented to, the agreement, or having committed ourselves to each other.

This third possibility is precisely the kind of agreement represented by paired declarations. After all, declarations are formally self-sufficient assertions, and it is this property that marks their unconditional nature. Formality functions for speakers the way that consent does for hearers. "I declare my intention to go to war," and "I consent to (your directive that I) go to war," are statements of comparable normative force—they both obligate me more than most other speech acts do—but their normativity comes from different directions, so to speak, and they constitute agreements of different kinds.

We might see agents' intentions behind acts of consent, just as we do with hostile acts, and call those acts policies. Of course, we can always be mistaken in such inferences. Alternatively, we might call assertions of intentions policy statements, and expect to see future acts consistent with those statements. Again, these expectations might be misguided, because these statements might well be bluffs or lies. When assertions of intention are given the formal completeness of declarations, and even more when agents intend them to coincide with other agents' declarations, they gain in normative force, and our confidence in them increases.

When, centuries ago, crowned heads conjointly declared their intentions, their agreements were not treaties on the model of contracts. Yet these agreements "were nevertheless considered sacred and binding," not simply "on account of religious and moral sentiment" (Oppenheim 1955: 878), but more specifically because exalted beings had given their word. Typically they did so in the form of an oath. "The practice of concluding a contract by oath-taking and inserting expressions of oath in treaties is believed to have continued until the eighteenth century" (Onuma 1993: 198, footnote deleted; also see Akashi 1998: 52). Intentions thus declared are beyond doubt. Declarations of intention are policy statements of the most emphatic sort.

When agents of the highest status together issue declarations of intention, these agreements have normative effects perhaps more powerful than those that arise from exchanging promises. Indeed, by giving their word, they have exchanged gifts on an occasion charged with significance. To this day, agents of states put great store in ceremonial exchanges. Their treaties often contain general provisions, which, though declaratory in name or thrust, are fully as normative as specifically contracted obligations are.

Contemporary international relations offers other examples. The General Assembly seems like a lawmaking organ because some few of its resolutions, styled declarations, exhibit the normative force of a great many coordinated declarations of intention.[12] Although the Helsinki Final Act is expressly not a treaty, the normative force of its provisions is hardly lessened for this reason and perhaps enhanced.[13] Even if such instruments depend on acts of assent in the form of affirmative votes for their adoption, such acts do not indicate consent to be bound. Instead they create agreements that we might fairly call collective policy statements. As such, they set public standards and engender expectations about compliance. They do the work of formal rules, or law, whatever legal positivists might call them.

Whatever policies may be, policy statements assert or, more likely, declare agents' intentions. Sometimes agents may themselves prefer to make their assertions of intention highly formal in order to make their intentions altogether clear. The point of assertive speech acts is to persuade other agents that any proposed state of affairs is credible. In the instance of propositions about agents' own intentions, the point is to persuade other agents that speakers are sincere in their expressions of intention—they will do as they say. When agents declare their intentions, instead of merely asserting them, they signal an intention to be taken seriously, with a commensurate gain in the credibility of whatever they say about their intentions. If acceptance is the point, then declarations are more likely than assertions to succeed as speech acts.

Declarations are more formal than assertions by degree. Pledges, oaths and vows are declarations of intention expressed in the highest degree of formality that agents, as speakers, are capable of giving them. They possess all the normative force that speakers can give their commitments (as beliefs and as instruments) without the help of other agents. In other words, pledges do not have other agents as targets and are not intended to elicit from them speech acts, such as consent or an offer of a promise, that would confirm or increase the normative force behind whatever is pledged. When Searle (1979: 22–3) classified pledges as commissive speech acts, he was mistaken for this very reason: other agents need not accept pledges, oaths and vows for these speech acts to do their job.[14] Promises, for their part, cannot be promises without agents for indirect objects.

---

12 On the legal issues, see Falk (1966) and Onuf (1970); on normative force, see D.V. Jones (1992) and Onuf (1998b: 690–1).

13 Compare Lipson (1991: 533) and Kratochwil (1995: 88), for whom the Helsinki Final Act is "informal" because it is not a legal instrument. Kratochwil's assessment of the Final Act is nevertheless unassailable: "Having all nations solemnly declare, so to speak, unilaterally, the inviolability of post-war boundaries added considerable legitimacy to the status quo."

14 We might plausibly construe pledges as the best possible evidence of commitments as strongly held beliefs and then use the terms interchangeably. Robert Jervis (1997: 83)

Consider an example of Searle's (1979: 22): "I pledge allegiance to the flag." In expanded form, this sentence becomes "I declare publicly, but to no one in particular, my intention to perform a variety of acts associated with flag and nation." It could also become "I promise myself to perform such acts," I myself being the only plausible candidate for an indirect object. Agents often make promises to themselves and accept them for themselves, not publicly, but silently. Such acts are not social and usually limited in normative force, as evidenced by the likelihood that they will soon be broken. The sorry fate of most new years' resolutions makes the point. If we make our self-promises public, then we translate them into declarations of intention, thereby making our concerns for reputation a source of normativity.[15]

Searle's second example, "I vow to get revenge," would seem to supply an agent for the indirect object and therefore qualify as a commitment. In expanded form, this sentence could become, "I vow to you that I will get my revenge." If you (the indirect object) are also the object of my revenge, then your acceptance is irrelevant. If you are not, then there would seem to be little point in my offering such a promise and in you accepting it. Either way, the promise means little if anything. As an alternative, we could have this sentence say: "I vow publicly, solemnly, but to no one in particular, to take my revenge on you." Normative force depends on my vow, even though you are the focus of my intentions.

Pledges, oaths and vows are an integral part of social life and a significant factor in making it normative. They make gifts of words: "I give my word that I intend to honor the nation," "uphold the Constitution," "exact my revenge." Presents make their presence known; pledges, oaths and vows draw attention to speakers' intentions. When agents want their intentions to be known, assertions are the appropriate vehicle. Declarations are better than mere assertions, and pledges best of all. Ceremonial occasions, formal speech, the incidents of status: all of these enhance policy statements and make them more useful instruments.

---

did just this in a discussion of self-commitment in strategic interaction. When Zeev Maoz and Dan Felsenthal (1987: 187) defined a *self-binding commitment* as "a unilateral credible commitment to act in a certain way regardless of what other players do," they could have called this move, and the commitment behind it, a pledge.

15 While Searle failed to comment specifically on declarations of intention, J.L. Austin, who pioneered the analysis of speech acts, thought that declaring one's intention, giving one's word and pledging (not to mention agreeing and consenting) are all commissive speech acts (1975: 157–8). Note, however, that Austin's typology of speech acts has no place for declarations as such. Perhaps Searle considered pledges to be commissive speech acts, and not declarations (of intention), because he associated intentionality with commitment as a state of mind. Austin even thought that *intend*, as a verb, is a commissive speech act (1975: 158), but Searle corrected him: "Intending is never a speech act; expressing an intention usually, but not always, is" (1979: 9).

Observers

Sometimes agents do *not* want their intentions known. To achieve them, they plan strategic moves that work only if other agents do not know what their intentions are. Indeed, successful moves may depend on deception, both with respect to intentions and to the circumstances that agents have taken into account in forming their intentions. Occasionally, agents will make pledges that they intend not to honor, thinking a pledge may work better as a bluff than a mere assertion would. If, however, other agents call the bluff, a broken pledge can be a costly move.

Deceptive assertions tend to be informal in order to limit normative implications for future conduct. When agents cannot avoid speaking on formal occasions, they take refuge in generalities. Such statements afford agents the greatest possible interpretive leeway for whatever they say or do subsequently. In most such situations, saying nothing, or as little as possible, is the best "policy."

Agents will have relatively fixed intentions, or policies, that they have never announced and endeavor to hide. Other agents are forced to make inferences about those policies from limited and often misleading evidence in order to choose their moves. Observers are in the same position, even though they often feel that agents have an obligation to disclose policies or even seek approval for them. Obligation may stem from electoral promises, parliamentary practices, statutory requirements or indeed policy statements that agents had reason to make at other times. Close observers tend to feel that their own professional status and responsibilities suffice to obligate agents to explain their conduct.

Faced with agents' reluctance to make policy statements in some situations, observers will claim that their inferences fairly represent agents' policies. If agents were to declare themselves, to say anything at all formal about their intentions, then, observers assert, this is what they would say. Agents in their turn can ignore these assertions, only to have observers interpret silence as assent. Or agents can repudiate words that observers have put in their mouths, at risk of disclosing more than they like about their intentions. Sometimes, of course, agents benefit from the cacophony of claims about their policies, because it gives them the cover they need to act on their undisclosed intentions.

However agents respond, policy statements of obscure provenience and questionable content will proliferate. Casual observers will assume that agents have policies that bear a systematic relation to the many policy statements to which everyone is constantly exposed. As observers look more closely, they discover that many policy statements are fictions, and that many agents are not talking. The closer they look, the less they find. In the end, observers are left with what agents want observers (and other agents) to know about agents' intentions, as manifest in their pledges and declarations, singular and collective, and the confusing evidence of their strategic moves.

In the wide space between glittering generalities and indecipherable events, there may be no policies to be found—at least, no *foreign* policies. (Students of public policy who assume that governments adopt formal policies openly and carry them out routinely will find little relevance in this discussion. That same assumption limits any contribution on their part to discussions of foreign policy.) Even in the absence of policies, there is much else to be seen and heard. Agents may refuse to declare their intentions publicly, but they still have to rely on other agents to carry out their moves. At minimum, agents must convey their intentions to subordinates through the medium of directive speech acts.

Information that moves up and down a chain of command is often hard to keep from public view. Multiple chains in complex organizational arrangements, and the opportunities for leakage also increase, no doubt exponentially. Directive speech acts intended only for subordinates' ears provide far better evidence of agents' intentions than their strategic interactions are likely to. Inferences about agents' intentions are more plausible, and they are harder for agents to repudiate without confusing their subordinates.

Keeping one's policies from view is frequently difficult. Disclosing policies may be a good move for practical reasons. As we have seen, agents also have principled reasons to declare their intentions. They make policy statements with the intention of being held to them. Oaths of office, major speeches, summit oratory, resolutions of public bodies, agreements as coordinated unilateral declarations are just some of the many examples of such policy statements. On all such occasions, agents treat all hearers as observers, and all observers as judges. When agents take these occasions to speak, they tend to be sincere in what they say.

Furthermore, they are likely to remain so for the sake of their reputations. Observers find it easy to draw inferences from policy statements—inferences that they, as agents, can rely on. In the absence of evidence to the contrary, highly formal policy statements, as declarations of intention, *are* policies. Even though these policies are often highly general and therefore permissive in practice, they have the normative force to make the world—any world of agents and intentions—what it has become and can ever be.

8

RULES IN PRACTICE

(2010)

Fritz Kratochwil has longed talked about *practice*. In an early, important essay, he identified "the problem of praxis" as "the necessity of choice in situations where no logically compelling solution is possible" and thus a problem of "practical reasoning" (1983: 40). In the shadow of Aristotle's *Nicomachean Ethics*, linking *praxis* and *phronêsis* is plausible but, as I argue below, hardly sufficient. A later paper has a several-page section headed "Understanding Praxis" (Kratochwil 2000: 59–63), which speaks of "practical matters" and "practical problems"—as if this were ordinarily understood ordinary language—in the context of theory-building. Only recently, Kratochwil presented a paper at a conference on The Practice Turn in International Relations (and see Pouliot 2008: 265–9). Since that paper (which he graciously made available to me) is a preliminary, untitled draft (now published as Kratochwil 2011), I will allude to it only in general terms.

In the field of International Relations, many of us use the term *practice* just as generally and loosely as Kratochwil did in his 2000 paper. In my own case, I often refer to "rules and related practices" with no elaboration. No doubt Kratochwil and I are influenced by legal practice, where the sense of the term *practice* is taken for granted (see below). Some of us speak of practice, at least some of the time, to signal critical or post-positivist allegiances. Again, I do not doubt this is so for both of us, if not always as a conscious practice (again, see below). Insofar as recent discussion exhibits any coherence at all, it suggests a turn to pragmatism (a major concern in Kratochwil's now published paper; also see Bauer and Brighi 2008, and Kratochwil's paper therein; Kessler 2010). If indeed a practice turn is underway, then Kratochwil will in some measure be responsible by virtue of adopting this turn of phrase.

Always concerned with use and meaning, Kratochwil strongly resists any effort to troll usage, discriminate senses of any abstract term and fix meanings by reference to ideal types or formal templates—practices he identifies with formal reasoning, rationalist theorizing and positivist science. On this we differ, perhaps more deeply than on any other issue. I prefer to identify categories and devise models (including taxonomies), and then refine them on the evidence. Here I will identify two general models of practice in circulation and then show that their terms are so poorly specified that the two models collapse into a single incoherent concept of practice.

In its place, I propose a pair of related but strictly differentiated models that offer complementary enticements for research. Next I consider Stephen Turner's telling critique of practice as generally conceptualized in social theory (1994, 2002: Chapters 1, 8), to which, I might add, Kratochwil is exceedingly hostile. I affirm Turner's claim that the concept of practice results in bad theory, but only if the source of the concept is the mixed model in general use. Then I try to show how the concept of practice, once clarified, relates to the concept of *choice* (to which Kratochwil alluded in 1983).

Choice is as central to positivists (not to mention the philosophical defense of free will, most conceptions of agency and intention, and liberal ideology) as practice is to critical and post-positivist thinkers. Here I suggest that there are two models of choice strikingly analogous to the two models of practice. I conclude with some very brief remarks on whether these two pairs of models complement each other.

Action and activity

In social theory, the term *practice* is a legacy of Marx. The young Marx defined *praxis*, and as "sensuous human activity" ("*menschliche sinnliche Tätigkeit*") and further claimed that "social life is essentially practical" (1969a, b). He also invoked the distinction between theory and practice (specifically, revolutionary practice), thus seeming to suggest that theory is *not* one of the many practices making up social life. Ever since, Marxists have invested a great deal of effort in developing theory about the relation of theory to practice and distinguishing such a theory from theories that fail to take their own practical implications into account. I prefer to think that Marx's greater legacy was his emphasis on an inclusive conception of practice grounded in the material conditions of everyday life. Today, the best example of this way of thinking is perhaps Michel de Certeau's *The Practice of Everyday Life* (1984).

Writing in 1845, Marx may have read Kant's essay, "On the Common Saying: This May Be True in Theory, but It Does Not Apply in Practice" (*Über den Gemeinspruch: Das Mag in der Theorie richtig sein, taugt aber nicht für die Praxis*, 1793). Here is how Kant began:

> A collection of rules, even of practical rules, is termed a *theory* if the rules concerned are envisaged as principles of a fairly general nature …
> Conversely, not all activities are called *practice*, but only those realisations

of a particular purpose which are considered to comply with certain generally conceived principles.

(Kant 1991a: 61; emphases in translation)

Kant went on to say that this spare description of theory implies not just understanding—the ability to generalize from particulars—but also "an act of judgment whereby the practitioner distinguishes instances where the rule applies from those where it does not" (Kant 1991a: 61).

Understanding and judgment are two of the higher faculties, or powers, that human beings are said to possess. In the *Critique of Pure Reason*, Kant systematically reconsidered these faculties, to which Aristotle had given a privileged position as applied forms of reason. By contrast, Marx's emphasis on "sensuous activity" shifts attention to the lower, bodily faculties of motor activity, perception, and emotions so pervasively affecting what we actually do from one moment to the next. Marx's view of practice includes the exercise of the higher powers. Yet it does seem to emphasize the importance of judgment, and not our knowledge of the rules, in how we carry on as sensuous beings.

If we look back beyond Marx, Kant and their early modern predecessors, all roads lead to Aristotle. Aristotle's *De anima* (*On the Soul* II, 414a29–415a13) considers the range of powers—"the nutritive, the appetitive, the sensory, the locomotive, and the power of thinking" (Barnes 1984: 659)—that together make us what we are. *Nicomachean Ethics* considers theory in relation to practical reason (II, 1103b28–32; also see *Politics* VII, 1325b14–23). And yet Jürgen Habermas (1973: 2) has claimed that the "Aristotelian distinction between *praxis* and *technê* serves as the connecting thread" for a critical reconstruction of theory's relations to practice.

Something is amiss here. Aristotle never used *theôria*, as in looking at something carefully, and *technê*, or *craft*, as interchangeable terms. Quite the contrary: as "sensuous" activities they seem entirely different (see *Nicomachean Ethics* I, 1098a30–33, on the different way geometers and carpenters use right angles). Nor is it clear why "the skilled production of artifacts and the expert mastery of objectified tasks" (Habermas's definition of *technê*, 1973: 42) would not count as *praxis*, at least in a Marxian sense.

Reading Aristotle closely, we can see where Habermas has gone wrong. *Nicomachean Ethics* (1094a1–2) begins as follows: "Every craft and every line of inquiry, and likewise every action and decision, seem to seek some good ..." (Aristotle 1999: 1). *Action* here translates *praxis*, and *decision* is the translator's term for *prohairesis*, literally "choosing before." Aristotle's parallel construction suggests a distinction between action and craft too obvious to require comment.

The text continues: "But the ends appear to differ; some are activities, and others are products apart from activities" (1094a4–6; Aristotle 1999: 1). The term *activity* is not simply an variant of the term *action*. Instead it translates *energeia*. The translator, Terence Irwin, has argued that Aristotle used *action* as an inclusive term and *activity* as one kind of action (Aristotle 1999, Glossary: 315). All human action has an end—a good end from the agent's point of view. Activity has as its end some result beyond the activity itself. To use two of Aristotle's examples of activities, shipbuilding has a ship as its end, and household management has the good of the household, or wealth, as its end (*Nicomachean Ethics* I, 1094a7–9).

By contrast, action construed in a more limited sense has no end or result beyond itself. In Irwin's interpretation, action in this sense "is not done exclusively for the sake of some end beyond it. It aims at 'doing well (or 'acting well', *eupraxia*) for itself … " (Aristotle 1999: 315). Consider eating. If this is something we do because we are hungry, then it is an action that is its own end. Yet we all know that eating is never just for its own sake. Eating also constitutes an activity with our survival as its end. Immediate ends contribute to larger ends and, from Aristotle's teleological point of view, ultimately to nature's ends.

Rules and powers

For Aristotle, actions are merely an observer's incomplete characterization of some larger activity. If, however, we construe ends as intended results, and not instantiations of nature's purposes, then it may seem plausible to count actions and activities as generically separate categories. Some actions are intended to be nothing more than what they are. Much of what we do unreflectively and routinely fits here, and not just the accommodation of bodily needs and urges.

In our time, Pierre Bourdieu (1977, 1990) is particularly well-known for adopting such a view.

> Practical sense is a quasi-bodily involvement in the world which presupposes no representation either of the body or of the world, still less of their relationship. It is an immanence in the world through which the world imposes its immanence, things to be done or said, which directly govern speech and action. It orients 'choices' which, though not deliberate, are no less systematic, and which, without being ordered or organized in relation to an end, are none the less charged with a kind of retrospective finality.
>
> (1990: 66)

Actions of this kind result in "the orchestrated improvisation of common dispositions" (1977: 17). Such a claim makes practice both deep and fluid, and it emphasizes "practical mastery"—"tact, dexterity, or savoir-faire," as against "precepts, fomulae, and codified cues" (p. 10). Indeed Bourdieu insisted on the distinction between "savoir-faire" and "codified cues" as a formal opposition (as has Pouliot 2008: 269–78). "In contrast to logic, a mode of thought that works by making explicit the work of thought, practice excludes all formal concerns" (1990: 91; see Bourdieu 1984: 467–79, on how and why we turn distinctions of degree into categorical distinctions—just as he has done here).

Bourdieu's distinction between "savoir-faire" and "codified cues"—between norms and rules—in characterizing practical mastery does not stand up to scrutiny. *Savoir-faire* involves knowing (what the rules are, especially the informal ones) and doing (some activity within the rules' constraints). All norms are rules—informal, internalized rules—and all rules are normative—even instructions (Onuf 1989: 78–90; 2008: 243–51, 443–50). Nevertheless, Bourdieu seems to have codified two views of practice: practice in accordance with shared norms *versus* practice in accordance with known rules, practice as doing *versus* practice as saying. Not least because saying *is* doing, this is a bogus distinction. Bourdieu's formulation also conflates what we do (practice) with how we do it (mastery). What we do accords with norms (internalized rules), while how we do it involves judgment, which is a faculty of mind, a cognitive power.

On Aristotle's account (*Nicomachean Ethics* II, 1103a27–8), powers come first, competence precedes performance: "if something arises in us by nature, we first have the capacity for it, and later perform the activity" (Aristotle 1999: 18). The Greek word for capacity is *dunamis*, which also means *power* or *potentiality*. In Aristotle's way of thinking, the actual is always the realization of some potential, whether in nature, of mind, or by design. Actions depend on the exercise of our various powers.

Repeated and imitated, these actions eventuate in normativized habits or routines (in Aristotle's Greek, *ethos*). We learn, and we are good at it. Activities also depend on our powers, in the process yielding goods, rules and skills. We use rules and skills to refine our powers—our own or others'—and to become good at what we do. This is craft, or *technê*, and it is the result of training.

It would seem that Aristotle developed the two models of practice that we found Bourdieu relying on. One highlights action, norms and habits, and the other highlights activities, skills and products. But I think we can read Aristotle to different effect. There are indeed two models of practice. One highlights rules and their internalization as tacit knowledge, and the other highlights powers and their externalization as skills and goods. One might call them the performance model and the competence model (cf. Certeau 1984: xiii). Given my own craft and associated discursive habits, I prefer calling them the rules model of practice and the powers model of practice.

I have already accused Bourdieu of conflating the rules model and the powers model. I would suggest that we keep the two models analytically separate—as Kant did—in order to show how they specify the terms of the agent–structure relation.

1 Agents have powers, powers produce rules and rules enhance powers.
2 Agents use powers, rules and skills to produce goods.
3 Related rules, skills and goods constitute a field of objects, which an agent observer could describe as a practice.
4 Patterns of practice constitute social structure.

5 Observing such patterns (the activity of theorizing) turns structures into institutions by giving them normative content (as per 1).
6 Institutions are ensembles of rules that impose practical limits on agents and the exercise of their powers.

I would also suggest that the rules model of practice, has, in its several forms, dominated social theory, and it has done so ever since the rise of positivist science and its critique by Marxist thinkers. Early modern thought shows a definite tendency to favor the powers model—a tendency that reaches its epitome in Kant's philosophical program and endures in the liberal preoccupation with rights (see Onuf and Onuf 2006: Part I). While this is not the place to show how deeply and normatively the liberal mind has interpreted the primacy of our productive powers over society's confining rules, consider how thoroughly the liberal identification of practice with craft colors the sense of the term *practice* in ordinary language. The practice of law, medicine or scholarship offers pertinent examples.

Process and content

At this point it would be nice to thank Aristotle for his help and move on. Unfortunately, Aristotle complicated matters quite a bit when, later in the *Nicomachean Ethics*, Book VI (1139a18–9, b15–8), he claimed that our minds in action—our sensory abilities, reasoning powers and desires (wishes, urges and feelings)—produce different kinds of knowledge: technical knowledge (*technê*), scientific or systematic knowledge (*epistêmê*), prudence or, in most translations, practical reason (*phronêsis*), wisdom (*sophia*) and understanding (*nous, dianoia*) (1139b15–1144b1).

Aristotle's text is puzzling at best. It would seem, however, that technical knowledge involves theory (1140a11) while practical knowledge is more limited, since its concern is action as its own end (1140b1–4). Scientific knowledge starts with general principles (1140b30–1) and practical knowledge is necessarily concerned with particulars, as is understanding (1143a25–8). Wisdom is understanding plus science (1141a19); by implication it takes wisdom to move from general principles to particulars and back again. It also takes wisdom to use technical knowledge to its fullest potential (1141a10–1).

Taken together, these distinctions collapse into two categories—practical knowledge and understanding *versus* technical and scientific knowledge—with wisdom presiding over them as some sort of higher knowledge. By associating *praxis* and *phronêsis*, Habermas could oppose *praxis* and *technê*, and he is hardly alone in making this association. While this would seem to be a category mistake (for Aristotle, reasoning gives us reasons for acting), the bigger problem is that it ratifies the unhelpful distinction between action and activity.

Recall that Aristotle made this distinction only provisionally, and that his philosophical system does not sustain it. Nor does any contemporary philosophical treatment of action and intention. In other words, practice always involves wisdom. Or perhaps we can say, practice is the interplay of Kant's faculties of understanding and judgment, played out in normative settings.

Both models of practice I offer here—the rules model and the powers model—emphasize a different aspect of this process without forcing us to prejudge the content of a practice. By contrast, the action model and the activities model stipulate a different content to practice. If practice is action, then the relevant power is being adept with particulars, and the content of the practice comes to include shared knowledge, common habits and a fluid ensemble of norms. If practice is activity, then the relevant powers are being adept with generalities and being able to see the eventual consequences of immediate actions. The content of practice therefore includes the rules, skills and goods that activities end up producing.

Turner's question

To summarize, if we start with the idea that practice is a process, and that we can approach this process either by looking at rules or at powers, then we do not start on the same page, but we can see the possibility of ending up there. If we start with the idea that practice is either a matter of action or of activity, then we can end up on the same page only by running the two models together—just as Bourdieu did. Then the content of practice is shared ideational stuff, much of it immanently normative, and yet it takes the form of actual things—institutionalized routines and communicable skills to which we impute causal significance.

Let me use Stanley Fish's *Doing What Comes Naturally* (1989: Chapter 7) as an example. If we follow Fish and define practice by reference to an interpretive community, then the ensemble of interpretations constituting such a community is the shared ideational stuff of the action model. At the same time, those interpretations are the identifiable products of the skilled use of rules of interpretation. Actions fold into activities, and activities dissolve into actions; the two models merge. And this is the very point at which Turner has asked his troubling question (1994: 44–5; 2002: 33–4): Can we have practices in the sense of shared ideational stuff, and can we then impute to them the causal force that we take for granted when we think of practice as a craft?

The problem disappears if we limit practice to an ensemble of objects—things that some set of activities has produced and an observer can identify as such. The practice cannot be said to cause these objects to *do* anything, even if agents thereupon put these things to use in some other set of activities. Thus delimited, practice is no more than a state of affairs noted as such by an observer. Furthermore, when we impute structure to this state of affairs, we have smuggled in a causal claim that we cannot sustain.

The problem also disappears if we simply assume that we actually do share ideas, in the sense that we come to have the same ideas in our minds by virtue of the way our minds work. The implicit claim here is that our powers are so powerful—so causally efficacious in the same way—that they swamp differences in experience and situation. Turner has no patience with this kind of argument, which is absurd as soon as it is made explicit. To say that we share in a practice, and to say in the same breath that this practice has an effect on the world, is an unreflective excursion into ordinary language, or a rhetorical move perhaps, but not a philosophically defensible claim. And this is what we—as scholars—all too often *do* say.

Now, it should be clear that I think Turner's problem is an artifact of giving too much attention to the contents of a practice. Even then, the problem only arises when we treat the contents of a practice as a whole—a thing in itself possessing causal powers of its own. If, however, we think of practice as a process, then we can go on to ask how powers and rules constitute the causal mechanism we call agency, and we can ask how the interplay of empowered agents creates the illusion of shared ideational stuff. When we encounter collective fictions that seem to have causal effects, we should go on to ask what rules authorize agents to act on behalf of the fictive whole.

It might seem from what I have just been saying that I am a methodological individualist and thus a conventional positivist. With positivists (and against philosophical realists: see further Chapter 6), I resist the attribution of causal powers to entities that cannot be observed. Instead, I would direct attention to the specific statuses, offices and roles that turn us (and derivatively, our institutions) into the social agents we do see in action (Chapter 1). These conditions of agency result from the application of rules and speak to the pervasive presence of what I earlier called a normative setting and here call an institutional context.

In my view, norm talk puts too much emphasis on internalization and too little on institutionalization. (For more on both processes, see Onuf 2008: 453–5.) Whether we emphasize rules or powers, the related practices must be processes. Beyond those just mentioned, constitution and structuration come to mind in relation to rules, and imitation, argument and training in relation to powers. Above all is production (*poiêsis*): this is Aristotle's most powerful, if implicit, claim. As the most general of processes, making and doing depend on the interplay of rules and powers.

Production and consumption

If production is a process of the most general order for social beings, we might want to ask what this makes the process of consumption. Obviously, production depends on the availability and then the consumption, or utilization, of resources, but these resources have themselves been produced as such. It would seem then that using resources are actions embedded in more general productive processes, and Aristotle's claim stands unchallenged. There is, however, a conceptual advantage to treating production and consumption as different, if complementary, kinds of activities: we can highlight *choice* as a distinguishing property of agency.

Aristotle himself assigned an important place to choice, or decision. We need only recall the first words of the *Nicomachean Ethics*, as quoted above: "Every craft and every line of inquiry, and likewise every action and decision, seem to seek some good." The Greek term for decision, *prohairesis*, suggests that one deliberates and then chooses before acting. Another recent translation renders *prohairesis* "rational choice" (Aristotle 2000: 1). We should recall, however, Bourdieu's remark, quoted above, that our sense of having deliberated before choosing is often enough a retrospective invention.

We make rational choices—at least some of them deliberate—in the process making things. As Aristotle suggested, each choice is itself an action (or is necessarily followed by an action; I am not sure Aristotle thought deciding not to act would be an action in itself). Many such choices involve the consumption of a good, or resource, that ongoing activity makes available for use. More than this, every action depends on a choice about the use of resources broadly defined; any general conception of production as activity depends on an equally general conception of consumption as rational action.

Aristotle offered no such general conception of consumption. It remained for early modern thinkers such as Grotius, Pufendorf and Locke to situate productive individuals, as sensuous beings, in a grid of rights and duties enabling them to make choices, consume resources, and exercise their powers. The gradual emergence of a general theory of unconstrained consumption and unintended consequences is, of course, a hallmark of liberal practice and duly eventuated in the conceptual edifice of microeconomic theory (as argued in Chapter 10).

Nor did Aristotle have a general conception of *strategic choice*—choice that takes into consideration its effect on someone else's actions. (On strategic choice, see Chapter 7.) In other words, he had no worked-out view of that class of activities we call games, and thus of those actions that we think of as moves in a game. While he thought of process as movement (*kinêsis, metabolê*), his metaphors are physical, not social. Strategic interaction is a pervasive kind of social activity, but one whose indeterminacy is difficult to reconcile with Aristotle's teleological worldview.

The conceptual developments necessary for theorizing about strategic interaction are one of the most impressive achievements of modern thought (see Hardin, 2003, for an accessible treatment). In my view, microeconomic theory only became possible with these same developments, beginning with abstract ideas of utility and ordinal scaling, as against subjective conceptions of worth and worthiness. These same developments have produced two models of rational action.

One model emphasizes the goals, tastes or preferences that rational agents are equipped with. Thus microeconomics starts with a general view of consumption. Individuals make choices in accordance with their tastes, and their tastes are stable enough to be taken as given. The other model of rational action emphasizes rules and institutions. Rules narrow choices and form institutions within which agents act on their preferences; in turn the choices that agents make have an impact on rules and institutions.

These two models are strictly differentiated. Yet they call on each other for satisfactory assessment of individual conduct and collective consequences. Agents have tastes, they makes choices in situations for which rules are always relevant. Consequences follow for agents' welfare, their tastes and the rules affecting subsequent choices.

Obviously the rational choice model oriented to goals or tastes parallels the practice model oriented to human powers: both start with the individual agents. Just as obviously, the rational choice model oriented to rules and the practice model also oriented to rules are closely related. Indeed these two models converge if we conceptualize rules as deontic propositions which, as a class, have relatively stable institutional implications. I have undertaken to show this elsewhere (in discussions of means, ends and interests: Onuf 1989: 270–83; policy statements and their relation to rules: Chapter 7; and consistency, proportionality and reciprocity as master rules of social construction: Onuf 2008: 458–66).

Scholars show little interest in bringing the two rules models together. I suspect that at least some of them are deterred from doing so because, in their view, rules are either as exogenously fixed algorithms having direct causal effects or shared beliefs making the world intersubjectively meaningful, but not both. In other words, bringing the models together would effectively relocate Turner's problem from practice to the rules guiding practice. Yet moving the problem from practice to rules *could* make the problem go away by giving due attention to the deontic, and thus normative, properties of rules as such.

To make a larger point, choice is integral to action; action always involves consumption of resources; at the same time, action contributes to productive activity. Agents have goals and powers, and they act in ruled settings. Goals and games are nested. Every assessment of action depends on a theoretical or explanatory model of consumption, and every assessment of activity depends on a model of production (even if both kinds of models are folk theories).

In the most general terms, neither set of models can do without the other. If rational choice achieves its logical coherence by dissociation from larger context of productive processes, this achievement is only provisional. If students of practice disregard rational choice, this exclusion undermines the empirical richness that an inclusive point of view makes so attractive. Ontological differences and methodological preferences always affect scholarly practices and limit choices. Nevertheless, we should never lose sight of the productive processes situating choices, rules and practices and eventuating in social construction.

9

FRIENDSHIP AND HOSPITALITY

(2009)

An odd conjunction

Associating *friendship* and *hospitality* may not seem especially odd. After all, the organizers of a conference on international political theory (for which I wrote this essay) conjoined these terms as an "indicative theme." Yet treating friendship and hospitality as comparable categories seems to me, as a scholar in the field of international relations, to be a mistake. Clarifying what I think is wrong points up the needlessly arbitrary, altogether odd limits that scholars in two fields—international relations and political theory—have imposed on themselves (and each other).

In the field of International Relations, the series *friends, rivals, enemies* functions as a convenient, seemingly "natural" classification for the relations of states as sovereign equals—relations that are allegedly anarchical by virtue of states' formal independence.[1] Even if the parallel series *kin, neighbors, strangers* functions as an informal classification system for social relations in general, it has no place whatsoever in the field. That the term *neighbor* (or more especially *good neighbor*) frequently turns up speaks to its metaphorical power. That we may owe foreigners the *hospitality* due to strangers has become a matter of much recent discussion, thanks largely to the way political theorists with cosmopolitan predilections read Kant's *Perpetual Peace*, but only at the margins of the field of international relations (see for example Shapiro 1998: 695–713; Benhabib 2004: 25–48; Benhabib 2006: 20–6; Hayden 2005:15–22). From my point of view, the odd and puzzling conjunction of *friendship* and *hospitality* begs for a conceptual

---

1   See notably Wendt (1999: 257–9), where friend, rival and enemy are roles producing familiar cultural forms or, in the context of international relations, distinctive "cultures of anarchy." On (Kantian) friendship, see pp. 298–9, (Lockean) rivalry, pp. 279–83, (Hobbesian) enmity, pp. 260–3.

assessment that speaks to scholars in my field but necessarily draws on sources more familiar to political theorists.

Looming over any discussion of friendship and hospitality today is the intimidating figure of Jacques Derrida. A good deal of Derrida's later work touches political issues (some of them transparently "international"). Yet Derrida has never had a substantial audience in a field where most scholars take the anarchical relations of states to bind their concerns and adopt the model of science to investigate these relations. Derrida has fared better among political theorists, few of whom have any interest in the properties of anarchy or the field of International Relations, even as they share Derrida's concern for issues that are manifestly political and transparently international. By taking us back to Aristotle and Kant, long before the emergence of autonomous scholarly fields and their anarchical social relations, Derrida's substantially unrelated treatments of friendship and hospitality help in identifying and clarifying just such relations—social relations that are anarchical in some formal sense of the word, thoroughly political, yet hardly confined to states.

If international political theory is to succeed in bringing two conceptually remote fields within "speaking distance," then Derrida's treatments of friendship and hospitality offer an obvious place to start. I do not propose to gloss these treatments, much less to situate them in the body of his work or subject them to critical assessment. Indeed, I make no claim to have combed his work—a vast, learned and (to the casual visitor) inhospitable archive—for relevant materials. Since I regard Derrida as a conceptual provocateur, I approached some few of his late texts in search of provocation.

Four texts gave me what I was looking for, one on friendship, three on hospitality: *The Politics of Friendship* (Derrida 1997a), *Adieu to Emmanuel Levinas* (Derrida 1999), *Of Hospitality* (Derrida 2000) and "Hostipitality" (Derrida 2002; also see Benhabib 2006: 155–8, for a lucid summary of Derrida's views on hospitality). These provocations are not, however, the *aporia*, or conceptual paradoxes, that seem to have provoked Derrida himself. One of these paradoxes is embodied in Montaigne's words, attributed to Aristotle: "O my friends, there is no friend" (Derrida 1997a: vii). The other is contained in "the hidden contradiction between hospitality and invitation" (Derrida 2002: 362).

What has provoked me in these texts is considerably more mundane, and less due to Derrida than confirmed by him. In thinking about friendship, I, too, start with Aristotle. Yet I do not dwell on an oxymoronic, surely ironic phrase that Aristotle may not have uttered at all. Instead, I start where Derrida ended up (1997a: 306), with a "phallogocentric schema" for relations within and among households that Aristotle paradigmatically developed in *Nicomachean Ethics*, Book VIII, *Eudemian Ethics*, Book VII and *Politics*, Book I, and Kant effectively reproduced in "The Doctrine of Virtue" (Kant 1996: Part II; see Derrida 1997a: 252–63).[2] In thinking about hospitality, Aristotle offers little and Kant, despite a

---

2   I should emphasize here that I read Aristotle's works (all of them lecture notes or transcriptions) as forming a relatively seamless whole. While specialists point to numerous inconsistencies, for example, between the two *Ethics*, which overlap

large literature to the contrary, not much more. Here Derrida's provocation lies in the way he developed the relations in a family of terms: host, guest (in French *hôte*), hospitality, hostility and hostage.

oikia d'esti tis philia

According to Aristotle, friendship (*philia*) should be understood as a relation between two or more people who bear good wishes for each other (*Rhetoric* II, 1380b36–1381a1). There are three kinds or forms (*eidê*) of friendship, respectively based on excellence, utility, and pleasantness. While fleeting pleasures gives rise to shifting friendships among the young, the majority of adult friendships emerge and endure because they are useful. Nevertheless, the primary form of friendship is grounded in and directed toward excellence or virtue (*aretê*) (*Eudemian Ethics* VII, 1236a17–b1).

Aristotle's three forms of friendship might seem to resemble, or even derive from, the three parts of the soul or mind (*psuchê*)—spirit, reason or calculation, and appetite—that Plato identified in human beings and then used to differentiate the three kinds of citizens needed for a properly ruled city (*Republic,* 440a–441a). Despite frequent allusions to the mind's parts, Aristotle expressly rejected Plato's tripartite scheme (*On the Soul* III, 432a22–b7). Instead he viewed the human mind as an ensemble of co-functioning faculties (Koziak 2000: Chapter 3; Lebow 2008a: Chapter 2). As we shall see below, these faculties are unequally distributed by nature but subject to development, through and for friendship, in and for the *polis*.

In Aristotle's scheme, each kind of friendship is further divided. The very term *friendship* implies equality (*isotês*), and Aristotle made an important distinction between two kinds of equality. The first he called numerical equality and the second proportional equality—an inequality that is nevertheless in proportion to the natural differences between kinds of people (*Eudemian Ethics* VII, 1238b15–21; on the justice of proportional equality, see *Nicomachean Ethics* V, 1131a10–b24). Thus there are friendships between equals; each friend counts for one, and what each contributes to the friendship is, formally speaking, the same. If I am your friend, then you are my friend: reciprocity rules. And then there are friendships between inferiors and superiors; each contributes unequally and perhaps incommensurately to the relationship because everyone has different faculties and performs different functions for the whole—friendship, family, *polis*, each as a whole composed of lesser wholes.

Indeed for Aristotle, "the family is a friendship": *oikia d'esti tis philia* (*Eudemian Ethics* VII, 1242a27; Derrida's translation 1997a: 200). In keeping with Aristotle's general ontological stance and his discussion of friendship by kinds, I would expand this overly concise formulation. The family functions

---

in content but were evidently prepared at different times, none of these problems render Aristotle's views on friendship unintelligible.

as such in a household (*oikía*). Since the household consists of a number of people whom Aristotle thought were naturally held together by functionally differentiated relations (parents and children, husband and wife, brothers and sisters, masters and slaves), it must be composed of different kinds of friends. By the same reasoning, a political society is composed of households (*sunkeitai polis ex oikiô, Politics* I, 1253b2), whose members may be friends with members of other households. As Derrida remarked, friendship is "thoroughly political" (1997a: 200): *en oikiai prôton archai kai pêgai philias kai politeias kai dikaiou* (*Eudemian Ethics* VII, 1242b1–2)—"in the household first we have the sources and springs of friendship, of political organization, and of justice" (Barnes 1984: 1969).

Within the household, Aristotle held that the friendship of brothers is a relation of equals, while the friendship between father and son is a proportionate relation of inequality. Based on utility, the relation of husband and wife is also unequal (*Eudemian Ethics* VII, 1242a31–6). Aristotle was conspicuously silent on the basis for the other relations in this scheme, and Derrida took these other relations to be primary.

> If the feminine figure seems exterior to the determining centre of familial friendship (father/son/brothers), this does not mean for Aristotle that all friendship is excluded, in general, between man and woman, husband and wife. It means only—and here is the exclusion—that such a friendship belongs neither to properly familial or syngenic friendship nor to friendship in the highest sense, primary or virtuous friendship.
>
> (1997a: 201)

I do not think Derrida is entirely right here. While Aristotle's scheme is undeniably "phallogocentric," other passages in Aristotle's discussion of family friendship suggest that friendship between spouses is properly familial, and not just because the family constitutes a household and thus an economic enterprise (*Politics* I, 1253b2–14). If the relation of husband to wife is instrumental (and unequal, in Aristotle's opinion), it is no less the case that the relations of father to son and brother to brother (the first unequal and the second equal) constitute partnerships of a political kind.

Aristotle claimed quite emphatically that all kinds of household relations are political.

> For the association [*koinônia*] of a father and his sons bears the form of monarchy [*basileias echei schêma*: echoes or models of kingship] … The association of man and wife seems to be aristocratic [*aristokratikê*] … The association of brothers is like timocracy [*timokratikê*: rule by people of worth].
>
> (*Nicomachean Ethics* VIII, 1160b24–1161a3, quoting Barnes 1984: 1834; also see 1161a18–29)

Again:

> The government of the children by the father is royal [*basilikê*], the relation of
> husband and wife aristocratic, the relation of brothers that of a commonwealth
> [*politeia*: for Aristotle a general term for an established political arrangement
> or, in this case, a synonym for timocracy as a form of rule].
> (Eudemian Ethics VII, 1241b29–32; Barnes 1984: 1968;
also see 1242a31–6)

All such relations exemplify the forms of rule that Aristotle canonically
identified for political society (*Nicomachean Ethics* VIII, 1160a32–b22, *Politics*
III–IV, 1279a23–1279b10, 1289a26–b26), and not just the good forms. Paternal
rule may thus turn into tyranny. Aristotle held this to be true of Persians, for
whom sons are slaves. That masters rule over slaves makes them tyrants, though
appropriately, because slaves lack the necessary faculties to be ruled any other
way (*Nicomachean Ethics* VIII, 1160b29–33). The rule of a man over his wife
may become oligarchic when he denies her the opportunity to function in the
household as her nature suits her (1160b35–7). The timocratic rule of brothers
seems not to have a perverse form, perhaps because, not ruling the household,
they cannot rule it badly. If no father were present, then the brothers (or perhaps
the eldest among them) would rule in his place, perhaps badly, although Aristotle
appears not to have considered these arrangements. Instead he suggested that
households having no head take a democratic form because everyone is equal
and, we may infer, in need (1161a6–7; on democracy as rule by the many in
need, see *Politics* III, 1279b19–1280a6).

Aristotle was not entirely consistent. Reprising the family scheme in *Politics*,
he asserted that a husband rules his children royally (*basilikôs*) but his wife
timocratically (*politikôs*) and not aristocratically (*Politics* I, 1259a37–b2). I take
this to be a simple error in word choice, perhaps even a transcription error.
More telling is his discussion in *Nicomachean Ethics*, which, in good Aristotelian
fashion, proceeds in functional terms. Man and woman come together

> not only for the sake of reproduction but also for the various purposes
> of life; for from the start the functions [*erga*] are divided, and those of
> man and woman are different, so they can help each other by throwing
> their peculiar gifts into the common stock. It is for these reasons that both
> utility and pleasure seem to be found in this kind of friendship. But this
> friendship may be based also on excellence, if the parties are good; for each
> has its own excellence and they will delight in the fact.
> (Nicomachean Ethics VIII, 1162a21–7, quoting Barnes 1984: 1836; also see
1158b17–20)

This line of reasoning is inconsistent with Derrida's reading of *Eudemian
Ethics*; the relation of husband and wife is not simply instrumental. Even more,

it is inconsistent with Aristotle's claim that there are three kinds of friendship. It would be better (and more consistent with Aristotle's functional ontology) to say that every friendship mixes an appreciation of excellence, utility and pleasure in some measure. Furthermore, the functional properties of friendship can reinforce or undercut each other, depending on circumstances—not just contingent events or natural developments (growing up, growing old)—but on the way individual human beings respond to circumstances, given the functional properties of their minds (spirit, reason and appetite).

What then is left of Aristotle's scheme? Families depend on three kinds of relations: father and son, husband and wife, brother to brother. Households add a fourth kind of relation—master and slave—not clearly a relation between friends. On this point, Aristotle equivocated: one cannot be friends with a "slave *qua* slave," but one can be friends with a slave "insofar as he is a man" (*Nicomachean Ethics* VIII, 1161b3–8, quoting Barnes 1984: 1835; also see *Politics* I 1259b21–9). Whether slaves are living tools no different from livestock, or men and women, their function is to serve the household, just as it is the wife's function. Yet the head of the household also has an important function in household management (*oikonomikê*).

Aristotle's discussion of this function is substantially devoted to the need to provide for the household's well-being *(chrêmatistikê*: making money; *ktêtikê*: acquisition) (*Politics* I, 1253b24–1254a17, 1256a1–1260b23) and by extension, the good of the *polis* as an aggregate of households (1257b36). Clearly implied but never fully specified is a division of labor. Wives manage households as such, following orders from their husbands, by giving orders, on their behalf, to children and slaves. Conversely, heads of households give orders delegating duties to wives (on this point, Aristotle is clear: *Nicomachean Ethics* VIII, 1260b35). Doing so enables them to attend to business outside the household, where they must deal, as equals and like brothers, with other heads of households.

At the same time, heads of households rule their families as kings rule cities and Zeus rules the gods: by exemplifying the excellence of those who are naturally superior and garnering the respect of all those who are inferior. This is the same kind of respect that the younger should show to their elders and that we acknowledge in the titles and tokens we confer on those whom we admire for their excellence. Since wives who do well in their household duties earn the respect of others, including their husbands, they earn the titles and tokens of respect appropriate to their stations (*Politics* I, 1259b7–17). Even younger brothers owe their older brothers the respect of age, and if the difference in age is great enough, then they are indeed no longer equals (*Nicomachean Ethics* VIII,1151a5–6). We can generalize Aristotle's position on royal rule. Kings and household heads need not rule in any active sense, because they are ruled by the kinds of duties and correlative emblems of respect their stations confer on them. In due proportion, so is everyone else.

Despite appearances, Aristotle's scheme for ruled relations is not predicated on the three forms of rule elaborated in *Politics*—rule by one, few or many.

Nor, conversely, are the forms of rule predicated on the three forms of family friendship—father and family, husband and wife, brothers. Instead, rather inductively, Aristotle arrived on a general model of social relations in three forms, each of which instantiates itself as a stable, functionally mandated system of rule in a variety of circumstances. Nothing makes this clearer than Aristotle's treatment of the relations of brothers.

According to Aristotle, the basis for numerical (formal) equality in friendship is similarity *(homoiotês)* (*Nicomachean Ethics* VIII, 1159b2–7). Brothers are friends because, as sons, they have the same formal relation to their father (Aristotle takes this for granted—birth order seems not to count—just as he takes for granted that sisters are not their brothers' equals) and, as brothers, they are "born of the same parents and brought up together and similarly educated," and thus "more akin in character" (1162a12–13), quoting Barnes 1984: 1836; also see 1161b29–33). Brothers are closest when close in age. Conversely, cousins are less close in family ties, less likely to be similar, and less close as friends (1161b34– 1162a3; also see *Eudemian Ethics* VII, 1242a5–6). More generally, companions or comrades *(hetairoi)* are like brothers; "familiarity makes for comradeship" (*Nicomachean Ethics* VIII, 1161b34–35, quoting Barnes 1984: 1836).

> Yet there is more to friendship between comrades than similarity and familiarity.
>
> Every form of friendship, then, involves association, as has been said. One might, however, mark off from the rest both the friendship of kindred and of comrades. Those of fellow-citizens, fellow-tribesmen, fellow-voyagers, and the like are more like mere friendships of association, for they seem to rest on a sort of compact [*homologia*: agreement].
>
> (*Nicomachean Ethics* VIII, 1161b8–16, quoting Barnes 1984: 1835)

One might interpret this passage as distinguishing kinship and companionship because the former is a matter of birth (and thus primary) and the latter a matter of choice (and thus instrumental).[3] I would suggest, however, that Aristotle meant to distinguish all formally equal friendships from all those that are functionally proportionate. As we have seen, friendships mix excellence, utility and pleasure, and this includes family relations. Brothers can agree not to be close, despite their common parentage and upbringing. Voyagers may have been brought together by choice, but their circumstances make them close, whether they like it or not. And in Aristotle's world, it is an honor for household heads to be citizens but not a choice.

The friendship of formal equals, whether brothers or comrades, is always implicated in the life of the *polis* (*Eudemian Ethics* VII, 1242a1–2). Civic friendship (*politikê philia*) rests not just on formal equality but also on utility (*chrêsimos*: that which is good for use); "just as cities are friends to one another, so in the like way

---

3   See for example Terence Irwin's note on this passage in Aristotle (1999: 285).

are citizens" (*Eudemian Ethics* VII, 1242b22–3, quoting Barnes 1984: 1968). Again equivocating, Aristotle distinguished between two kinds of agreement—legal and moral (*nomikos*: conventional; *êthikos*: reflecting good character)—evidently differentiating business partners and comrades. Legal agreement is voluntary and temporary, while moral agreement depends on trust. Often business partners will claim to be comrades too, only to fall out because they do not trust each other's professions of comradeship, "for friendships based on utility and based on excellence are different" (1242b30–1243a2, quoting 1242b39; Barnes 1984: 1970). Yet business relations always depend on the generalized trust—the willingness to trust—that makes political arrangements workable and the *polis* a functional whole. Without this sort of trust, no household could flourish and no father could secure his family's respect.

The result of discretionary agreements between formal equals is a reciprocity that, by being cumulatively "proportionate," holds them together (*Nicomachean Ethics* V, 1132b34–6; on "proportionate reciprocity" and the function of money in expediting it, see 1133a7–b7). Trust arises from and depends on the reciprocity that every such agreement presupposes. In effect, every such agreement is an exchange of promises, backed up by the normative presumption that promises should be kept, by the practical consequences of reciprocity when promises are broken, and by the sheer weight of innumerable agreements. All three factors in backing up agreements support the assumption that formal equals, and they alone, can exchange promises. As far as I can tell, Aristotle had little to say about promising, although what I have just said is easily inferred from his remarks about reciprocity, agreements and trust.

Relegating Aristotle to the distant past, early modern writers made the exchange of promises a central theme in their social theories. When they did so, they forgot that Aristotle made the relations of formal equals a form of rule based on their capacity, as friends, to make choices, promises and agreements. So too had he made the relations of father and son, husband and wife, forms of rule, well known today as *hegemony* and *hierarchy*. The third, less visible form of rule, identifiable in the relations of brothers, of companions, of householders and of cities, I have called *heteronomy* (Chapter 1).

Aristotle's general model of social relations ineluctably leads to forms of rule. Yet it starts in the mind, with *philia*, which is experienced as an emotion (*pathos*), developed as a faculty (*dunamis*), evinced as a disposition or character trait (*hexis*) and practiced as friendship (see Solokon 2006: 16–19, for helpful discussion). On Aristotle's account, for every emotion there is a contrary.[4] If *philia* is wishing good for others (or love, broadly conceived), its contrary is wishing bad for them (hate: *misos, ekhthra*); friendship's contrary is enmity. Between these contraries are any number of emotional states and their social concomitants (on contraries, see Chapter 4).

---

4   In *Rhetoric* II, Aristotle identified several pairs of emotions besides love and hate, including anger and pity, and fear and confidence. See generally Sokolon (2006), Lebow (2008a: Chapter 2–3).

Where there is heteronomy, or the rule of many partners bound together by agreement, reciprocity and the exercise of choice within the limits of reciprocity, more or less stable and thus identifiable social categories will correspond more or less to the way we feel about our various partners. As friends, we are partners in friendship. As producers and consumers, we are partners in the exchange of things we value. As rivals, partners in a rivalry that we have agreed to conduct among ourselves. As enemies, we are partners in enmity.

For liberal thinkers, autonomous individuals, bound together by their reciprocal rights and duties, choose their partners and, in doing so, constitute kinds of partnership (Chapter 10). Yet the process works both ways. Already constituted, kinds of partnerships effectively select individuals to serve as partners. Households may be partners, and so it is with any other institution that individuals form through friendship.

Thanks to the principle of sovereignty and the practice of recognition, states have made themselves partners (friends of a sort) in an exclusive club. They are formal equals, possessed of rights and duties, always free to choose their friends (of another sort), rivals or enemies. When one partner no longer wishes to be a rival, for example, then the rivalry ends, but not the underlying partnership. Clearly this is not anarchy, whatever scholars in the field of International Relations want to think.

Hospitalität as philanthropie

Strangers have no place in a world of brothers, of friends, rivals and enemies, of partners. When strangers appear, different rules apply—including rules telling strangers and citizen-householders alike what hospitality requires. Different rules apply because fathers rule the household and thus the city as a collection of households. Among friends, hospitality is beside the point.

In Aristotle's conceptual world of friends, strangers hardly matter. That we might love strangers he barely acknowledged. Regard for one's own kind is as natural for human beings as it is for birds and most animals, "whence we praise lovers of their fellow men": *hothen tous philanthrôpous epainoumen* (*Nicomachean Ethics* VIII, 1155a16–21, quoting 1155a20 and Barnes 1984: 1825). Against this rather oblique praise for the sentiments that would come to be associated with Stoicism, Aristotle expressly doubted that "some races of distant foreigners" (*enia genê tôn porrô barbarôn*) even qualify as human. By nature, they "are thoughtless and live by their senses alone" and thus live as beasts: *zontê thêriôdeis* (*Nicomachean Ethics* VII, 1149a9–11, quoting Barnes 1984: 1814).

In Aristotle's actual world, the world of the Greek cities, citizens had families, kin and neighbors. As neighbors, most citizens would know each other and each other's character. And there were strangers *(xenoi)*—in larger cities, people who did not know each other personally, with bad political consequences for the conduct of public life (*Politics* VII, 1326b13–20), and people from distant lands with goods to exchange (again, in Aristotle's opinion, with bad consequences

(Politics I, 1257a31–b16). Obviously, people who engaged in any given act of exchange could be complete strangers and become only slightly less so for having been partners in such an act. Even if the relations of strangers are hospitable, and, in the case of ongoing relations, partners cease to be strangers, none of these acts reflects a concern for the welfare of strangers because they are human beings.

From Hugo Grotius to Adam Smith and Immanuel Kant, many early modern writers invoked a Stoic conception of an ordered cosmos and the world as a city. The apogee for this kind of thinking is not Kant, as many writers today take for granted, but Christian Wolff (Onuf 1998a: Chapter 3; Cavallar 2002: Chapters 3–4). In Georg Cavallar's words,

> there is little new in Kant's cosmopolitan right, in spite of the fact that some contemporary scholars, not knowing its prehistory, are overly enthusiastic … Wolff's universal commonwealth … can be read as an anticipation of Kant's rational ideas of an original contract and original community.
>
> (2002: 367)

Cavallar has also shown early modern writers, including Samuel Pufendorf, Wolff and Kant, to have been preoccupied with the right Europeans claimed for themselves to be received in distant lands, without threat or danger, and to engage in trade.

This is a call for hospitality in the limited sense of friendly relations among strangers that Aristotle accepted, though grudgingly. There is in this way of thinking little sense of *philanthropy*—a duty to love humanity as it is—for which Aristotle had such faint praise. Whether we can or should impute a Stoic ethical sensibility to Kant, its early modern expression hardly results in a strong claim of love for humanity (see Nussbaum 1997 on Stoic influences on Kant's late work, chiefly by way of Cicero, and Gould 1999: 32–4, for an incisive critique of Nussbaum's position). Nor can it be inferred from Kant's treatment of the "natural right of hospitality" enshrined as the Third Definitive Article of Perpetual Peace.

Here is how the Third Definitive Article begins:

> As in the foregoing articles, we are concerned here not with philanthropy [*Philanthropie*], but with *right* [*Recht*: law, right]. In this context, *hospitality* [*Hospitalität*; Kant added *Wirtbarkeit* parenthetically] means the right of a stranger not to be treated with hostility when he arrives on someone else's territory. He can indeed be turned away, if this can be done without causing his death, but he must not be treated with hostility, so long as he behaves in a peaceable manner in the place he happens to be in. The stranger cannot claim the right of a guest to be entertained [*Gastrecht*], for this would require a special friendly agreement [*ein besonderer wohlthätiger Vertrag*] whereby he might become a member of the native household

[*Hausgenossen*] for a certain time. He may only claim a right of resort [*Besuchsrecht*], for all men are entitled to present themselves in the society of others by virtue of their right to communal possession of the earth's surface.

(Kant 1991b: 105–6, emphases in translation)[5]

After affirming Aristotle's distinction between a principled love for everyone and practical relations among relative strangers, Kant alluded to the welcome traditionally accorded a complete stranger. Yet he did so negatively, by denying that strangers have a right to such a welcome (*Gastrecht*). Receiving a stranger would seem to be discretionary (is the stranger evidently harmless, in need, unaccompanied?), not obligatory—an act of charity. Kant's "special friendly [*wohlthätiger*: charitable] agreement" is tacit in the stranger's unexpected appearance (appearing at one's door, appearing to be harmless, needy and alone) and the householder's welcome. Once welcomed, the stranger becomes a member of the household, but only "for a certain time"—the time needed to rest and be refreshed. No longer a stranger, the guest becomes a visitor, perhaps returning later to the welcoming household, perhaps remaining in the community, but only, by right, as a transient engaged in trade and other useful activities.[6]

Perhaps Kant viewed love for all, including strangers, a virtue approximating a universal duty (but not a categorical imperative). Perhaps he viewed charity toward strangers a virtue that becomes a local duty by convention. Given Kant's cosmopolitan reputation, he was oddly silent about the obligation to love strangers in general (as compared, for example, to his fierce condemnation of lying under any circumstance). If there is any such an obligation, exempting the stranger at one's door from the general category of those to whom love is owed in principle makes no sense.

Yet Kant was clear on this point: no stranger at the door could expect hospitality in every circumstance. As I just suggested, receiving a stranger into

---

5 The term *Wirtbarkeit* is not in common use, but see Derrida (1996), where he associated Kant's *Wirtbarkeit* with *oikonomia*.

6 This is not the usual reading of this difficult passage. Compare my reading, for example, with Seyla Benhabib's (1991: 43):

> Kant distinguishes between the "right to be a permanent visitor", which he calls *Gastrecht*, from the "temporary right of sojourn", from *Besuchsrecht*. The right to be a permanent visitor is awarded to one through a freely chosen special agreement which goes beyond the call of moral duty and legal right; Kant names this a "wohltaetiger Vertrag".

While this reading comports with the Lewis White Beck's well-known translation of *Perpetual Peace* (the relevant passage of which Benhahbib quoted), it assumes that Kant was contrasting temporary and permanent visitors, when I believe he was contrasting hospitality as a charitable act (strictly limited in duration) with hospitality as a regime of friendly relations (imposing various, instrumentally defined limits on visitors).

one's home may nevertheless be an obligation because custom makes it so. What for Kant was a matter of discretion, the head of a household could interpret as a customary obligation. Not knowing what local custom requires, the stranger has cause to expect hospitality only insofar as such customs are to be found in many places.

Wherever there is a customary obligation to welcome the stranger at one's door, custom will also qualify one's obligation by reference to circumstances. Typically, the head of the household (and only he) *must* invite the stranger to enter his home, if (as I said earlier) the stranger is evidently harmless, in need and unaccompanied. We find no better illustration of this suite of obligations than Homer's tale of Odysseus washing up on Corcyra, the land of the Phaeacians (Homer 1900: Books 5–8). On that shore he lay asleep, naked and alone. When Nausicaa, daughter of the local king, discovered him (with some divine assistance), he awoke and asked himself, "to the land of what mortals am I now come? Are they cruel, and wild, and unjust? Or do they love strangers [*philoxeinoi*] and fear the gods in their thoughts?" (6.119–121).

Odysseus had nothing to fear. Nausicaa provided him with fine clothes and brought him to her father's house. There her father and his host, Alcinoos, gave Odysseus a great banquet even before asking his guest's name. Indeed he is addressed throughout as "stranger," the word itself a title of distinction, and on occasion as "father stranger" (*xenie pater*: Homer 1900: 7.29, 7.48, 8.408). A naked stranger has no status beyond that which gender and age accord; the many rules that assign status in such societies are suspended at the moment of his appearance.

When the father decides to extend hospitality—*must* decide and, in this circumstance, *must* extend it—the stranger is granted the respect due the head of a household. His status for that occasion is a gift, which only a father may bestow and only a father may receive. When the stranger departs, his status is as it was before his arrival. If indeed he is a man of his host's stature, they will part as brothers.

This familiar episode tells us a great deal about hospitality. Perhaps it is too familiar, too easily "read" by convention and as convention, for Derrida to have considered it. Nevertheless, Derrida's treatment of hospitality brings Odysseus to mind.[7] For Derrida, hospitality comes in two forms, one conditional and the other absolute or unconditional. The former is a matter of convention—"it is inscribed in a right, a custom, an *ethos* and a *Sittlichkeit*"; it "presupposes the social and familial status of the contracting parties, that it is possible for them to be called by their names, to have names, to be subjects in law ..." (Derrida 2000: 23). If this is the kind of hospitality to which Kant gave his attention in *Perpetual Peace* (Derrida 2000: 27), then

---

7 I am not alone. See Naas (2003: 156–9) who, in recounting this tale, paired it with Odysseus's encounter with the Cyclops Polyphemus. The latter tale is "a parody of sorts of the rites of hospitality, an inversion of roles" (p. 156) so assiduously honored by Alcinoos and Odysseus.

> absolute hospitality requires that I open up my home ... to the absolute, unknown, anonymous other, and that I *give place* to them [emphasis and plural pronoun in translation], that I let them come ... without asking of them either reciprocity (entering into a pact) or even their names.
>
> (Derrida 2000: 25)

This other kind of hospitality would be Kant's *if* a love for strangers were the categorical imperative he could not make himself believe in.

For Derrida, the two kinds of hospitality do not preclude each other. Though opposites, each "becomes hospitable to its other" (Derrida 2002: 362). Instead, the one is "strangely heterogeneous to" the other, much "as justice is heterogeneous to the law to which it is yet so close, from which it is in truth indissociable" (Derrida 2000: 27). The two forms differ in duration and immediacy or perhaps intensity. Unconditional hospitality demands a suspension of time and, with it, a suspension of all of the conventional obligations that would otherwise be in force. This act of suspension, this interruption, closely resembles the bracketing, as a phenomenological procedure, that any deconstructive reading of a text also depends on. "Hospitality is the deconstruction of the at-home; deconstruction is hospitality to the other, to the other than oneself, the other than its 'other,' to another who is beyond any 'its other'" (Derrida 2002: 364).[8]

Notwithstanding all the attention that Kant's brief discussion of hospitality has occasioned, Kant gave us little help in spelling out the content of conditional hospitality. We get considerably more help from Derrida, but I am not sure we need it. Where he has helped is in explaining what happens when the stranger comes to the door and all convention is suspended for the moment. According to the "implacable law" of unconditional hospitality,

> the *hôte* who receives (the host), the one who welcomes the invited or received *hôte* (the guest), the welcoming *hôte* who considers himself the owner of the place, is in truth a *hôte* received in his own home. His home does not belong to him; the *hôte* as host is a guest. The dwelling opens itself to itself, to its "essence" without essence.
>
> (Derrida 2002: 41)[9]

Accompanying this radical instability in roles and even of place is radical uncertainty as to the intentions of either *hôte*. Etymology reveals the uncertainty

---

8   Also see Naas (2003: 160–5), on hospitality as deconstruction by virtue of their "undeniable structural similarity" (p. 162).

9   Derrida further claimed that "[t]his absolute precedence of the welcome, of the welcoming, of welcom*ing* [*accueillance*], would be precisely the femininity of 'Woman,' interiority as femininity—and as 'feminine alterity'" (2002: 43). I think this claim is regrettable because it validates a phallogocentric view of the household as woman's proper sphere of life and untenable because it fails to acknowledge the phallogocentric thrust of both laws of hospitality as instantiated together in historical experience.

at the moment at the door. In Latin, *hostis* is stranger: the one whose arrival is unexpected, intentions undisclosed, capacities yet to be assessed, one who is other than the other others, an alien (as if from another planet), a hostile (as North American natives came to be known to settlers), "the foreigner (*hostis*) welcomed as guest or enemy" (Derrida, 2000: 45). But enemy (*inimicus*, not-friend) is not right, for one's enemies are already known for their enmity; they are enemies by agreement.[10] Etymology says it all: "Hospitality, hostility, *hostpitality*" (Derrida 2000: 45, read *hostipitality*; the French text has "*hostipitalité*", Derrida 1997b: 45; also see Derrida 2002: 419).

Host and guest have no grounds for trusting the other. When the stranger enters, the host may harm or enslave the guest, and the stranger may attack the host and pillage the household. Even if both are naked and thus stripped of their status, each remains a potential threat to the other. This is indeed the thrust of Hobbes's theatrical, and very effective, representation of the state of nature (1991: Chapter 13; on the state of nature as Hobbesian theater, see Onuf and Onuf 2006: 118–27) and the core of the security dilemma so well known to students of international relations: with no information to the contrary, a rational being must impute the worst possible intentions to other rational beings, because they have no choice but to do the same. If anarchy there be, this is it, pure and simple.

According to Hobbes, the only way out of the security dilemma is agreement, with its presuppositions about the formal equality of partners and their capacity to make and keep promises (Chapter 14; see generally Booth and Wheeler 2008). Host and guest have the strongest possible incentive to enter into Kant's "special agreement" to end the moment of uncertainty and bring convention back into force. To do so is to reaffirm heteronomy as rule by many partners. In this view, heteronomy is the *sine qua non* of social life, and anarchy an imagined condition or perhaps a fleeting aberration—an instance of the "first encounter" so vividly imagined if rarely experienced (Todorov 1984; also see Inayatullah and Blaney 1996; Wendt 1999: 326–36).

Extrapolating from Derrida, there is another way out of the security dilemma. At the moment of welcome, with its radical uncertainty and rational fear, before any agreement to end the moment, to exchange names and courtesies, host and

---

10 The suspension of conventional obligations at the moment of unconditional hospitality bears a marked resemblance to Carl Schmitt's rationale for the suspension of a state's constitution at the moment that enemies mount an existential threat to the state. In this context, the term *enemy* suggests a category mistake, perhaps stemming from the absence in German of readily distinguishable terms for *enmity* and *hostility*. Nevertheless, Schmitt's claim that enemy is "the stranger, the other," someone who is "in a specially intense way, existentially something different and alien, so that in the extreme case conflicts with him are possible" (1996: 27), suggests instead that translators should use *hostile* and its cognates whenever Schmitt used *Feind* and its cognates. Appropriately, one of the chapters in Derrida's *Politics of Friendship* substantially devoted to Schmitt is titled "Absolute Hostility" (1997a: 112–37).

guest might be said to have taken each other hostage. The terms *host* and *hostage* may not be etymologically related—the latter term may come from the former, or it may come from the Latin *obses*, which links the condition of being held as hostage or under siege and the condition of being haunted or obsessed (also see Derrida 1999: 56–7). Indeed the roots seem tangled (Derrida spoke of "a semantic, if not etymological, kinship between *host* and *hostage*," p. 57). The fear experienced by both is fixed not just in time but also in place. The host's home, "which, in the end, does not belong to him" (Derrida 1999: 41) is under siege— it would seem by both host *and* guest.

> The host [*hôte*] is a hostage insofar as he is a subject put into question, obsessed (and thus besieged), persecuted, in the very place where he takes place, where, as emigrant, exile, stranger, a guest [*hôte*] from the very beginning, he finds himself.
>
> (Derrida 1999: 56, brackets in translation)

By making each other hostages, host and guest use the other's fear as a deterrent, which, in the absence of better information, is *prima facie* credible (on the logic of deterrence, see Morgan 2003: Chapter 2). When nothing unexpected happens, host and guest have an opportunity to size each other up, assign statuses, come to (some sort of) agreement.[11] If the guest is a father and household head, then, as formal equals, host and guest may agree to act as brothers, to become friends or rivals or enemies. Or, if the guest is an absent father's son, then the host as father may invite the guest to remain in the household, as if the host's own son, and the guest is more or less free (as hostage) to accept this invitation, or to leave the household with all of the assistance that a son might expect.

In short, there are only hostages. If this seems like anarchy, then it rules only for the moment. Between host and guest, among us all, the Stockholm effect goes to work. In circumstances where radical uncertainty and rational fear extends beyond the moment, hostages can no longer resist their takers. Indeed, hostages begin to identify with those whom they fear, in effect shamed by being vulnerable, "naked" and alone into abandoning their otherness. Instead, they begin to live the fiction that they are at home with their brothers. The household shelters and duly domesticates the hostages within its walls.

The deterrent value of holding hostages is, of course, well-known. So is the practice among warlords of sending a son to live, as if a son, in a rival's household. Well-treated hostages serve as insurance policies.[12] Dynastic marriages are

---

11   This sequence of events is long familiar, made so by David Hume and his discussion of the emergence of convention in *A Treatise of Human Nature*, III, ii, ii (1978: 489–91). On conventions and their relation to rules, see Chapter 1.

12   "Hostages are defined as persons who are delivered as security for a debt, namely that an agreement will be performed or a debt will be paid" (Wolff 1934: §497, p. 256). Those for whom a debt is mostly likely to be paid should be given as

structurally similar. Princesses are compelled to marry princes whom they do not know and take their place in households far from their father's; in time they come to think of themselves as sons and daughters of their hosts. We can generalize this state of affairs to the early modern warlord system of Western Europe, where the reciprocal placement of well-born hostages in rival households presaged the exchange of diplomats. The immunities and privileges afforded diplomats enable them to identify with their hosts in order to improve relations between households (later, governments) and identify themselves as a community of hostages whose shared experience in foreign lands serves a common good.

philia xenikên

Throughout this essay I have insisted that *friends* and *strangers* belong to unrelated conceptual schemes. Casually lumping these terms together is, as I have suggested, a category mistake. To speak of "strangers who are friends" or "friends who are strangers" points up the absurdity that such a mistake can lead to. Only the Stoic ideal of an abstract love for humanity escapes this absurdity, and only because the philanthropic ideal is so highly abstracted from a world where people who are connected to each other experience friendship and enmity, and strangers experience hospitality and hostility.

Yet Aristotle may seem to have made this very mistake in *Nicomachean Ethics*. Twice in talking about kinds of friendship he included *philia xenikên*—the friendship of strangers—among the useful kind (*Nicomachean Ethics* VIII, 1156a31, 1161b16). Translators have preferred other formulations—"the friendship of host and guest" or "family ties of hospitality among foreigners."[13] And they have done so for good reasons. In these passages, Aristotle was referring not to strangers (*xenoi*) but to ritually bonded friends from autonomous social groups (also *xenoi*).[14] As an institution, "ritualized friendship" (*xenia*) antedated the Greek cities, included relations with and among barbarians, and constituted networks of obligation, including hospitality, preempting civic duties. While these relations were clearly between formal equals, they were not instrumentally motivated, as Aristotle implied, even if they expedited

---

hostages, including women and children, and especially people of high rank (§508–9, p. 262).

13 The friendship of host and guest: Terence Irwin (Aristotle 1999: 122, 132), and W.D. Ross (trans., Barnes 1984: 1827, 1844); family ties of hospitality among foreigners: Horace Rackham (Aristotle 1934: http://www.perseus.tufts.edu/cgi-bin/ptext?looku p=Aristot.+Nic.+Eth.+1156a+1; +1161b+1).

14 As Irwin has suggested in his note on the first of these passages (Aristotle 1999: 276). Also see *Politics* II, 1263b6, on the pleasure of helping "friends or guests [*xenoi*] or companions" (Barnes 1984: 2005). There may of course be other occasions in which Aristotle alluded to *xenia* and *xenoi* that I am not aware of; Derrida did so at least once (2000: 29). The following discussion relies on Herman (1987), as does Koziak's (2000: 188–31); on *Politics* II, 1263b6, see Herman (1987: 122n).

"the circulation of resources" (Herman 1987: 73, chapter title). At least in the first instance, they were forged between warrior-kings and heroes in mutual recognition of excellence (or at least standing), and they passed from father to son.

As a widespread, enduring institution, *xenia* takes us into the world of the fathers, replete with kin and strangers, marked by the hospitality of the household and danger from all sides (see further Lebow 2008b, 480, on honor and the obligations of "guest friendship" as one of Homer's central themes in the *Iliad*). The world of the fathers came before the world of brothers, of the citizens whom Aristotle extolled and the merchants whom he decried. Yet the Homeric world of the fathers never disappeared.

We might even say that the fathers—the privileged few of high birth, many resources and great honor—became ritual brothers to help each other, and they remained so to keep their place in a changing world. Father to son, Cicero affirmed as much for their world (*On Duties*, Book II, §64): "It is most seemly … for the homes of distinguished men to be open to distinguished guests" (Cicero 1991: 89). Seemliness is a cardinal virtue; "this seemliness of which I speak relates to the whole of honorableness …" (I, §95; pp. 36–7).

Indeed the institution, or perhaps the cultural memory, of *xenia* persisted into the early modern world. How else can we make sense of this curious passage from Kant's *Metaphysics of Morals* ("The Doctrine of Virtue," §47)?

> A *friend of human beings* [*Menschenfreund*] as such (i.e., of the whole race) is one who takes an affective interest in the well-being of all human beings (rejoices with them) and will never disturb it without heartfelt regret. Yet the expression *"friend of human beings"* [*Freundes der Menschen*] is somewhat narrower in its meaning than "one who merely loves human beings (a *philanthropist*)" [*Menschenliebenden (Philanthrop)*]. For the former includes thought and consideration for the *equality* among them, and hence the idea that in putting others under obligation by his beneficence he is himself under obligation, as if all were brothers under one father who wills the happiness of all.—For, the relation of a protector, as a benefactor [*Beschützers als Wohlthäters*], to the one he protects, who owes him gratitude, is indeed a relationship of mutual love, but not of friendship, since the respect owed by each is not equal.
>
> (1996: 217)

The one who loves humanity in the abstract (*Philanthrop*) Kant commended, but rather abstractly (just as in *Perpetual Peace*, Definitive Article Three). Those who make friends of others by treating them as equals—*as if* brothers—Kant found to be needing a protector and benefactor—*as if* their father. Here again, Aristotle's phallogocentric scheme does the work. The father owes his sons protection and the benefits of the household (as he does strangers by "special agreement"; recall Definitive Article Three), while the sons owe their father gratitude and assistance. The result is mutual love (*Wechselliebe*) or Aristotle's functionally proportionate friendship, as against the friendship (*Freundschaft*) of Aristotle's formal equals.

The world of the fathers is a world in which every father must have a retinue of kin and as many companions as his standing and resources allow (Herman 1987: Chapter 5). In such a world, there are factions and followers, patrons and clients, but few strangers and few occasions for unconditional hospitality. Fathers are brothers, partners in a vast enterprise, whether allies, rivals or enemies. As fathers, they are bound by the many ceremonies of friendship that suppress the potential for hostility that resides in the very moment of unconditional hospitality. At the same time, visits, banquets, toasts and initiation rituals affirm their standing in the world they have created for themselves and, they would say, their families and followers, their tribes, cities, countries—indeed, everyone to whom they are somehow connected.

Ceremonial ties and expressions of friendship have always informed international relations, and continue to do so in our own time. Yet theoretically inclined scholars in the field of International Relations ignore these ties, and so do moral and political philosophers who would universalize the concept of conditional hospitality. Summit meetings and state visits are not simply or even chiefly public demonstrations of pomp and power. Like fathers, heads of governments welcome each other into an old and exclusive club. Even after they come to know each other personally, they treat each other as honorary strangers, unconditionally due the beneficence of the household during their brief times together. Assisting them are retinues of ministers and functionaries who also stand in for their heads on lesser occasions. Like sons, diplomats present their credentials, attend ceaseless rounds of diplomatic receptions, and await the summons of their surrogate fathers while they live the lives of pampered hostages.

Punctuating the daily conduct of international relations, ceremonial occasions and ritual ties constitute a lifeworld for initiates. Such occasions reaffirm the largely unseen network of obligations that supervene the formal entailments of sovereign equality. They calibrate standing in the process of conferring it. Cumulatively they stratify social relations from the top down. They are instantiations of hegemony in a world—an allegedly modern world— by appearances given over to hierarchy and heteronomy.

A few scholars in the field of International Relations talk about hegemony, but typically as the dominance a powerful state exercises over its neighbors and more rarely the world. So construed, hegemony takes place in an anarchical world. When political theorists, sociologists and sundry other scholars talk about hegemony as cultural phenomenon, they also tend to make the same assumption, though less explicitly. Anarchy is the modern world's default or baseline condition; what happens, happens in a world of states that are, formally speaking, sovereign equals.

In this essay, I reject anarchy's conceptual hegemony. Instead I show that what I call heteronomy better describes the relations of friends, rivals and enemies, all of whom, as partners, are formal equals. States are hierarchies in form and their relations are heteronomous in the first instance. Yet governments consist of people for whom status always matters. These people live in a world in which a great variety of social relations, in every degree of formality, embody Aristotle's proportionate equality. This is hegemony, and it is the condition within which hierarchy and heteronomy take place—the human condition, where all inequalities have their *raison d'être*.[15]

---

15   Here I am paraphrasing N.M. Fustel de Coulanges, *Recherches sur quelques problèmes d'histoire* (1885: 3), on slavery (as quoted in Finley 1980: 67): "it has its roots in an age of the human species when all inequalities had their raison d'être."

PART IV

Making sense of modernity

For those of us influenced by Foucault, the choice of topic and time may be biased.

(Ian Hacking, *Historical Ontology* 2002: 104)

10

INSTITUTIONS, INTENTIONS AND INTERNATIONAL RELATIONS

(2002)

"We students of international affairs need a better theory of institutions." So said Robert Keohane (1993: 293, his emphasis), who is a principal in recent discussions of institutions and their importance. Liberal scholars of an earlier time made institutions the primary subject of their largely descriptive and patently normative inquiries: institutions mattered to them. A new generation of scholars, realist and liberal, start with states as rational agents, and not institutions. They ask whether institutions matter, not to themselves as scholars, but to states making choices consistent with their goals.

The best theory would tell us when institutions *necessarily* matter to states, and *why*. A general explanation of this sort is hard to foresee and almost certainly not what Keohane had in mind. Next best, and better than anything we have now, would be a systematic point of view, a frame of reference, a theory in a much looser sense of the term. It would help us understand the ways in which institutions *possibly* matter by telling us *how* they come about, have the properties that they do, and come to be used.[1]

Economists have also experienced a renewed interest in institutions (Langlois 1986; Rutherford 1994). Thanks chiefly to Friedrich Hayek, they also have a systematic point of view, a "better theory," by which to understand the ways in which institutions matter to rational individuals. Hayek's influence is inestimable. A giant among liberal economists, a polemicist of great power, Hayek was unwavering in his convictions and relentless in espousing them over three decades.

Hayek invariably presented his point of view as a story about Western social thought. By making sense of complex intellectual developments, the story makes his theory plausible. There are, however, other ways to tell the story, and an even better theory to be gained.

---

1   See Wright (1971), on the difference between "why necessary?" and "how possible?"

Hayek went back to the ancient Greeks, and their famous debate over *nature* and *convention*, to show how the terms of that debate inhibited modern Europeans from thinking systematically about institutions. The latter simply assumed that people devise institutions to suit their needs and should design them for everyone's benefit. Hayek blamed Cartesian rationalism for this lamentable reliance on social engineering. As an alternative to institutions by design, there are those that arise as the unintended consequences of self-interested human action. First noticed in the Scottish Enlightenment (mid-eighteenth century), this process had monumental implications. Nevertheless, it remained for an Austrian economist, Carl Menger, to spell them out a century later and for another Austrian, Hayek himself, to bring the message back to Britain.

Taken out of time, this story functions as a sorting device. There are only two possible positions, each of which carries ideological freight. *Either* one believes that institutions are too important to be left to chance because they limit people's choices, for good or bad. Political arrangements exemplified by the modern state fit this description. *Or* one believes that it is important to leave institutions alone because they give people the room that they need to make rational choices. Markets illustrate the point.

By dividing institutions into two sorts, Hayek's story would seem to offer something to any scholar who assumes that agents make rational choices. Yet recent discussions of institutions in the field of International Relations have far more to do with system properties and agent goals and then with the cumulative effect of agents' choices on institutional conditions and the specific effects of institutions on agents' choices (Baldwin 1993: 3–11; Keohane 1993: 269–83). Given Kenneth Waltz's endorsement of markets as "spontaneously generated" and his strong claim that the international system is "structurally similar" to a market, indifference to Hayek's story may seem surprising. Perhaps Waltz's insistence that "the market is not an institution or an agent in any concrete or palpable sense," but instead a "structural cause," is the reason (1979: 90–1; also see Chapter 6). More likely, scholars in the field of International Relations have overlooked Hayek's work because they see economics as a repository of analytically useful concepts (for example, transaction costs) but not of stories by which to understand the ways of the world.

Indifference has its rewards. Hayek's story could not have given International Relations a better theory until it is better told. In substantiating this claim, I identify a third way of looking at the origin and character of institutions. To do so, I follow Hayek back to the ancient Greeks, whose dispute over nature and convention I interpret as having consequences dramatically different from those that he described. While he saw "convention" as the source of 2,000 years of confusion, I see "nature" as the source of a position that he ignored altogether. Nature has its own design, which serves as a template for institutions that human beings make and use for their own purposes. Unacknowledged by Hayek, this was Aristotle's position.

My first large task in this essay is to set out Hayek's magisterial but misguided rendition of institutional possibilities. I turn then to the missing possibility: nature's design as a template for institutions that we design for our own purposes. Over time, nature receded from view, along with Aristotle and any overt acknowledgment of nature's guidance. Left behind is a conception of institutions at two or more levels of generality, linked by purpose.

My second task is to apply this enlarged scheme to contemporary International Relations as a field of study. I focus discussion on liberal scholars, because they are the ones today who most keenly feel the need for a better theory, but I also draw realists into the discussion, because they, too, are liberals. Martin Wight and Hedley Bull, as leading members of the English School, saw institutions as spontaneous developments. By contrast, liberal scholars in the United States typically start with institutional design. If we take Keohane himself, Oran Young and John Ruggie as exemplary figures, we soon find that they are not merely Cartesian rationalists. Each has identified elements in what I have called the third way of construing institutional possibilities.

Unintended consequences

Hayek's thoughts on institutions can be traced to his famous polemic in the great debate of the 1930s and 1940s over planning and freedom, and they were very much shaped by his *laissez-faire* commitments (Hayek 1994). After years of additional reading and reflection, he articulated those thoughts with exceptional cogency (Hayek 1967: 96; footnote deleted).

> The belief in the superiority of deliberate design and planning over the spontaneous forces of society enters European thought through the rationalist constructivism of Descartes. But it has its sources in a much older erroneous dichotomy which derives from the ancient Greeks and still forms the greatest obstacle to the proper understanding of the distinct task of both social theory and social policy. This is the misleading division of all phenomena into those which are "natural" and those which are "artificial." Already the sophists of the fifth century b.c. had struggled with the problem and stated it as the false alternative that institutions and practices must be either due to nature (*physei*) or due to convention (*thesei* or *nomo*); and through Aristotle's adoption of this division it became an integral part of European thought.[2]

Hayek's construction of the "dichotomy" is itself "erroneous." The terms *nature* and *convention* refer to the conditions under which our regular practices acquire the normative force that we routinely ascribe to them. The ancients did

---

2   Also see Hayek (1973: 20), p. 20, where we learn that *nomo* does indeed mean "by convention" but *thesei* "means roughly 'by deliberate decision'."

not uniformly divide all phenomena into these two categories. Depending on which position they adopted, they assigned all *social* phenomena to one category or the other. Naturalists saw no fundamental difference between nature and society: The one gives rise to the other. Conventionalists saw just such a difference: human action gives rise to convention and thus to society. Starting from a naturalist stance, Aristotle tried to accommodate the conventionalist position, but the effect of his efforts was to codify the two positions as alternative ontologies, one identified with Aristotle and the Stoics, the second with the sophists (Onuf 1998a: 31–7).

The Aristotelian position holds that nature has a design which people fulfill by doing what comes naturally—by being social. The thrust of this position favors spontaneous development but *not* as an unintended consequence of self-interested conduct. As reasonable beings, people know that nature has designed them to work together for common good. For the most part, working together works well enough and deliberate planning is necessary only occasionally. When it is necessary, people have nature's design to guide them. There is no opposition between spontaneous development and deliberate design. Instead, they are mutually compatible elements in an ongoing process in which nature follows its purpose and fulfills its potential.

Hayek argued that the terms *nature* and *convention* have resulted in much confusion. Indeed, his story requires the terms *nature* and *convention* to have been a source of confusion until he came along to set the record straight. Yet people were never confused by these terms, and everyone preferred one position to the other: social institutions follow nature's design, or they stand apart from nature. Aristotle's enormous prestige in medieval and early modern Europe assured the dominance of the former position. Only gradually did people become indifferent to the ontological issue that these terms so aptly point to, and only then could they wonder whether it was better to design institutions or to let them happen.

To think of institutions apart from nature, we must be able to think of ourselves apart from nature. Only then is it possible to separate our intentions from nature's design. We may intend that our actions result in or conform to a design. We may not. We may recognize design in the actions of others, whatever their intentions. We may not recognize design in the constraints on our actions. None of these possibilities are required, or prevented, by the move to Cartesian rationalism.

Hayek held, to the contrary, that "the new rationalism of Francis Bacon, Thomas Hobbes and particularly René Descartes contended that all useful human institutions were and ought to be the deliberate creation of conscious reason" (1967: 85). Freed from nature's grip, some early modern thinkers may have been "naïve" (1967: 85) about the human capacity to design good institutions, although I doubt that Hayek's trio deserves the epithet. Indeed, Hayek was less interested in them than in the fact that Descartes was French, and thus in Cartesian rationalism as a French pathology.

From Descartes the new rationalism descended to Rousseau, who "fired the enthusiasm of the successive revolutions which created modern government on the Continent and guided ... the approach to totalitarian democracy in the whole world" (1967: 120). If these connections were not tenuous enough, Hayek could for convenience even drop Rousseau from the sequence, as when he spoke of "the extreme rationalism of the Descartes-Hegel-Marx school" (1967: 95). Ever the ideologue, Hayek read inevitability, and thus necessity, into the history of ideas by reading Continental history backwards. The practical advantage of blaming a rationalist faith in institutional design on the French was to put "the British moral philosophers of the eighteenth century" in the most favorable light possible. It is they who "built up a social theory which made the undesigned results of human action its central object, and in particular provided a comprehensive theory of the spontaneous order of the market" (1967: 99).

The first figure in this development is Bernard Mandeville, who emigrated from Holland to England as a young man and whose *Fable of the Bees* (1714–24) stirred much controversy in its time. An admirer of English institutions, Montesquieu also counts. Most important are the Scottish thinkers, David Hume, Adam Ferguson and Adam Smith. Edmund Burke is less important only because he was not a systematic theorist (Hayek 1973: 22).

Ferguson provided Hayek with the epigram, "the result of human action but not of human design" (1973: 22). Smith most clearly identified the individual's self-interested conduct as the mechanism for promoting society's interest. Yet Hayek bestowed his greatest attention on Hume, who did more than any other writer of his time to show exactly how conventions arise without need of promises—of the institution of promising—through which we so often put our intentions to work. "For even promises themselves ... arise from human conventions" (Hume 1978: 490). So do language, money, ideas of justice and property (Hume 1978: 490; also see Hayek 1967: 111).

Hayek paid little notice to Hume's explanation for the vast array of institutions that characterize society. For good reason: Hume made habit, not self-interest, the centerpiece of his social theory. Instead Hayek identified an evolutionary logic in the sort of institutions Hume deemed basic to society. "In effect, he [Hume] proclaimed a doctrine of the survival of the fittest among human conventions—fittest not in terms of good teeth but in terms of maximum social utility" (Hayek 1967: 111, quoting Bay 1958: 33).

I find no such logic at work. The "peace and security of human society" depend on the development of three conventions: "stability of possession," "transference by consent," and "performance of promises" (Hume 1978: 526; Hayek 1967: 113). Once these "three fundamental laws of nature" are in place, people will follow their many routines and pursue their interests. Society for its part will develop additional institutions of no particular character. Hume's story gives every society the same start, and then allows each to follow its own path.

While Hume's story speaks to conservative liberals and pre-liberal conservatives alike, Hume was no Darwinist ahead of his time. Hayek's forced interpretation of Hume parallels his refusal to see Hobbes as a theorist of unintended consequences. Hobbes indeed saw the war of all against all as an unintended result of fearful people acting rationally to protect themselves. The state of nature is an institution that cannot become something else. Hobbes concluded that deliberate action is the only hope. On ideological grounds, Hayek could never admit that Hobbes might have been right about any institution that develops spontaneously.

It was far easier for Hayek to discredit Hobbes for his rationalist manner of exposition, even though Hume proceeded in the same vein. Hobbes started with nature (the very first word in *Leviathan*) and ended up with the commonwealth as an "Artificiall Man" (Chapter xxi; Hobbes 1991: 147). Hume started his discussion of justice in his *Treatise* with "artifice" and ended up with natural laws (III, ii, i; 1978: 477; also see p. 491). If either analysis contributes to "the misleading division of all phenomena into those which are 'natural' and those which are 'artificial'" (Hayek 1967, as quoted above), then both do. Both started with the individual and ended up with society.

Menger

In Hayek's tragic reading of European history, Hume's social theory never found a Continental audience. Even in Britain, Jeremy Bentham and his utilitarian followers "did not escape the fatal attraction of Rousseau and French rationalism" (Hayek 1967: 94). Nevertheless, we see traces of Hume in the legal theory of Friedrich Karl von Savigny and the German historicalists. Inspired by their work, Menger finally retrieved "the conception of a grown order" from the margins of social thought in 1883 (Hayek 1967: 103–4).

Menger acknowledged that some social phenomena (social institutions, social structures: he, or his translator, used these terms interchangeably) are "the result of agreement of members of society or of legislation" (1963: 146). Starting with the stated intentions of their creators, their origin is easy to explain. With nowhere to start, the origin of much else that is social is impossible to specify. Nevertheless, it is possible to generalize about origins in relation to a defining characteristic of all such social formations: the degree to which they serve the common good.

> Language, religion, law, even the state itself, and, to mention a few economic social phenomena, the phenomena of markets, of competition, of money, and numerous other social structures are already met with in epochs of history where we cannot properly speak of a purposeful activity of the community as such directed at establishing them. Nor can we speak of such activity on the part of rulers. We are confronted here with the appearance of social institutions which to a high degree serve the welfare of society.
>
> (Menger 1963: 146)

For Menger, the task of science is to explain how this general result is possible without slipping into organic metaphors.

> [N]ot even the slightest insight into the nature and the laws of the movement of social phenomena can be gained either by allusion to the 'organic' or 'primeval' character of the processes under discussion, nor even by mere analogies between these and the transformations to be observed in natural organisms.
>
> (Menger 1963: 150)

Using money as an example, Menger concluded that this institution, and many others, including law, language and morals, came about "merely through the impulse of *individual* interests and as a result of the activation of these interests" (1963: 157, emphasis in translation). This elegant explanation repeats Smith's claim that the aggregate of self-interested conduct advances the interest of society and applies it to the range of institutions that Hume had explained as arising from convention.

Although Menger never defined the term *institution*, he clearly had in mind all those social phenomena that we do tend to think about organically, because we design them to function as if they are organisms. Organizations generally fit this description. He also had in mind "a large number of phenomena which cannot be viewed as 'organically' created 'social structures', e.g., market prices, wages, interest rates, etc." (Menger 1963: 158). These, of course, are the observable consequences of individual self-interested choices made in accordance with the rules of established institutions. If such outcomes are observed to be regular, they may, for the usual Humean reasons, become institutions in their own right. If such outcomes are observed to be irregular or otherwise undesirable, they may induce people to decide on rules fixing or changing them.

Menger saw that institutions are continuously subject to undirected development and periodically subject to alteration by design. They are the product of both processes, each fueling the other.

> The present-day system of money and markets, present-day law, the modern state, etc., offer … examples of institutions which are presented to us as a result of the combined effectiveness of individually and socially teleological powers, or, in other words, of 'organic' and 'positive' factors.
>
> (Menger 1963: 158)

This general pattern of development is more or less undirected. Nothing prevents Hobbesian consequences or solutions from entering the mix, or dropping from it.

On my reading of Menger, there is no mechanism of natural selection lurking behind institutional change. On Hayek's reading, what was true of Hume must also be true of Menger: spontaneous development depends on natural selection to prevent Hobbesian consequences. Menger quite possibly accepted the social Darwinism so characteristic of his time. Yet I see no evidence that Menger made a place for natural selection in his conceptual scheme, although he could easily have done so.

Whose design?

Writing thirty years before Menger, Francis Lieber had given institutions an especially thorough consideration. A German immigrant, Lieber was the first academic political scientist in the United States. His book, *On Civil Liberty and Self-Government* (1853) was much admired in its time. Yet political scientists in the United States have long neglected him and the institutional orientation that he pioneered.

Lieber carefully defined the term *institution*, and he followed his definition with an extensive discussion of its use (Lieber 1859: 304–15).

> It always forms a prominent element in the idea of an institution, whether the term be taken in the strictest sense or not, that it is a group of laws, usages and operations standing in close relation to one another, and forming an independent whole with a united and distinguishing character of its own.

Even today, it would be difficult to improve on this definition, which makes rules working together "through human agents" the central feature of any institution (Lieber 1859: 305).

Institutions are everywhere; they exhibit "the greatest variety in character and extent." Conceptually, things are simpler. Some institutions have been "instituted" or "enacted." Others are "grown institutions." Many are mixed.

> Most of the institutions which owe their origin to spontaneous growth have become in course of time mixed institutions. Positive legislation has become mingled with self-grown usage, as is the case with the institution of property, the jury, the bill of exchange, the Hindoo castes, money.
> (Lieber 1859: 305, 307–8)

Lieber and Menger had come to the very same conclusion about the actual situation of important institutions, such as property and money: they are inextricably the result of two quite different processes of development that prompt each other. Viewing the process of spontaneous development in Humean terms, Lieber did not remark on the role of self-interest. Nor did he seem to think that grown institutions were more likely to contribute to the common good than institutions designed for this purpose. Instead, he believed that countries varied in the degree to which their institutions flourished— especially their political institutions.

Lieber disliked France, as Hayek would a century later, for its institutional deficiencies and absolutist tendencies (Friedel 1947: 263–4). Indeed Hayek (1992: 216) approvingly referred to Lieber on this matter. By contrast, institutions prospered in the United States. First, it was the beneficiary of institutions that had spontaneously developed in Britain over the centuries. Second, circumstances in the United States favored a local disposition, which Tocqueville had emphasized (1960: 114–28), to form public associations for any conceivable purpose.[3]

There is, however, more at stake than institutional density. Deeply concerned over centrifugal tendencies within the United States, Lieber felt that "the tendency of localizing may prevail over the equally necessary principle of union"—"the union of the whole, whatever this whole, or Koinon, as the Greeks styled it, may be." Constitutions institutionalize the whole even as "they themselves consist of an aggregate of institutions." In the case of the United States, its "enacted" Constitution "consists of a distinct number of clearly devised and limited, as well as life-possessing institutions" (Lieber 1859: 343–6). In Britain's case, the absence of regional divisions (at least in Lieber's day) well suited the country as a whole to a constitution that had developed spontaneously and remained informal.

Lieber's concern with the institutional whole and its higher purpose is characteristic of political thought in the United States. So is his understanding of the whole as an Aristotelian *koinonia*, or association of parts which are themselves associations whose purposes fit within the whole's. The inspiration for this point of view is the federal union itself; its institutions frame a whole world of institutional possibilities (Onuf and Onuf 1993: Part I). Large social purposes, such as the protection of liberty and self-rule, dictate the general character of these institutions. If necessary, people of reason are capable of coming together to (re)design them, but this is a momentous responsibility and not often necessary. Furthermore, overarching institutions and their purposes always make their presence felt through the activities of particular institutions. The latter's purposes must be consistent with the former's, and this condition limits the possible range of specific institutional features. In these circumstances, "on purpose" design is often warranted, sometimes mandated, but always with the requirements of the whole or, in an earlier version of this position, with nature's design in mind.

As I read Lieber, people are ultimately responsible for carrying out nature's design as they understand it, and they cannot count on nature to do the job for them. Natural selection has no place in his conceptual scheme. Nor is social Darwinism an ideology that Lieber can have favored. Very much of his times, Lieber was a Romantic nationalist given to exceptionalist claims on behalf of his

---

3   Conversations that Tocqueville had with Lieber, who also provided him with materials, contributed to the development of Tocqueville's views. In turn, Lieber was "fired by Tocqueville's interest in American institutions" (Friedel 1947: 89–91, 97–9, quoting p. 91).

adopted country. Yet "manifest destiny" is no more required by his scheme than social Darwinism is by Menger's.

Lieber and Menger told how institutions come about, but not why they necessarily matter. Their conceptual schemes permit, but do not require, the extravagantly ideological stories so much a feature of their times. Such stories are theories—bad theories. They are bad in the largely methodological sense that I think Keohane had in mind when he called for a better theory. From the point of view of contemporary cosmopolitan liberals, they are even worse normatively. To conflate these stories with the conceptual schemes that Lieber and Menger developed, as Hayek does with Menger's, can only prompt us to dismiss their contributions by associating them with discreditable ideologies.

Liberal institutionalism in international relations

The story that liberal institutionalists told about international relations, from Lieber's time until Hayek's, featured spontaneous institutional development, chiefly in the form of customary international law, the movement to freer trade and the emergence of international finance. Yet this story also featured calculated institutional development, reflected in the codification of international law, the turn to arbitration, and a series of multilateral conferences to settle a variety of European political issues. Functionally specialized organizations proliferated. Culminating in The Hague Peace Conferences of 1899 and 1907, the combination of these many and diverse developments reinforced progressive sentiments among liberals, not to mention a strong sense of civilizational superiority in dealings with the rest of the world.

In this smugly told tale, rationalist undertakings added to the evidence of success in Darwinist terms. General war and depression shocked liberals out of their complacency. The balance between spontaneous development and conscious design shifted in the latter's favor, with the United Nations and the Bretton Woods system a conspicuous result. Responding to circumstances, the liberal internationalist story lost its coherence. Just as some liberals anxiously affirmed their faith in design, others gave voice to their Darwinist or conservative inclinations with no less anxious charges of utopianism.

Even the story of functionally limited organizations took a subversive edge. As an unintended consequence of their success in dividing tasks for efficient performance, these organizations would gradually replace the liberal world of states—a consequence those telling the story very much intended. The disintegration of the liberal institutionalist story coincided with the institutionalization of International Relations as a field of study. Indeed, we might say that the field institutionalized itself around that story's incompatible tellings. Keohane's call for a better theory is, among other things, a plea for a new story.

Waltz vs. Wight and Bull

Any assessment of the way that liberal scholars in the field today understand institutions must also take realists into account. They are the ones whom I just described Darwinist and conservative by inclination. Their world consists of independent, goal-oriented, calculating and highly competitive entities called states. This is, of course, a liberal point of view rigorously applied to states as if they were human individuals. Nevertheless, many realists are resolutely hostile to institutions—irrationally so, one might think, if indeed institutions matter as little as these same scholars allege.

Hayek despised social engineering because history shows that institutions *do* matter. Designed institutions have bad consequences, whether intended or not. Realists despise institutions because they tend to share Hayek's ideological preferences and tell stories much like his. Liberals in an elemental sense, they fear that institutions *might* matter.

With a better understanding of institutions, realists might be less hostile. Here Waltz is a case in point. Menger, Hayek and their followers in economics have had no difficulty thinking of the market as an institution. As we saw, Waltz rejected this view, I believe, because he confused the origin of the market with its current character.

Unintended, the market was initially unobserved—a structure but not an institution. Agents who are affected by such structures are disposed to act on them as soon as they realize they can, sometimes with the results that they intended, sometimes not. The market has become a complex institution, in some measure designed to work *as if* its results were unintended. As with all such institutions, it has rules, some arising as Humean conventions and some formally enacted. From an observer's point of view, these rules constrain participants so that they behave in ways appropriate to the market. None are more important than the complex of rules that confer access to the market by reference to property which participants are free to buy, use and sell.

The same reasoning applies to anarchy, which, as Waltz (1979: 107–16) defined it, is the dominant structural feature of the international system. While this structure may have had an adventitious origin in the self-interested activities of agents acting on behalf of institutions that we now call states, it did not go unobserved for long. Defining the institution that anarchy has become is a complex of rules making states its members if and when they meet a rather strict set of qualifying criteria. Waltz himself affirmed the operation of this complex of rules by noting that states are functionally similar (1979: 93–7). Homogeneity is institutionally reproduced. An institution such as this, whose large purpose is to insure the liberty and self-rule of states, is so dominant that all other institutions recede into the background.

For most liberals, the term *anarchy* conjures up a Hobbesian vision of unintended consequences that are deleterious and yet, perversely enough, institutionalized, and therefore self-reproducing, to the point that they seem inescapable. For those who believe that Humean institutions mitigating the Hobbesian condition have gradually emerged, again as the unintended result of agents' self-interested actions, some other term would seem preferable. *International society* is an obvious candidate, given its favored place in the work of the English School. However favored, the term escapes clear definition.

According to Wight, the very language historically available to describe European international society "is necessarily full of qualifications and imprecision" (M. Wight 1968b: 95). Wight saw no promise in conceptual clarification, presumably because such an undertaking would depend on concepts illicitly brought in from the sphere of domestic society and thus the state.[4] Instead, he claimed that international society "can be properly described only in historical and sociological depth" (1968b: 96). Historically situated activities call for detailed description.

Once we define international society by specifying its contents, we may subject these contents to generalization. By calling particular sets of activities "institutions," Wight and Bull did just this. From a sociological point of view, "institutions" are the mark of society: "where there are *institutions*, there is society" (M. Wight 1992: 140, his emphasis). Property and marriage are institutions consisting of "[r]ecognized and established usages between individuals or groups," and forming "an enduring, complex, integrated, organized behaviour pattern" (M. Wight 1992: 140–1, quoting Ginsberg 1934: 42). Marking international society is a small number of such general institutions. On Bull's short list, for example, we find "the balance of power, international law, the diplomatic mechanism, the managerial system of the great powers, and war." Bull had already, quite pertinently remarked that "states themselves are the principal institutions of the society of states" (1977: 74, 71).

Evidently, institutions consist of rules, for this is what "recognized and established usages" would seem to be. In the instance of international society, these rules presuppose that states are, and have, agents. Put into practice, these rules yield the "behavior pattern" that Wight used to identify institutions for what they are. While Wight failed to mention rules in this context, Bull was not so reticent.

In Bull's estimation, "rules by themselves are mere intellectual constructs. They play a part in social life only to the extent that they are effective" (1968: 55). Rules work because institutions create the circumstances that allow them to work. It takes institutions to make, communicate, administer, interpret, enforce and legitimize rules. Institutions also protect rules from changes in society and make it possible for rules to change with such changes (Bull 1968: 56–7).

Bull's formulation is ambiguous. Clearly the institutions in question consist of rules. Yet, by his reckoning, institutions exist only to make rules work. Bull adopted this view because he thought that rules have only one function that matters: they make order in society (1968: 57–76).

---

4   Bull (1968: 48; 1977: 46–51) forcefully articulated this concern in his well-known critique of the "domestic analogy."

Every society pursues "universal goals" that depend on orderly arrangements. Bull named three such goals:

> First, all societies seek to insure that life will be in some measure secure against violence resulting in death or bodily harm. Second, all societies seek to ensure that promises, once made, will be kept, or that agreements, once undertaken, will be carried out. Third, all societies pursue the goal of ensuring that the possession of things will remain stable to some degree, and will not be subject to challenges that are constant and without limit.
>
> (1968: 4–5, footnote deleted)

Bull claimed in the footnote to this passage (1968: 320n2) that "there are many sources for this analysis," citing the positivist legal theorist, H.L.A. Hart, who, in turn, had Hobbes and Hume in mind.[5]

It is hardly obvious that every society actually does pursue these goals. This is Hume's story about his own society. So central is this story to Britain as a deeply conservative, liberal society that most members of the English School simply take it for granted. The more important issue for our purposes is *how* a given society will pursue such general goals, when indeed societies consist of diverse agents and institutions with many competing interests.

Hobbes and Hume had different answers—contract and convention— yielding the same result: rules. Bull gave credence to neither alternative, to their combination, nor to their common result in the context of international society. Bull tried to cover himself in this respect. "I believe order in social life can exist in principle without rules" (1977: 7), but he never considered how this might be possible.

Rules are beside the point for Bull because "order is not the only value in international politics, nor is it necessarily an overriding one." The values motivating states in their political relations contribute little or nothing to society as such. On the contrary, agents pursuing them are likely to produce disorder. Thus any "description of it [international society] as a society at all only conveys part of the truth" (1977: 75). The rest of Bull's truth is the disorderly pursuit of diverse values. If such self-interested pursuits produce deleterious institutions as an incidental effect, these institutions will presumably also endure as long as the societal order manages to survive. In Bull's story about international society, disorder is tantamount to a goal to which that society has adapted itself.

To give some examples of institutions that are ambiguously related to the production of order in international society, we might add spheres of influence, arms races and collective intervention to the list. Why stop there? Short lists of international institutions belie claims of historical grounding, and they betray a narrow set of assumptions about what rules do and what institutions count.

---

5   See Hart (1961: 189–95) for an "empirical version of natural law" and p. 254 for citations to Hobbes and Hume. Bull mentioned Hume in passing.

Long, open-ended lists would honor the historical record, but they would also make any general pattern or developmental tendency impossible to discern. Not only is a "better theory" beyond hope. So is any story, even Hume's or Bull's.

Keohane, Young and Ruggie

As an alternative to lists of the institutions that make international society what it is, we might begin, as Lieber did, with the term itself. We could then proceed with conceptual clarification in order to judge the claims made on behalf of any list. Keohane has recently offered just such a clarification. He started with

> institutions that can be identified as related complexes of rules and norms, identifiable in space and time. This conception of the scope of my analytic enterprise deliberately omits institutions that are merely categories of activity, as well as general norms that can be attached to any of a number of rule complexes. It allows me to focus on *specific institutions* and *practices*.
> (1989: 163, emphasis in original)

It is entirely appropriate for Keohane to put a limit on the scope of any term. Every analytic enterprise depends on such choices. Nevertheless, his decision to eliminate mere "categories of activity" excludes the institutions that Wight, Bull and their followers focused their attention on, if only because these institutions are general. Indeed institutions such as diplomacy and the balance of power are attached to a large number of "rule complexes." Yet they are also rule complexes themselves, "identifiable in space and time," just as Keohane required. Wight and Bull deserve credit precisely for having made these identifications convincingly.

General rules complexes are nevertheless specific *if* their general properties can be specified. When Keohane proposed a general property for his specific institutions, it turns out to be the same property Wight and Bull had proposed for theirs: "Specific institutions can be defined in terms of their rules" (Keohane 1989: 165). It would be better to say that *all* institutions are defined in terms of their rules. We need more—an additional, general property of the institutions that Keohane would have us restrict our attention to. This Keohane provided by specifying the properties of "institutionalized rules." Such rules need not be formal, although they do need to be durable. They must also "prescribe behavioral roles for actors, beside constraining activity and shaping expectations" (1989: 165; also see Keohane 1990: 732).

Roles are key here. As ensembles of rights (entitlements and powers), roles depend on the sort of rules that must be found in any institution meeting Keohane's definition. Elsewhere I have called rules of this sort commitment-rules to indicate that they function the way that reciprocal promising does (Onuf 1989: 78–95; Chapter 1). They are central to such institutions as property and marriage.

Commitment-rules do not figure centrally in the general institutions that we find on short lists. In the context of international relations, the most general institution of all is anarchy, which prescribes roles collectively making states into agents. As such, states are largely free to conduct themselves as they (meaning the agents acting on their behalf) see fit. An unintended consequence of their self-interested conduct is the development of general institutions that do not further specify roles.

The general, often informal rules constituting these institutions tell agents what to expect from a particular course of action. Rules of this sort are Humean conventions; on functional grounds, I have called them instructions-rules.[6] The rule complexes, or specific institutions, attaching to them are far more likely to be outfitted with rules prescribing roles. For example, the balance of power may be a general, plastic but durable institution whose few rules work as instructions. In the nineteenth century, informal rules emerged to prescribe the roles of balancer and broker. Keohane would likely see these rules as constituting a specific institution attached to the more general one; Bull would have seen them as modifying the general institution.

An institution whose central rules assign roles is an association, *koinonia*, in the sense that Aristotle and, much later, Lieber used the term. At minimum, an association has members; membership is the one role common to all associations. As Aristotle taught, some associations may have people as members, but many others assign this role to associations, or associations of associations. Any such association is higher, greater or more general than the ones composing its membership.

The most general association—for Aristotle, the *polis*—frames lesser associations and grades them by level. Here generality is a property that Wight and Bull had no reason to concern themselves with. Instead British thinking makes institutions autonomous by virtue of their Humean origins. Although Keohane limited his attention specifically to associations, his decision to focus on specific ones prevented him from thinking about them in grades of generality or, in the conventional shorthand, levels.

Keohane has had good company in wanting to restrict institutions to those sets of rules in which roles figure centrally. Consider Young's definition. "Institutions are social practices consisting of easily recognized roles coupled with clusters of rules or conventions governing relations among the occupants of these roles" (1989: 32, and see Young 1994: 26, for a slightly altered version of this definition). By way of illustration, Young remarked that "[s]tructures of property rights, on this account, are institutions" (1994: 3). Citing Hayek, he noted that "all institutions are social artifacts created by human beings— consciously or unconsciously" (1994: 3). Young's environmental interests led him to generally Hobbesian conclusions about unintended consequences, and his work addresses problems in designing institutions.

---

6   Rules of a third sort, directive-rules, constitute organizations, defined as such by the chain of command, or offices, that such rules put in place. Anarchy permits no such general rules, but, by design, organizations are a familiar, specific institutional feature of international relations. Here again see Onuf (1989: 78–95); Chapter 1).

While Keohane sought to extricate institutions from more general patterns of practice, Young saw institutions giving rise to more specific practices informed by their own rules, some of which might in turn become institutions. For Young, institutions are nested. He divided them into "regimes" and "orders," the former specific, as Keohane's institutions are, and the latter general in the way that Wight's and Bull's institutions are. He defended the division of institutions into two sorts on practical grounds while conceding its imprecision (Young 1989: 13–14).

Young's institutions are associations. Although they are nested, this property seems to be unrelated to their membership rules. Missing from Young's discussion is any sense that associations are graded by generality. For Young, associations all have the same general purpose—"to cope with problems of cooperation that arise as a result of interdependencies among the activities of distinct individuals or social groups" (1994: 3, footnote deleted). By contrast, the Aristotelian conception grades associations through membership rules and by purpose. Associations of individuals must have different purposes than associations of associations.

In general, liberal scholars in the field today are reluctant to use the term *purpose*. Prevailing positivist sentiments make the term *function* almost as suspect. Ruggie has been an exception. In his well-known essay on embedded liberalism and international regimes, Ruggie considered "[c]hanges in the structure of social purpose' to explain differences between the liberal orders superintended by Britain before World War I and the United States after World War II" (Ruggie 1997: 63–84, quoting p. 69). According to Ruggie, the *pax Britannica* depended on *laissez-faire* liberalism at the domestic level, itself "planned," and then imposed on other states participating in the world economy (1997: 67, quoting Polanyi 1957: 141). The interwar period saw a shift in the role of the state. Previously the guarantor of the self-regulating market, it had become responsible for social welfare and economic stability at the market's expense. Social purpose had changed. The postwar *pax Americana* saw liberalism "predicated upon domestic interventionism" instituted multilaterally (1997: 69–73, quoting p. 73).

Like Young, Ruggie discriminated between *regimes*, such as for trade or money, and *orders*. Never defined, the latter term seems to refer to a number of regimes related by purpose. Some regimes may have had a spontaneous origin in Humean conventions—Ruggie had no reason to address this question—and they change in response to changes in power and purpose. Orders are different. States' leaders make them to accord with their visions of the world. Different visions imply different forms (Ruggie 1997: 79–81).

In later work, Ruggie returned to issues of institutional form. Following Keohane, he defined *institutions* as "persistent and connected sets of rules, formal and informal, that prescribe behavioral roles, constrain activity and shape expectations" (1997: 109, quoting Keohane 1990: 732). Then he identified "three institutional domains of interstate relations: international orders, international regimes, and international organizations. Each type can be, but need not be multilateral in form" (Ruggie 1997: 110). Two other forms are available: bilateral and unilateral (Ruggie 1997: 109).

Multilateralism is more than a matter of numbers. It has a *"qualitative dimension"* that distinguishes it from other forms (Ruggie 1997: 105, his emphasis). As Ruggie pointed out, Keohane had defined the term *multilateral* merely quantitatively (Ruggie 1997: 105; Keohane 1990: 731). Using any institution whose purpose is collective security as an illustration, Ruggie claimed that multilateral institutions depend on "'generalized' principles of conduct." These principles "specify appropriate conduct for a class of actions, without regard to the particularistic interests of the parties or the strategic exigencies that may exist in any specific occurrence" (Ruggie 1997: 109).

Some well-known, generalized principles of conduct are excluded by this definition. Sovereignty and its corollary, non-intervention, are said to be general principles undergirding Waltzian anarchy as a spontaneous institutional development. Yet Ruggie would not call this institution multilateral because these principles invite self-interested conduct on the presumption that the unintended consequences are either tolerable or subject to institutional remedy.

According to Ruggie, any multilateral institution must depend on principles reflecting common social purpose. Ruggie had earlier treated orders as necessarily planned, whether unilateral (*pax Britannica*) or multilateral (*pax Americana*). On further consideration, he concluded that an order of the latter sort need not be planned, because his definition of *multilateralism* "says nothing about *how* that order is achieved" (Ruggie 1997: 111). If indeed an order arose spontaneously yet reflected common social purpose, it seems reasonable to surmise that such an order reflects what used to be called nature's design, which people are capable of recognizing when they step back from their particularistic concerns.

If people thought that a multilateral order that had developed spontaneously did not accord with nature's design, presumably they would deliberately design and constitute a new order for themselves, or they would design regimes and organizations to correct an order's deficiencies. For Ruggie, a *regime* "refers to a functional or sectoral component of an order," and it is "more concrete than an order" (1997: 111). Not said, but strongly implied, is a central place for rules prescribing roles. A regime is an association of associations and organizations. Each part, or level, has its own purpose and all of them linked by common purpose and constitute a whole. As wholes, regimes are linked, as parts, by higher purpose—more general principles—in an order, which constitutes a greater whole.

Conclusion

Ruggie started with a strong preference for design. He built his position almost entirely with conceptual materials provided by his liberal contemporaries in the United States. He ended up with a scheme whose foundations are plainly Aristotelian and, as such, potentially subject to criticism from positivists. Turning to constructivism, Ruggie abandoned the language of "social purpose," with all its teleological resonances. In its place is "collective intentionality" (Ruggie 1997: 20–1).

Ruggie borrowed this term from John Searle (1995: 23–6). I think that he made a mistake to do so. According to Searle (1995: 23, 25), beliefs, desires and intentions are all "intentional states," which people share and from which they derive their individual beliefs, desires and intentions. Collective intentionality yields social facts. Although Searle called "institutional facts" a "special subclass of social facts" (1995: 26), the distinction melts away in subsequent discussion.[7] Searle's story turns out to be Hume's story: when people do what they do, they produce institutions within which they proceed to do what they do.

It is hard to imagine any social scientist, even the most ardent methodological individualists among us, arguing with Searle's general claim that social facts *are* facts. Yet *this* fact tells us nothing about intentions as such, much less about their collective form or other properties. From a constructivist perspective, we can only agree with Ruggie (1997: 20–1) that collective intentionality gives social facts their meaning and supplies them with normative force. This is, however, a minimalist, Humean conception of what human beings can do for themselves. Lost is any sense that people are capable of thinking about themselves and their relations as a whole, formulating their ideas by reference to common purpose, and joining together, level by level, to put some order in their affairs.

Ruggie need not have stopped with Searle. Social construction, or constitution, is a pervasive process producing, and taking place within, constitution as a condition. As Lieber taught, institutional abundance produces a constitution understood as an ensemble of general rules framing the social whole in relation to its parts. Some constitutions are designed of a piece. Others are not. Nevertheless, agents will always see purpose in any such ensemble of rules and treat them as matters of design.

Few scholars have thought much about the constitution of international society. There are exceptions, including myself (1998a: 163–90; also see Stone 1994; Reus-Smit 1997; Weiler 1998; Ikenberry 1998).[8] If pressed, most realists would argue that sovereignty is the only rule that matters for the constitution of anarchy. They tell a version of Hayek's story about freedom and, by implication, the perils of planning. Indeed, we should view Morgenthau (1946) a polemic, along with Hayek (1946), in the great debate, then coming to an end, over freedom and planning.

---

7   Searle defined an institution as a product of "constitutive rules" (1995: 27–30), leaving us to surmise that social facts are social by virtue of the operation of "regulative rules." Searle (and Ruggie 1997: 22–5) notwithstanding, the distinction between constitutive and regulative rules is untenable (see Onuf 1989: 50–2). Since all rules are simultaneously constitutive and regulative, it should come as no surprise that social facts are indistinguishable from institutional facts in practice.

8   I should also note that Christian Reus-Smit's *The Moral Purpose of the State* (1999) appeared after this essay was submitted, revised and accepted for publication. His "final word on Aristotle" (p. 170) suggests some points of agreement between us.

For most liberals, other rules join sovereignty in the constitution of international society. These rules are the product of arduous political interaction. This is design the hard way. Their purpose collectively is the common good, for the whole and its parts. If liberal scholars in the field of International Relations are to have a better theory of institutions, then it must take common purpose into account.

To do so means accounting for organizations as institutions designed for specific purposes, whatever their unintended effects. It also means accounting for the constitution of international society. Here again, design matters. Because it always matters to people as a whole, and not just to liberal scholars in particular, it necessarily matters to states.

11

CIVIL SOCIETY, GLOBAL GOVERNANCE

(2005)

One world

The idea that the whole of humanity *is* a whole, with properties of its own, has ancient roots in Western thought. As Aristotle declared in *Politics*, Book I (1253a19–20), the *polis* "is by nature clearly prior to the family and the individual, since the whole is of necessity prior to the part" (Barnes 1984: 1988). Despite the Aristotelian logic of wholes and parts, not to mention Aristotle's conviction that the gift of speech and a sense of what is just and unjust sets humanity apart, his *polis* is never a global whole. Instead the *polis* is always a definite place with a distinctive past and destiny of its own: a city and its environs, a civil society, a political society. If none of these terms adequately conveys what the term *polis* or its Latin equivalent, *civitas*, meant to the ancients, all of them together give us a sense of what they had in mind.

Stoic philosophers took the same logic of parts and wholes and extended it notionally far beyond anything Aristotle contemplated in the *Politics*. Because the faculties of speech and judgment set the whole of humanity apart from other living beings, this whole has identifiable, specifically social properties. It is a city, a civil society, a political society in its own right, a *cosmopolis*, standing above all other cities and including them all—a city of cities. And why stop there? The inclusive logic of wholes as parts of yet larger wholes makes the universe the ultimate whole (as Aristotle said, the whole of nature) and gives it the properties of a city (as Stoic thinkers averred). As if a city in its functional relations, the cosmos itself *is* a cosmopolis (Schofield 1991).

Stoic ideas had a powerful effect on early modern thinkers from Hugo Grotius to Adam Smith. Perhaps the most obvious evidence of this phenomenon is the unending discussion of universal reason augmented by an Enlightenment fascination with the course of universal history. Furthermore, these concerns were inextricably related to the revival of ancient republican ideas and practices. Among the political arrangements known to humanity, only republics provide in principle for the common good; nesting whole republics as parts in ever greater republican wholes can have the effect of universalizing political arrangements for the common good; a *civitas maxima*, as Christian Wolff strikingly claimed, or great republic, is not just a vague aspiration but a normative reality underwriting human development as a whole (Onuf 1998a: Chapters 2–4).

The French Revolution forever altered the comfortable belief that republicanism is the only road to moral progress. Liberal ideas and practices emerged in the nineteenth century as an engine of social change and an index of moral improvement—or for Marxian critics—of willful moral blindness. Republican ideas and practices receded into the background, all the while providing institutional support for the rise of what came to be known, rather euphemistically, as the liberal democratic state. Throughout the nineteenth century, liberal internationalists advocated free trade and the development of international law as the twin pillars of an emerging world order whose most important members were the liberalizing, democratizing states chiefly responsible for unprecedented material prosperity. Already by the turn of the twentieth century, governments had devised numerous international institutions to expedite their peaceful relations, accommodate the functional demands of industrial capitalism and respond to at least some of the social problems transcending state borders. Universal institutions were the next step; some progressive thinkers emphasized the universalizing potential of federal republican arrangements.

The twentieth century witnessed world wars, the rise of the total state, the birth of universal international organizations, decolonization and the belated emergence of a global society of states, resurgent liberalism, capitalist penetration of the world's every nook and cranny, massive embourgeoisement and immiseration, technological revolutions affecting every aspect of daily life, environmental degradation on a staggering scale, fierce debates and frequent violence over the direction of social change, heightened moral awareness and appalling atrocities committed against whole peoples. Some of us think we can pick out the path of material and moral progress in these developments, identify their large causes, and summarize these large causes and selected consequences as a process of *modernization*. Others see catastrophe looming—material and moral. Either way, the context is global. The Stoic prophecy finally has borne out: there is now, finally, just one world. Just or unjust, that world is a city.

Two views of civil society

In early modern usage, the term *civil society* was a frequent vernacular translation of the Latin term *civitas*. At a time when *state* was not a term used as it is today, this usage was inclusive; the *city* was always something more than an agglomeration of people. For John Locke, civil society and political society were one and the same. For Immanuel Kant, civil society and *civitas* were synonyms, and he translated the latter into the vernacular as *state*. In broad terms, the city exists for the good of the people; it is, in English, a commonwealth or republic, in French, a *république*.

It would seem then that the term *civil society* bespeaks of a republican view of politics and society, one that looks back to antiquity, and especially to Aristotle. Indicatively, G.W.F. Hegel took this view in *Philosophy of Right* (1991; also see Onuf 1998a: Chapter 10). Nevertheless, Hegel identified civil society (*bürgerliche Gesellschaft*) as a category clearly on a par with the family and the state. One can find these three categories in Aristotle's *Politics*. There the *polis*, or state in most translations, and the *oikos*, or household, left space between them for the many associations enriching city life for the Greeks. In liberal social and political thought, this space and the many activities taking place within it constitute civil society.

What Aristotle had in mind gives little support to the liberal conception of civil society as a space populated by freely formed groups of people pursuing their diverse interests and concerns under the protection of the state as a public order. The *polis* is an association and, as such, a natural whole (see Chapter 10). Within this whole all other associations, including households, naturally fit as necessary parts. *This* is civil society, and, for Aristotle, it was an inclusive category. So it was for Hegel, and so it must be for any republican.

To clarify the difference between these two views of civil society, we should also notice that neither Aristotle nor Hegel made a hard and fast distinction between public and private worlds. If republicans generally make no such distinction, liberals insist on it. In the liberal view, families are conceptually privileged as a private world. The state is no less privileged as a public world. Between these two worlds, liberals locate private individuals performing all those roles that take them out of their households, involve them in diverse pursuits, including the production and exchange of goods and services, and allow them to engage, shape and buffer the state. Obviously these activities are public in different ways and degrees; private initiatives have public consequences, just as public undertakings have private implications.

By contrast, Hegel defined civil society as a "system of *needs*." We satisfy them by working, generally together, yet in "the most diverse processes" (1991: 226, 231). Such a definition recalls Aristotle's conception of the *polis*, in which a functional division of activities—work, in Hegel's scheme—fulfills human needs and nature's purpose. Hegel conceptualized civil society from two points of view. Seen from the outside, civil society exists in its own terms, and so does the state. Seen from the inside, however, civil society exhibits inclusive institutional tendencies. The state has its place in the system of needs that constitutes civil society.

On Hegel's account, "mediation of need and the satisfaction of the individual" lead to "the protection of property through the administration of justice" and "care for the particular interest ... by means of the police and the corporation." The need to protect property brings the state into civil society, in the limited way that liberals favor. Care for particular interests implicates the state more substantially. Hegel used the term *police* (*Polizei*) more broadly than we would use it today, either in German or English. "The police should provide for street-lighting, bridge-building, the pricing of daily necessities, and public health" (1991: 226, 262). Today, we would be inclined to call these diverse activities public administration, but even this underestimates their importance in stabilizing social arrangements.

Corporations share in responsibility for the care of particular interests. According to Hegel, the corporation is an association whose members' skills are appropriate to "the trade which is the corporation's proper business and interest ..." Corporations constitute one of three estates, through which all interests in a society are advanced. Corporations selected deputies to represent trade and industry in legislative bodies. The other two estates—agriculture and public service—also selected deputies to represent their constituent interests in the same legislative bodies. "Viewed as a *mediating* organ, the Estates stand between the government at large and the people in their division into particular spheres" (Hegel 1991: 270, 342, emphasis in translation).

In the old-regime societies of Europe, there were generally three estates consolidating many more specific status gradations into three broad ranks or stacked levels. In Hegel's system, the estates are hardly equal in status; their very existence has ordering implications for civil society as a whole. Beyond this function, however, the estates also mediate between individuals and "the organic state" (Hegel 1991: 342). To do so, the three estates stand side by side. Conventionally visualized as columns, they give civil society an enduring institutional architecture responsive to unchanging human needs.

In this conception, the corporate column has local associations at its base, upon which there are secondary associations, and upon them tertiary associations. Given the mediating function and vertical organization of the three estates, they constitute chains of command that are vertically *and* horizontally linked. As we saw, Aristotle is the ancient source of this way of thinking. In the early modern period, it gave rise to federal republicanism and, more recently, to corporatist practices.

Globalized civil society

With Hegel, liberals see civil society in relation to the concrete needs of individuals. Again with Hegel, they make much of associations. Modern liberals have long held that a pluralist society is a necessary condition for the liberal democratic state. They also hold that a civil society rich in voluntary associations fosters democratic practices and social justice. In both cases, associations are seen to arise autonomously, coexist in egalitarian terms, compete for private resources, form partnerships and rivalries depending on their goals, and apply pressure on state institutions to achieve those goals.

In the liberal imagination, it matters what these goals are. For progressives, associations that underwrite the state work to limit democracy. In contrast, associations that confront the state help in democratizing it. Most significant in this respect are popular social movements. As self-identified associations of the like-minded, movements respond to those deeply felt needs and concerns not met by the state or society's other institutions.

Social movements conceived in just these terms date from Hegel's time. Indicatively, romantic intellectuals were drawn into the cause of Greek independence in such numbers that the movement, and not the cause, is what we remember. Just as this movement depended on local voluntary associations, so must they all. Because the causes to which movements are dedicated tend not to be localized, additional, loosely linked associations take up the cause, thereby spreading the movement. Civil society has become a global phenomenon, only weakly segmented and rapidly articulating, because social movements know no boundaries.

For progressive liberals, movements define themselves against states, and the arena in which they do so is civil society. Most studies of globalization make their frame of reference just as clear. Expedited by spectacular technological developments, the production and exchange of material and cultural goods move freely across state boundaries, whether state officers like it or not. It seems that we are faced with an unspoken division of conceptual space—on the one side there are active civil societies and on the other autonomous global processes—where Hegel taught us to look for one space within which diverse processes are functionally related.

Europe today offers just such a space. Longstanding corporatist practices and long developing functional arrangements effectively reproduce a Hegelian conception of civil society by giving the region an inclusive and not very well formed structure consisting of ascending levels of association and side-by-side functional sectors of activity. Furthermore, this structure constitutes a variable segment of an even more inclusive structure. At global and regional levels, institutions that have states as members—commonly known as international regimes—link public offices in administering the global system of needs. States occupy the next level in the structure, where their many functioning parts forge vertical links with institutions at other levels.

Obviously the administrative presence of territorially demarcated states introduces massive structural irregularities. Yet this presence is consistent with the Hegelian model of civil society, where public administration is prominently featured. While functional sectors need not line up neatly from level to level, stratified networks help to make the overall structure more regular than formal variations, invocations of sovereignty and state organization might suggest. Forming institutions into ascending levels and side-by-side functional sectors, however misshapen, this structure gives the world today a Hegelian character.

If civil society today has globalized, this is, for most observers, an inevitable consequence of modernization. Ever since the Enlightenment, discussion of civil society has been integral to the larger discussion of modernity's triumphs and discontents. In the first instance, modernization meant challenging, and eventually overcoming, the old regime, understood as any highly stratified society, saturated in rules that define and confer statuses. In this way of thinking, a stratified society cannot be a just society. Modernization also meant the rise of a new regime, normally constituting the government of a state, defined as the territory over which the government has exclusive control and within which a just society can fulfill its developmental potential.

In the process of modernization, new rules rationalizing administration and enumerating individual rights and duties replaced the old, customary rules conferring status. In a virtuous circle, new rules strengthened those institutions responsible for these rules. In contemporary liberal parlance, the result is *good governance*. With the indispensable help of a vigorous civil society, this is presumably what governments do in modern liberal democratic states: they practice good governance. And this is presumably what governments in states with modernizing societies need help in doing.

In my opinion, this account of modernization is incomplete. Stratification is perhaps more subtle than it used to be. Nevertheless, institutionalized status relations are so obviously important that observers comment on them endlessly. If we construe civil society inclusively, as Hegel did, then it will include institutions of every stripe—today as in Hegel's time. Furthermore, governance takes place in any civil society, and it will take place everywhere in civil society. Whether good or bad, just or unjust, governance is never simply what governments do with support from civil society. When governments form international institutions to assist in them in governance, this is indeed *global governance*, but hardly the whole of it. Global governance suffuses global civil society.

Three modes of global governance

Hegel insisted that civil society is an inclusive set of functional relations, and that these relations are structured, vertically forming the functional sectors, or columns, of civil society and laterally forming into ascending levels of institutional development. Agents locate themselves in these crisscrossing arrangements by reference to the rules constituting them as agents. Yet this suffices neither to give civil society its structure nor to give agency the continuity that we generally see it as having. There are additional processes at work, which firm up civil society as an inclusive structure of functional relations by simultaneously actualizing agency and activating institutions in regular and predictable ways.

These processes are ongoing, rule-related practices—social processes are always this and nothing more. Taken together, processes of this sort constitute governance, not in the limited liberal sense, but in the more expansive sense that I have identified with Hegel and the republican view of civil society. These processes also approximate what I think Anthony Giddens *might* mean when he uses the term *structuration*. Giddens has been maddenly elusive on this subject. In his two most sustained statements of "structuration theory," I find nothing even approaching an actual definition (1979: Chapter 2; 1984: Chapter 1).

Free from any constraints that a definition might have imposed, I suggest that the terms *participation, representation* and *recognition* broadly describe the three ways in which agency instantiates in particular human beings, institutions come, at least metaphorically, to life and society constitutes a structured totality of relations. In other words, participation, representation and recognition are the generic modes by which any society achieves and sustains what, for lack of a better term, we call its structure. More concretely, they are the primary modes of governance in any modern civil society, manifest in the activities of governments and associations. In the context of civil society at its most inclusive, global governance resolves into these same three processes, however much they are obscured by formal properties of an international society consisting of independent states.

Participation

The term *participation* occurs frequently in recent discussions of civil society. Its use is highly normative, almost always introduced to identify modernization with democratization or to make democratization more authentic by freeing it from organizational constraints. Interpreters of Alexis de Tocqueville's *Democracy in America* (1835–1840) have linked "active participation … in civil associations" to "the democratic character of … political culture" (1992: 19). Carole Pateman's "participatory theory of democracy," drawn from Jean-Jacques Rousseau, John Stuart Mill and G.D.H. Cole (1970: Chapter 2), is a more recent source of inspiration for many participants in these discussions. Lately, the continuing exclusion of status groups broadly connoted by such terms as race, class and gender from participation in democratic processes has gained a good deal of attention. The emphasis on democracy is hardly surprising. Yet it masks those properties of participation that make it a generic mode of structuration and a primary mode of governance.

Rules assigning statuses tell agents which strata of society they are free to participate in and, by the same token, which ones are not open to them. The extent to which agents take advantage of participatory opportunities is no doubt variable. Yet it is probably the case that *being* and *doing* are largely indistinguishable—at least in traditional societies. Where passive participation is an active form of agency, transgressive participation, by which I mean an active defiance of status markers, will normally prompt an active response from agents in the transgressed stratum. Even then participants will often feign passivity as they silence or exclude the offending agent. If they act as if nothing happened, nothing happens.

In this light, we can see why modernizers have always called for the dismantling of the old regime of status relations. Yet globalized communications fosters the creation of new networks and increases participatory opportunities. These activities may make existing strata more inclusive. More likely, they contribute additional strata to an ever denser structure of status relations. The proliferation of strata creates the impression that agents control the statuses available to them and that society more readily accommodates change than it once did.

It would be better to say that proliferating strata make it possible for agents to pick and choose among them and participate more actively in some than others. Perhaps this is what we should mean by the term *democratization*. Exercising these choices, agents swell some strata and make them more important in relation to other institutions, and they shrink others, which then seem to diminish in importance. The totality of these choices add significantly to the mechanisms of change already institutionalized in the general process of modernization. With so many changes, participation has also changed as a primary mode of structuration. Democratization suggests that participation performs a broader function than it once did.

Representation

If participants in recent discussion of civil society speak of participation with too casual abandon, then the term *representation* is under-represented in these same discussions. Early-modern modernizers made no such mistake. Thomas Hobbes is the key figure. His point of departure is the *person* (recall Chapter 5). Either an actor speaking on behalf of someone else or an author speaking for herself, the person is not simply the biological isolate whom we typically describe as a human being.

Every person is a "civil person" and a "representative"; civil persons may be human individuals or they may be institutions. Civil society is the largest body of civil persons. As such, it is indistinguishable from the *body politic*—a civil person consisting of many such persons, for whom someone (a representative) or some body (a representative institution) acts as "the person of the Body Politique" (Hobbes 1991). The latter person is an officer, or an institution organized to speak in a single voice, whose acts consist of binding directives issued on behalf of the body politic and carried out by subordinate officers. At the bottom of the chain of command are the most numerous of these officers, and they are the citizens.

For Hobbes, civil society must have the organization of a body politic, a sovereign head and citizens as subjects, if it is not to descend into civil war. Someone (or thing) in charge, a head, represents the body by acting in its collective interests, and the body makes its interests known to the head through authorized channels. Directives move in both directions, up and down the chain of command. Hegel also made institutionalized representation an integral feature of civil society. For federal republicans, its relevance was obvious. In *The Federalist* (1787), Alexander Hamilton called it one of a very few "great improvements" in the "science of politics" since ancient times (1961: 51).

As worked out by Montesquieu, David Hume and the framers of the United States Constitution, a federal body politic consists of an association of associations matched to an arrangement of offices. These associations occupy levels by virtue of being organized as a chain of command, thus enabling directives to flow up and down, through levels. Institutionalized representation regulates the flow of directives, first, by assembling and fusing them at each level on the way up, and, second, by disaggregating them at each level and distributing them across organizational branches on the way down. Federal arrangements formalize levels, and levels function as platforms for additional institutional developments. As a primary mode of structuration, representation helps to stabilize civil society as an inclusive structure.

Representation in both directions makes states into democratic republics, and it makes them more effective organizations. Modernizers were, or could be, persuaded that democracy meant the extension of the "rights" of political "participation" to more and more citizens, independent of status considerations. While I think the terminology is confusing, the idea is simple enough. If citizens cannot assemble, speak their minds, vote freely and stand for election, then they cannot represent themselves, and no other officer is likely to represent them to their satisfaction. The key to adequate representation, and thus to effective states, is procedures that make it possible for citizens to join together and decide on officers to represent them at the next level.

At the citizen's level, voting procedures get most attention. At higher levels, officers are more likely to send formal directives than elected officers to represent their interests at the next level. Voting will recede in importance, as rules of assembly and debate shape the upward movement of directives. Procedural formalities aside, modern political practice emphasizes the connection between representation and group interests. We see this emphasis in both pluralist and corporatist theory. Recent discussions of civil society devote much attention to the procedural requirements of democracy and, of course, to the associational milieu that makes these procedures effective. There is much hand wringing about active citizenship.

In these discussions, the ways that officers represent their interests at the higher levels of association go relatively unnoticed. Thanks to pluralist and corporatist theory, we had, perhaps, a clear enough picture of these processes of interest mediation when the sovereign state occupied the highest level in the inclusive structure of civil society. In a globalized context, global and regional levels complicate this picture enormously. Institutional vehicles for representing interests at higher levels are likely to be an informal consequence of bargains that officers strike out of public view. How well these bargains represent lower-level interests, and how well they work in shaping the upward flow of directives is impossible to say, at least until observers learn more about the organization of global civil society at its highest levels. I for one am skeptical.

Recognition

Recent discussions of civil society make recognition a favorite theme. Typically they do so by taking Hegel's brief remarks on recognition (*Anerkennung*) in *The Phenomenology of Spirit* (1807) as a point of departure. The context for Hegel's claim is self-consciousness, which depends on recognition of the other as a self-conscious being. Conversely, the other must recognize her recognizing other in order for that other—the one initiating recognition—to be able to recognize herself. Hegel's demonstration that selves require reciprocal recognition leads to his famous analysis of forced recognition and failed self-consciousness in the relation of master and slave.

Freed from Hegel's subjectivist philosophy, the concept of recognition points to the role of mutuality in commitment, agreement, rights and duties, and association. In contemporary discussion of civil society, these themes are conspicuous. Others join together voluntarily—they associate—just as "we" do. By associating with us, others obtain the same rights and duties that we have. Exercising our rights individually and collectively, we make commitments that others accept, and, when we make those commitments formal and reciprocal, we make contracts. In the absence of reciprocal commitments, we invite others to associate with us, thereby constituting voluntary association of formal equals.

Agents can withhold recognition, just as they can refuse to negotiate reciprocal commitments. When they do so, others are excluded from association. Voluntary associations with exclusionary rules are clubs. When clubs reinforce existing social strata, often by supplying them with identifying slogans and insignia, we may commend them for the solidarity and self-esteem that they encourage, or criticize them for aggravating the sense of exclusiveness that stratified arrangements produce on their own. Social movements frequently form in response to exclusionary practices. Claims about universal rights foster a sensitivity to clubs and their particular practices, and yet these same claims enable agents associating in movements to avoid coming to terms with the exclusionary logic of a stratified society. As I have suggested, stratification is a pervasive institutional feature of any civil society.

Not all clubs are so exclusive that they incite movements to form against them. Yet many, if not most, associations are clubs because they have membership rules specifying status requirements. They also impose any number of other requirements on candidate members, such as sponsorship, membership fees, ceremonial expressions of commitment and probationary periods, all of which are intended to show that candidates acknowledge the goals that associations seek to fulfill. Admission to any club is an act of recognition, implying a reciprocal act of recognition. Agents not willing to reciprocate in this fashion are excluded by their own choice.

International society provides a compelling example of recognition at work. States join this society when they meet status requirements by exercising internal sovereignty *and* when other states recognize them, thereby acknowledging external sovereignty in their relations. As members of a club, a rather exclusive club at that, states (meaning, of course their agents) may decline to recognize candidates. Yet they cannot easily prevent other states from doing so, if status requirements are met and candidates acknowledge the club's rather limited but singularly important goals and a willingness to live by club rules.

In my opinion, it is no coincidence that Hegel began to write about recognition at the very time that states took on their fully modern character and formed themselves into a club. They did so by formalizing recognition as a ruled practice. At this time, states' agents systematically began to invoke the rights and duties of states in their mutual relations—more systematically, I might add, than any so-called liberal society did for its members until quite recently (also see Onuf and Onuf 2006: 40–2). Once in the club, states are free to associate as they wish and to undertake reciprocal commitments, formal and informal.

Over time, club members have committed themselves collectively to the organization of sectors of activity more or less corresponding to the usual branches of governmental organization. Another of Hamilton's "great improvements" was the "distribution of power into distinct departments" (1961: 51). Widely mimicked, this improvement carried over to international society, and it now provides global civil society with its vertical structuring. Not only do functional sectors define tasks for officers at every level, but they give associations a basis for common action.

Acts of recognition in all degrees of formality normalize relations among associations at every level. Collectively, they confirm and support functional differentiation along existing lines. Vertical boundaries are the product of many agreements and cumulative recognition. Without them, global civil society would barely exist and agency, as we have come to know it, would be severely curtailed.

Conclusion

In my view, civil society has taken on global dimensions because a general, multi-faceted process called *modernization* (for lack of a better term) has substantially succeeded in imposing a *kind* of order, at least indirectly, on the totality of human relations. In this essay, I have tried to indicate *what* kind of order this inclusive social arrangement is, how it differs from the liberal conception of social relations on a global scale and, more briefly and impressionistically, where it came from.

Embedded in contemporary discussions of civil society and global change are a number of related assumptions about the general process of modernization over the last several centuries. Let me summarize these assumptions.

1   Modernization depends on ideologies and moral systems emphasizing individual autonomy, aspirations and achievements.
2   Modernity provides people with the personal security and material support that they need to fulfill their individual potential.

3   Modernity cultivates instrumental rationality and organizational efficiency.
4   Modernity displaces the old regime of stratified social relations and strips away stultifying status markers.
5   Modernity demystifies nature and reins in identification with clan, tribe, nation or any other allegedly natural social arrangement.
6   Modernization produces long-term moral and material improvement as people outgrow their atavistic tendencies and pre-modern prejudices.
7   Nevertheless, modernization is slow and uneven because of the continuing resistance of pre-modern social formations, tensions inherent in the process itself, and the skepticism, dissatisfaction or alienation of its presumed beneficiaries.

The liberal conception of civil society makes it a spatially conceived zone, neutral and unstratified. In this zone, the tensions inherent in the process of modernization work themselves out. Most obvious are the tensions between individual choice and productive activity on the one hand and mandated behavior and collective need on the other. The generally good results that follow from the existence and proper functioning of this zone have additional, unintended consequences. They reinforce the recognized boundaries between individuals, households, markets, productive enterprises and states, and they support the coextensive development of these autonomous entities within their respective spheres of competence.

At the same time, reinforced boundaries perpetuate civil society as a notionally empty zone. Within this zone, concerned citizens and social movements address the ever-shifting agenda of problems brought forward by the process of modernization. With the globalization of markets, productive enterprises, and organizations constituted by states to serve their collective needs, not to mention the development of space-reducing communication and transportation systems, multiple civil societies have transcended state boundaries and merged to form a space that liberals would have us visualize as a global playing field. As such, it is cordoned off, level and open to view, as any well-formed civil society must be.

I reject the liberal conception of global civil society for two reasons. First, it seems like a fanciful exercise in liberal logic to claim that modernization produces a huge variety of institutional features yet manages to leave an empty zone called civil society. I maintain instead that the general process of modernization calls on processes of structuration, concretely manifest as modes of governance. Structuration operates everywhere and at all levels; processes of structuration operate in every society and order any society as a totality of human relations. Thus they order the institutional products of modernization in a discernible pattern that we identify with governance in modern societies.

As a globalized totality of relations, the world today exhibits the familiar structure of a modernizing society. One world means a world everywhere affected by intricately connected processes of participation, representation and recognition. It also means that centuries of changing ideas about good governance and just societies have altered these processes. Even more they have altered—at least in the liberal view—the relative importance of these processes. And this takes me to a second reason for rejecting the liberal conception of global civil society.

Ever since the Enlightenment, progressive thinkers have thought of modernization as a two-step process. First, modernization requires that the status-ordering of the old regime be dismantled. Then it requires that a new regime based on some combination of Lockean rights and Hobbesian offices be installed in its place. Whether the process is gradual or abrupt, it is presumed to eliminate status and stratification as the basic means for ordering the totality of relations in a society.

The Enlightenment campaign against inherited privilege and for equality of treatment is, of course, something that most of us admire a great deal. Yet it is wrong to think that, once dispatched, status ordering and stratification will never return, or that they can never matter very much in a society where modern institutions are fully functional. Indeed, I would suggest that we conceptualize modernization in three steps. First, the old regime of status is dispatched, and then modern institutions are put in place. Finally, status markers are adapted to new circumstances, rules for participating in modern society are selectively broadened, and stratification resumes its place in giving society its structural integrity. (Chapter 12 continues this discussion of modernization.)

In a world made modern, valued skills confer status, rules for participation continue to operate selectively, and stratification yields a relatively impermeable boundary between those with skills and those in need. This division is a general, globally manifest property of civil society. Reinforced by enduring status markers associated with gender and race, it anchors the social arrangements of modernity in material conditions that are only marginally susceptible to change. Wealth and poverty are not just a convenient way of describing these conditions. Wealth and poverty are the primary status markers of the world we live in.

12

ALTERNATIVE VISIONS

(2012)

Participating in a seminar in Rio de Janeiro on "visions from the periphery"—or, more precisely, on visions of international relations theoretically sensitive to the situation of the periphery—raises a very personal question. Will a scholar who is not from the periphery have a blinkered vision of international relations, one that peripheralizes the periphery? Behind this question lurk others. Is the periphery an objective state of affairs, a contingent, historically situated construct, or a state of mind that only someone from the periphery can appreciate? Is it all three, but only for a time that may already have passed? If the periphery is conceptual in the first instance (as I believe it is), does the very act of bringing it front and center contribute to making the world an asymmetrical territorial arrangement reflected in the terms *center* and *periphery*? Is this what scholars "from the periphery" want? Is it what I want?

These are sobering questions. It is certainly possible for scholars who are not from the periphery to envision a field of study called International Relations in which the periphery barely figures. A number of us did just this in a book called *Visions of International Relations* (Puchala 2002; see Chapter 2 for my contribution). None of its contributors lives in the periphery. Indeed all of us reside in the United States, at the very "center of world power" (to use a phrase much used in the Rio seminar). Despite some limited discussion of culture, difference and the other, *Visions of International Relations* effectively dispatches the periphery as an obsolete concept. In effect, the book's vision from the center takes the center's centrality for granted.

Yet the alternative is no better. Affirming the conceptual power of the center-periphery distinction also affirms the asymmetric relation of the two terms. This in turn contributes to the social construction of the periphery as an unwanted state of affairs, perpetuates a division of labor in which scholars from the center produce theories and scholars from the periphery consume them, and devalues the lived experience of billions of people and not just a few scholars. I believe there is a way out of this impasse. I proposed it some years ago in my book, *World of Our Making* (1989).

There I developed a theoretical framework oriented to a very large world of experience that I referred to as social relations. By not limiting this framework to what we in the field call international relations, I had hoped to move beyond the field. More to the point, I had hoped to leave behind an impoverished, auto-limiting apparatus for thinking and talking systematically about international relations as an odd, perhaps unique *kind* of social relations. Instead we must think about the social relations of the world we know, the world we have made—the modern world. We must also think about the social relations of a world in transition—for lack of a better term, the late modern world.

I still believe that *World of Our Making* offers a robust theoretical framework that makes the field and its received theories superfluous—unless the latter are reworked so as to find their place in the more inclusive framework that I had developed (something I tried to do at several places in the book, most notably perhaps in the last chapter). Yet in the years since, much has changed. International Relations has rapidly globalized and in the process become more entrenched as a field of study. Indeed, it looks ever more like a discipline, and this is what growing chorus of voices, not least from the periphery, are calling it.

If I failed in my project to rewrite the book on International Relations, the question animating the Rio seminar nevertheless inspires me to try again. Here is my rendition of that question: Can scholars from the periphery of world power envision a world that would centrally implicate them in world-making? I take this question to disaggregate into three closely related questions:

1   At this moment, is there only one way that *anyone* can think and talk systematically about international relations?
2   Must International Relations make the center of world power the center of world-making?
3   If so, can scholars from anywhere in the world think and talk systematically about the social relations of the modern world without reproducing International Relations by another name and, in the process, reverting to center and periphery as organizing concepts?

The first question calls on us to consider "conditions of possibility," to borrow a key phrase from "the figure whom we call Foucault," as Michel Foucault himself might have said (1971: xxii).[1] These conditions put limits on our capacity to envision alternatives to the world we think we know. For Foucault, they are

---

1   Although the phrase "conditions of possibility" is Immanuel Kant's (1965: 126–7), Foucault's sense of it is not epistemological and not Kantian. According to Ian Hacking (2002: 90), "The figure whom we call Hume" (his quotation marks) is a phrase typical of Foucault. While I have yet to find this exact formulation in

the rules of scientific discourse—"rules that come into play in the very existence of such discourse …" (Foucault 1971: xiv; also see Foucault 1972: 46–9). The second question asks if International Relations imposes additional limits on the way we think and talk about the world. If it does, then it is exceedingly difficult, if not impossible, to disentangle world-making from "world power" (a concept that International Relations makes intelligible). Conversely, if we disallow the concept of world power, then International Relations ceases to exist as a would-be discipline. The third question calls on us to envision world-making without reintroducing the concept of world power and the asymmetrical territorial arrangement reflected in the ancillary concepts of center and periphery. Can we think and talk systematically about such a world as *our* world?

My short answers to these questions, are (1) perhaps; (2) yes; (3) yes, within limits that we do not yet know. I will try to make these answers more substantial and satisfying. Lacking space, I forego a full exposition of a claim that my answer to the second question depends on. Theoretical frameworks, fields of study and worlds of experience all operate on each other in ongoing constitutive processes. As a result, International Relations mandates a vision of world dominated by territorial arrangements of power. International Relations helped to create these arrangements, which made the world modern over a period of several centuries. Scholars in the field can envision the social relations of the late modern world in any other terms only by leaving International Relations behind. Otherwise they can only be implicated in keeping the world more or less the way it has become—a modern world of nation-states, some vastly more powerful than others.

Thus this essay has two sections. The first section addresses the general question of limits on science or systematic knowledge (that is, question 1) by drawing on the historical ontology that Foucault so brilliantly deployed in *The Order of Things*. Of particular interest is the role of transitional figures, among them Foucault, in opening up new conditions for what we can possibly think about the world. The version of this essay that I presented in Rio had a second section substantially drawn from other work (Onuf and Onuf 2006). To save space, I confine myself here to a few additional remarks on the co-constitution of fields and their worlds, with particular reference to International Relations in the making of the modern world (question 2). Given my claim that International Relations produces an increasingly irrelevant vision of the world, what is now this essay's second section identifies plausible features of an alternative vision (question 3). A theoretical framework suiting the social relations of the late modern world abandons center and periphery as organizing concepts, even as it draws attention to the asymmetrical social relations of this or any world. By implication, it no longer makes sense to think of scholars "from the center" as producers of theories and scholars "from the periphery" as consumers.

Foucault's work, it does convey his position quite nicely. See, for example, Foucault (1971: xii).

Historical ontology

When Foucault asked, "what is it impossible to think, and what kind of impossibility are we faced with here?" (1971: xv), the first question is rhetorical—how can we ever know what we cannot bring to mind?—but the second question is precisely what we need to address first, just as he did. To know what it is possible to think and talk about, we need to sort out the question of *kinds*. There are, of course, objective or natural limits (as we say) to what we can possibly experience. These limits are embedded in our physical, perceptual and cognitive faculties, which are themselves a product of evolutionary history. There are additional, if elastic, limits that we impose upon ourselves as social beings—rules to follow, or not followed at some risk or cost. Moreover, all of these limits variously play on each other so thoroughly and extensively that they become fused as the practical knowledge we all acquire in experiencing the world.

I am inclined to think that all knowledge is practical knowledge in this sense; the physiological and social determinants of what we know, the material and ideal constituents of human experience, are inseparable. Foucault thought otherwise. There is a kind of knowledge, unquestionably social, which is nonetheless not practical because it has no *direct* relation to what we do—to the ends we have and choices we make. Yet this knowledge constitutes a "system of thought" not thought about and imposes limits not known to us (Foucault 1971: 329). Indeed it is a "space of knowledge," and "epistemological field" or an "episteme" (in French, *épistémè*) (Foucault 1971: xi, xxii, xxiii, 344, 346 and many other places; also see Foucault 1972: 191–2).

The term *epistemological* is misleading here, for the knowledge in question pertains to what we (do not) know, and not, at least directly, to how we know it. The kind of knowledge that fixes and secures "the order of things" without our knowing that it does so constitutes an *ontological* field or space. Yet the term *episteme* seems right, I think because it echoes Aristotle's memorable discussion of the kinds of knowledge (also see Chapter 8). In *Nicomachean Ethics*, Book VI, Aristotle held that there are five kinds of knowledge: technical knowledge (craft, *technê*), scientific or systematic knowledge (*epistêmê*), practical reason (*phronêsis*), wisdom (*sophia*) and understanding (*nous, dianoia*). Foucault's "epistemological field" is not just science, or even scientific and technical thought together linking general principles and chosen ends. Nor is it wisdom, which in some measure each of us possesses individually. Aristotle's treatment of the kinds of knowledge takes for granted the space, or field, within which we act on, make use of, discover, put in order and store what we know.

This space is not neither epistemological nor epistemic. It constitutes an *ontological field*, but not one that is universal or necessary, open to science and awaiting discovery once and for all. Instead it is socially constituted, subject to change and manifest in history. If this field has rules and puts limits on what we can plausibly say, then these rules are ascertainable to an informed observer by inference from observed behavior and institutional effects. Foucault named the search for these rule-traces "the archeology of knowledge," as if it were a science devoted to the exploration of a universal and necessary state of affairs. With Ian Hacking, I prefer to call what I am doing *historical ontology* because any ontological field (and there are potentially many) is contingent on the particulars of historical experience and immanent in the kinds of knowledge that experience makes available to us.[2]

Foucault claimed that what I call ontological fields or spaces are stable for long periods and then transform suddenly. When they do, they radically alter the conditions of possibility for systematic thought. There have been "two great discontinuities in the *episteme* of Western culture: the first inaugurates the Classical age (roughly half-way through the seventeenth century) and the second, at the beginning of the nineteenth century, marks the beginning of the modern age" (Foucault 1971: xxii). The first rupture ended the Renaissance, which had emerged as a distinctive ontological space by 1500. Foucault's Classical age subsumes the Enlightenment, the last years of which mark the transition to the modern age.

The ontological space containing the modern age developed a significant discontinuity, if not a complete rupture, around 1900. As to the possibility of a modernist age beginning at that time, Foucault had nothing to say. This is quite possibly because modernist thought reaffirms "the strange figure of knowledge called man" and thus the ontological premises of the modern age. Instead Foucault foresaw "the disappearance of man" and, by implication, the appearance of a post-modern ontological field (and not merely a post-modernist age) in which this strange idea would make perfect sense (Foucault 1971: xxiv, 386).

Foucault emphasized that the ontological ruptures he had identified transformed some bodies of knowledge—"disciplines," "sciences," "fields of study," or, to use the term Foucault used consistently in *The Archeology of Knowledge*, "discursive formations"—but not others.[3] They were not changes in the way that everyone in the ambit of Western culture thought about everything (Foucault 1971: xi; Foucault 1972: 157–62). He did study three discursive formations that he thought had changed together at the close of the Classical age. With the advent of the modern age, around 1800, discussion of life, labor and language became the "human sciences" of biology, political economy and philology. Law is a fourth body of knowledge that Foucault could have taken into consideration.

As a discursive formation, law acquired the same general properties that life, labor and language had in the Classical age, and then transformed into a modern,

---

2   According to Hacking (2002: 2), "the historical ontology of ourselves" is a phrase Foucault used twice in his influential essay, "What Is Enlightenment?" "Historical Ontology is about the ways in which the possibilities for choice, and for being, arise in history" (Hacking 2002: 23). For a major study also adopting Foucault's historical ontology, see Bartelson (1995).

3   This and the next half dozen paragraphs closely follow Onuf and Onuf (2006: 30–2).

human science in tandem with biology, political economy and philology. Foucault seems to have recognized and substantially rectified this omission in his later work, in which law, the state and government figure prominently. "What is important for our modernity, that is to say, for our present, is not then the state's takeover (*étatisation*) of society, so much as what I would call the 'governmentalization' of the state" (2007: 109).

Foucault's account of the ontological space enclosing Renaissance thought starts with what we think our senses tell us about the world. Appearances are the key; treating like things alike is an organizational principle. Resemblance fosters repetition as the means by which to disseminate knowledge. The ontological space encapsulating the Classical age turns from the way things seem to be similar to each other to the fundamental nature that each thing uniquely possesses. To uncover any thing's nature, it is necessary to look for and, if possible, measure the ways in which it differs from other things.

That things have different properties but do not differ in every property makes it possible to sort them. Categories identify the ways in which different things are alike. Even if nature is a vast collection of different things, nature has an order that we cannot perceive directly. Classifying things is the way we make sense of nature. By speaking of some one thing as a representative member of its class, we are able to convey what we know about those things in relation to other things and thus about nature itself. In the process we reproduce nature's order in our minds, where it provides the reasons that we offer for ends we pursue and the choices we make.

Foucault's account of modern thought is more difficult to summarize. History takes order's place as "the fundamental mode of being of empiricities." History is not simply the accumulation of "empiricities"—things that happen to things or the changing properties of things. Historians find structure in the events they compile because things thus assembled have structure; they are like living things. "History *gives place* to analogical organic structures, just as Order opened the way to *successive* identities and differences" (Foucault 1971: 216, emphases in translation). One might think that Foucault was simply endorsing the familiar view that the end of the Enlightenment saw a shift from mechanical metaphors to the organic metaphors ushering in the Romantic era. I think he had something more in mind; the terms *empiricities* and *structure* do not suggest a Romantic sensibility.

Nevertheless, the term *organic* is crucial to Foucault's account of modern thought. In his discussion of modern biology, Foucault gave credit to natural historian and Parisian luminary Georges Cuvier (1769–1832) for a new way of thinking about living things. Before Cuvier, the classification of organs proceeded by reference to structure and function as necessary complements: for every function a structure, for every structure a function. Cuvier realized that life depends on the integrity of functional relations. Operating as a whole, "organic structures" are contingent solutions to functional needs, and this is what the classification of such structures must reflect. "From Cuvier onward, function, defined … as an effect to be attained, is to serve as a constant middle term and to make it possible to relate together totalities of elements without the slightest visible identity" (Foucault 1971: 263–79, quoting pp. 263, 265).

Even if the "totality of elements" is functionally interdependent, functions are hierarchically ordered. That some functions are more important than others "implies that the organism, in its visible arrangements, obeys a *plan*. Such a plan ensures the control of the essential functions and brings under that control … the organs that perform less vital functions" (Foucault 1971: 266–7, emphasis in translation). In the absence of a plan, the organism would not be able to function as a whole in an environment of which it is a part, and it could not survive. If its environment changes sufficiently, then none of its kind will survive. It is a short step from here to Charles Darwin's explanation for the extinction and emergence of species. These are unplanned changes that seem to obey some mindless natural logic. In the Classical age, no one could have talked this way.

Foucault's "empiricities" are the objects and events, the things, that the analytic procedures of modern science bring to view. In principle, positivist methodology puts the identification of things and measurement of their properties first. Observers are then free to make causal inferences about the relations of things thus identified. Where things are themselves composed of irreducibly complex relations and further analysis is thwarted, we often call these things of this kind organisms or, more abstractly, systems. We impute structure to them and make inferences about what we call functional relations.

If nineteenth-century physics typifies modern science in the positivist mode, Foucault's characterization of modern biology typifies the science of functional relations. Only after modern science took a Darwinian turn and the modern mind (if I am permitted this figure of speech) fully assimilated its implications, did modernism make its *fin de siècle* appearance and a new suite of human sciences—political science, sociology, psychology and anthropology—made their appearance. International Relations is a late product of this modernist partition of ontological space in the modern age. As in the other modernist sciences, contending modes of inquiry are reflected in the inconclusive debate over behavior and system, cause and function, as explanatory foci.

Nomenclature aside, Foucault's strong claim that successive ages possess distinctive ontological spaces and indicative discursive tendencies offers a tight and tidy interpretation of Western culture's last half-millennium. It would seem, however, that his archeology pays too little attention to the transitional moments between successive ages and underestimates what transitional figures can teach us about the colliding rules of discourse.[4] Hugo Grotius

---

4   In suggesting that Foucault "liked to find" discontinuities taking as little as a decade, Hacking (2002: 142) seems to have exaggerated. See, for example, Foucault (1972: 170). Also see Foucault (1980: 112) where the rupture in medical thought beginning about 1790 takes twenty-five or thirty years.

figured in the transition from the Renaissance to the Classical age. So did Thomas Hobbes and René Descartes; none of them is a fully Classical figure. According to Foucault, Adam Smith and David Ricardo bracket the transition to the modern age, and yet for most commentators, Smith's work marks the onset of the modern age, and not the end of the Classical age. In my own opinion, Smith's work reads both ways; it is a monument to a transitional moment (see Onuf and Onuf 2006: Chapters 2, 6). Immanuel Kant's discovery of "man" the moral legislator notwithstanding, his late work still affirms the providential plan of nature. Here again is a monumental collision of discursive trajectories.

Perhaps we should say the same of Foucault's work. Indubitably modern and highly idealized, his model of social change stipulates sudden changes in the way that we think and talk. These changes very much depend on what philosophers are prompted to say; they are ontological legislators or indeed "men" of the sort that Kant discovered. Their disappearance would close the ontological space of the modern age and open a new space for a post-modern age. It would seem then that Foucault's presentiment that the end of "man" is at hand (1971: Chapter 10) marks him as a transitional figure.

Just possibly Foucault was right about the future. Language, its uses and its rules may indeed displace the figure of "man" in defining what we can say and still be heard. More likely, however, is the dispersion of the "totality of elements" constituting both the figure of "man" and that figure's many institutional personifications. With this will come—has already come—the plasticity of human agency and the multiplication of agents, a philosophical preoccupation with intentionality and a theoretical preoccupation with unintended consequences. As Foucault would say in later work, power is dispersed, its predicate not self-legislating men and women but populations, infinitely divisible and subject to proliferating disciplinary mechanisms (2007: lecture 2).

The continuing dispersion of the "totality of elements" constituting the figure of "man" can only accelerate the modern dispersion of power along functional lines.

> Power's condition of possibility, or in any case the viewpoint which permits one to understand its exercise, even in its more "peripheral" effects, … must not be sought in the existence of a primary point, in a unique point of sovereignty from which secondary and descendent forms would emanate; it is the moving substrate of force relations which, by virtue of their inequality, constantly engender states of power, but the latter are always local and unstable. The omnipresence of power: not because it has the privilege of consolidating everything under its invincible unity, but because it is produced from one moment to the next, at every point, or rather in every relation from one point to another. Power is everywhere, not because it embraces everything, but because it comes from everywhere.
> (Foucault 1978: 93)

We may talk about center and periphery, but such talk is empty because, at least according to Foucault, it ignores what power is—what power makes possible—in the modern age.

What then *are* the limits to what we can talk about? Few indeed—that we *know* of. If we talk as we have for two centuries about things and their relations, the primary thing we talk about is the figure of "man," and the most important relations we investigate are necessarily relations of power, variously conceived by the human sciences in causal or functional terms. If this is a time of transition at the end of the modern age, then we can talk as if the figure of "man" will disappear into the play of words or disaggregate into the micro-organs of power, but it is still "man" of whom we speak.

Modern nations embody the figure of "man"; collective identity is a concept the human sciences pretty much take for granted (but should not; here see Chapter 5). Furthermore, the relations of nations are relations of power. This is, as I said above, a defining premise of International Relations as a field of study. Ever since Foucault, scholars in the field have had two ways of talking about what they do. We talk about the modern figure of "man" and its personifications, or we talk about the post-modern fate of that figure.

Constitution: a few remarks

As scholars in the Western world talked about life, labor and language (first as matters of philosophy and then as the human sciences of biology, economics and philology), they changed their mind about these things because they drastically revised their most basic ideas about what anyone would want to know. Add law and government to Foucault's list of discursive formations, and we find the same pattern. An old set of rules for making serious discourse intelligible colliding with a new set of rules produces a disorderly transition lasting for at least a generation.

Furthermore, the collision of discursive rules in a time of transition prompts scholars to talk about their assumptions, to explore the ontological space they can no longer take for granted and to formulate the latent rules limiting what they have been able to say. That Foucault could open up for inspection what makes the modern age ontologically distinctive—indeed what modern thinkers never needed to know—is precisely what makes him a transitional figure. That Foucault attached a good deal of importance to the ontological properties of two earlier ages suggests that a time of transition brings a more general awareness of historical ontology and even suggests that later ages dampened and diminished the ontological spaces of earlier ages without discrediting or displacing them completely. Rather than functioning as limits on what is possible to think about systematically, the ontological premises of earlier ages find expression in ongoing constitutive processes and social practices that condition what we want and do more generally.

In other words, old ontologies never die. They fade from view as the frame and fabric of the social furniture in which we sit and think our modern thoughts.

I would go further: that which Foucault thought was an unspoken constraint on what we can say is always manifest in practice, in the practical possibilities that we do know are open to us, along with the residual constraints of sedimented ages, again available in our ongoing, infinitely complex practices. Ontological consistency is hardly a problem except when we engage in systematic thought. The practical realities of our daily lives reside in a manifold of constitutive processes linked not by logic but history.

In practice, international relations exhibit features that are 500 years in the making. As a modern/ist discursive formation, International Relations bears the traces of Renaissance and Classical antecedents. In modern thinking, these developments suggests a one-way causal relation: changes in International Relations follow changes in international relations. In modernist thinking, international relations and International Relations are functional wholes, both shaped by the whole of their environments. For International Relations, the relevant environment includes university settings, intellectual fashions, personal politics, partisan activities and government ties, all of which swamp the field's ostensible, indeed contestable, subject matter.

In a time of transition, it is plausible to think that causal and functional claims are only part of the story, that International Relations and international relations are historically linked in the constitution of their enduring properties, and that the decisive moments of co-constitution coincide with successive ruptures in the ontological space of Western culture. If these claims are indeed plausible, then it would seem that transitional figures deserve our attention. They do so because they bore witness to great changes, and because they opened new ontological spaces to make sense of what they witnessed. Most of all, they deserve our attention because they made the world different in the very act of making sense of it.

Before International Relations became a modern/ist science, Classical thinkers talked about the society of nations. Traces of the way they did so linger on in the study of international law and in the self-styled English School, in both of which the figure of Grotius is the subject of an appreciation more rhetorical than substantive. Grotius was indeed an important transitional figure, but hardly alone. The transition from the ontological space of the Renaissance to the Classical age also involved Hobbes reacting to Grotius and, even more, Samuel Pufendorf reacting to Grotius and Hobbes. Marking the half-century transition are Grotius's *De jure belli ac pacis* (1625), Hobbes's *De cive* (1642) and *Leviathan* (1651), Pufendorf's *De jure naturae et gentium* (1672): works that few scholars in the field of International Relations think of as an ensemble.

The linked figures of Grotius, Hobbes and Pufendorf gave International Relations its constitutive moment at the dawn of the Classical age by standardizing moral personality in the form of nations rendered equal by the reciprocities of rights and duties among them (Onuf and Onuf 2006: Chapter 4). Such nations have sovereignty as an expressed entailment of their most important rights, just as their duties to other nations impose limits on their sovereignty. They are implicated in an enduring system of relations *and* a legal order: the system and the order depend on each other, and the continuing existence of nations on both. Peace and war define the primary categories of well-ordered relations among nations. In effect, International Relations furnished international relations with a large and accommodating room at the very moment that the transition to the Classical age made space for International Relations. Equipped with an antique template and the raw materials of European life, International Relations fashioned something new and different—something for the field to be about, a continuing supply of constitutive energy, a striking feature of the modern age.

The modern age made a "proper space," as Foucault has said, "for the human sciences" (1971: xxiv). The Classical age had made such a sturdy space for International Relations/international relations that two waves of human sciences (first political economy and positivist law, then political science, sociology, psychology and anthropology) washed up against it without affecting its defining Classical properties: nations equal in their rights and duties, their relations playing out in a simple, expansive and self-sustaining legal order. Only when the twentieth century cratered international relations with catastrophic world wars did International Relations take on the modern features of a human science. It did so, however, without abandoning its Classical pedigree of nations and their ordered relations.

This could hardly be otherwise. Modern nations combine the positive legal powers of the state with affective and normative power of nationalist ideology and popular sovereignty. Modern international relations always seem to bounce back from catastrophes. The legal order among nations appears to be as supple (or slippery) as it is robust. If the modern age and the invention of an ever more differentiated figure of "man" have made new space for the human sciences, they made International Relations late. And they made it a human science without making it leave its old space. If the constitutive symbiosis of International Relations and international relations breaks down, if the space closes, then both will cease to exist, and some other coupling will fill the void. In a time of transition, we can only begin to guess what this might be: one (or more) of the established modern/ist sciences and its preferred figuration of "man," a transitional, late modern, ironically self-aware way of talking that enlivens the figure of "man" in the very act of calling it the dominant discursive artifact of the modern age, or finally a post-modern account of social relations after the banished figures of "man" and "nation" have well and truly vanished.

The future of international relations

There is, of course, a great deal of speculation that international relations are finally, after three and a half centuries, giving way to some other kind of social relations. We tell each other that the canonical division of social space between the level of "man" (the site of human relations and the human sciences) and the level of "nation" (the relations of nations as space reserved for International

Relations) is breaking down, that sovereignty is eroding, that International Relations has lost its focus. We "dignify" these claims—fuel their constitutive potential—even by rebutting them or qualifying them or putting them in perspective. If (people are saying that) international relations are somehow undergoing a fundamental change and becoming something else, then so must (what we in the field are saying about) International Relations.

I have already claimed that the co-constitution of the International Relations and international relations got its start in the transition to the Classical age and that the reconstitution of International Relations as a human science came late in the modern age. More specifically, realism embodied in the figure of Hans Morgenthau registered *and* reinforced the vitality of modern nations and the potency of their struggles. Functionalism embodied in the figure of David Mitrany registered the rise of needs-oriented public bureaucracies and reinforced their transnational reach. Statistical analysis embodied in the figure of L.F. Richardson (Quaker and meteorologist) gave international relations their measure and reinforced the problem-solving ethos of modern science. Positivism embodied in the figures of Morton Kaplan, David Singer and Kenneth Waltz enforced the ontological unity of nature and society by endorsing it, ratified the Comtean compact dividing nature and organizing science into levels, and raised the stakes on theoretical rigor. Even if these constitutive events inspired debate and often worked at cross purposes, International Relations/international relations made the center of world power, itself shifting, the center of world-making; and world-making made the newly consolidated center of world power seem historically inevitable, inseparable from the development of the modern world and, as such, warranted by nature.

No less inevitably, the first significant challenge to International Relations as a human science came from the periphery—more precisely, from figures who adopted the geometrical imagery of center and periphery to characterize relations between global regions and who came to identify themselves with the periphery even as they trafficked between regions. Dependency theorists identified a structure of dependency relations that already existed, but only in diverse institutional manifestations not counted as the kind of international relations that International Relations is about. Once observed, the structure of dependency took on a "life" of its own; agents apprised of its existence acted as if it were a something requiring an intentional response on their part; a whole new set of institutional manifestations came into being; International Relations made dependency relations into a kind of international relations; the Classical space for International Relations/international relations broadened at some cost to the field's capacity to order the contents of that space. If dependency theory ended up as a classificatory issue for a Classical science, world system theory embodied in the figure of Immanuel Wallerstein represented a more substantial challenge.

World systems theory drew on the modernist human science of sociology, locating it in the center of world-making. Advocates presented it as an alternative to International Relations because the structure of relations they identified already had a powerful, coherent institutional history as global capitalism and could not be assimilated to or subsumed by the relations of nations. Just as the Marxist view of the modern age made the nation structurally irrelevant, the Marxist underpinnings of world systems theory gave the structural properties claimed for the world system instant ontological credibility. It was an alternative to International Relations/international relations, institutionally available for agents to act upon, but only if those agents possessed a modern sensibility that was nevertheless not liberal. As Marxism exerted an ever diminishing appeal, this very feature of world system theory proved to be its fatal flaw. Despite the overwhelming presence of global capitalism, the modern world is a liberal society operating at two levels—within nations and among nations—because so many people continue to think it is.

The correspondence of rights and duties, whether among nations or within nations, survived the transition from the Classical to the modern age to become a central feature of liberal society. Liberals take for granted that institutions of all kinds occupy a notionally empty social space that is divided both by level and so-called public and private sectors, and that the occupants of these divided spaces are free, by right, to move about those spaces and form relations with each other. Conspicuously occupying both levels and indeed both sectors are the many institutions, identified as the structure of global capitalism, which constitute and differentiate global markets for goods, services, capital and labor. Another important set of institutions constitutes a buffer zone liberals call civil society, which mediates conflicts between capitalist institutions, large populations and needs-oriented public bureaucracies. In other words, the spread of liberal sentiments and capitalist institutions has also meant the spread of civil society within and among nations. All of these processes are mutually constitutive, as is the process of naming this phenomenon globalization and re-orienting the human sciences to account for what is happening.

By flooding the ontological space of the modern age and washing over all social and conceptual boundaries, globalization offers a challenge to the human sciences as a whole, and not just to International Relations as a Classical science become modern. In International Relations, interest in globalization and the arrival of a global civil society coincides with claims that sovereignty is eroding and the field has lost its focus. Yet the nation remains a primary frame of reference for all discussion, and not just discussion in International Relations. Given the liberal ascendancy and the way liberals order space by levels and sectors, we should expect nothing else. Elsewhere I have developed a more refined view of what I call late modern civil society, in which I try to show that the emergence of additional levels and sectors put limits on the nation and its level without defining it out of existence (Onuf 2005; Chapter 11). Here I want to comment, however, briefly, on the technological correlates of globalization, all of which I take to be integral to the constitution of ascendant liberalism and its institutional correlates, not to mention strong evidence of a transitional moment in the ontological space of Western culture.

The technological correlates in question are glaringly visible to all observers. We see them materialized in computers and cockpits, modems and cables, browser screens and game consoles, cellular telephones and GPS navigation systems—the list seems endless. We stand in awe of the computational power of these machines, their capacity to retrieve, relay and organize information, their ever smaller size and ever greater impact on transportation, the production of goods and provision of services, the movement of wealth. We recognize their astonishing capacity to alter space and time as limits on our activities, and readily extrapolate these effects to society at large.

Anything more that I might try to say about these developments will be incomplete, uninformed and ill-formed. Instead I rely on Manuel Castells' monumental trilogy, *The Information Age*, and especially Volume 1, *The Rise of the Network Society*. Not a work of social theory as such, Castells' comprehensive exposition follows from a philosophical stance that I find congenial, not least with respect to "material support" for what Castells has called "the space of flows" (2000: 440–8, quoting p. 442, emphasis deleted).[5] Flow connotes process. Whatever counts as social always flows, even the space of flows—a space that includes the ontological space that Foucault may be accused of having unduly dematerialized.

The figure of Castells is hardly likely to displace the figure of Foucault as a transitional object.[6] Nevertheless, both figures have the same kind of general, evocative impact on contemporary discourse. As we saw, Foucault suggested that the age after the modern age would displace "man" with language. Castells has identified the new age by what I think will be its canonical name: the information age.

Language is but one vehicle for the coding, storing, communicating and acting on information, which is, by itself, limitless, weightless, infinitely manipulable and potentially timeless. We deploy our cognitive capacities as information makers and users to form institutions and control the flow of events, even events about which we do not have information. Technical-material limits on the production and distribution of information has always imposed limits—conditions of possibility—on its use. To the extent that the technical-material properties of the information age lift these limits, the eventual result may be to reverse the historic relation between us and our world. Instead of our cognitive capacities providing us with the information necessary to act in and on the world, a self-organized world of information (adumbrated in the model of a "perfect market") effectively deploys our cognitive capacities without reference to our intentions. Any such state of affairs would indeed signify the disappearance of "man"—an event already presaged in the structural dopes and

---

5   For my view of the relevant philosophical issues, see Onuf (1989: 60–5); Chapters 4–6.

6   I use the term transitional object to suggest, as D.W. Winnicott has in the case of children (1971:104–10), that these figures help us through the ontological uncertainties of what may be an epochal transition.

rational calculators of modern/ist human sciences, not to mention the cyborgs of science fiction and virtual war.

And all of this is speculation. A reversal of relations between "man" and "machine" may indeed await us on the other side of the transition. Given the conditions of possibility granted us by the successive ontological spaces, the sedimented ontological fields, of Western culture, we cannot know until we get there. Until then, we must give our attention to the transitional potential of the moment, whether it is a transition to a post-modern age, or merely a transition like modernism within the age. And here again Castells has identified the moment in what I think will be canonical terms: the rise of the network society.

Networks in society depend on flows of information. They always have; networks are nothing new. Every so-called traditional society is a network society saturated in information and tightly bounded by technical-material and institutional limits on the reach of that information. Yet these societies never consist of a single homogenous network; only the simplest, most transitory or schematically imagined society—for example, a secret society whose members invent information known only to themselves—might fit this description. Where there are many networks, there is stratification.

By definition, networks occupy parallel planes in a fixed space. While I do not think this claim is especially controversial, it tends to be left implicit. Consider Castells' elegant formulation: "A network is a set of interconnected nodes. A node is the point at which a curve intersects itself. What a node is, concretely speaking, depends on the kind of concrete networks of which we speak" (2000: 501).

From Castells' Euclidian point of view, an intersecting set of curves must occupy the same plane. Any curve not intersecting that set occupies some other plane, and the planes themselves must be parallel or the curves on those planes would intersect. Speaking only somewhat more concretely, social networks have members (whether individual human beings or institutions formed by them). Membership is a status; stratification describes the parallel planes of a network society such that each plane is valued relative to all other planes; status is the value assigned to each member (node) of a given plane relative to the members of other planes.

Speaking even more concretely, traditional societies are highly stratified. Individuals are members of the society by virtue of their multiple status assignments, which grant everyone in the society all the information needed to know where everyone stands on every occasion. In other words, this information tells every member of every network what all members of the society can, may and should do. Status confers agency, albeit in different measure and to different effect for each member of society. However defective as a concrete description of any actual society, this idealized description of traditional society constitutes the point of reference for what we think it means to become modern.

As a transitional moment, the Enlightenment marked the advent of manifold social, economic and political changes that we have only recently come to call modernization.[7] Indeed, the discussion of what it means to be modern has taken place in tandem with these changes. That they do so is a preeminent example of the co-constitutive processes that have made and filled the ontological spaces of Western culture. In this discussion, modernity and tradition stand in opposition. Thus framed, the process of becoming modern is a challenge to the highly stratified societies that tradition both produces and depends on. Traditional societies have an abundance of rules that define and confer statuses; in aggregate statuses give people standing; where people stand in relation to each other determines the distribution of privilege. From a modern perspective, no such society can be just, because tradition offers no choice, no possibility of change and only itself as a good reason for this state of affairs.

If traditional society consists of a multiplicity of embedded networks, modernization requires their replacement with newfound, or newly founded, organizations and associations. Offices and roles displace statuses as the source of agency.[8] Modernization results in a rationalization of political arrangements. Powers of office are delegated from the next higher-office, ultimately reaching an office above which there is none. Within the confines of the nation, the state replaces the old regime.

The modern nation is an elusive abstraction, consisting as it does of people tied by place, history and sentiment, a bounded space called the state—so recognized by other states—and a rationalized, coordinated ensemble of offices called the government, which is presumed to act on behalf of the state and its people. For this purpose, the government has access to the state's resources and control over some specified range of people's activities. Over time, the government replaces old rules conferring privileges and immunities with a new rule making people formally equal. Additional rules allow them to associate with whomever they wish and organize their activities in whatever way they find useful, thereby fixing the necessary conditions for a just society. As an organization, the government works better too. People prosper, and their faith in the nation and confidence in their political arrangements deepen. A virtuous spiral ensues, and the modernizing society "takes off" (Rostow 1960).

Thus conceptualized, modernization is a two-step process. First the traditional rules assigning statuses and stratifying society are abolished. Then new rules providing for rational administration, formal equality and the right to associate are adopted. Yet it is naive to think that status ordering and stratification will never return, that the process we call modernization simply comes to an end. Given enough time, informal rules assigning statuses find their way back into society. As these rules proliferate, they compromise rational administration and

---

7 I have adapted this and the next several paragraphs from Onuf (2007: 6–7), having taken this material from an early version of this essay and put it there for a somewhat different use. Also see Chapter 11.
8 On statuses, offices and roles as constituents of agency, and of the properties of networks, organizations and associations as the institutional forms within which agents exercise their powers, see Chapter 1.

undercut equal treatment. Stratification returns, at first insidiously and then as a matter of course.

Nothing reveals the return of stratification so clearly as the distinction between *ascription* and *achievement* as grounds for status assignment. Modernizers hold up merit as the only justifiable basis for stratification. In this view, status is an incentive for excellence in competitive circumstances and a reward for success. For society, the stratification that results is structurally inconsequential because status of this sort is constantly subject to reassignment and therefore never accumulates.

Not only do modernizers believe that one should and can be judged by one's achievements.[9] No less do they believe that earned status reinforces rational administration and equal treatment. Yet earned status turns out to be a vague criterion for assigning status. After all, the measure of one's achievements is the value ascribed to them by those others whose status makes their judgment relevant. Ascription gives achievement its meaning. Stratification ends up giving society its coherence and durability, just as it always has.

Modernization has always met with resistance. If modernization disperses power, as Foucault claimed, then globalization disperses the modalities of modern power by making technologies of information, communication, transportation and destruction accessible and affordable. Old, localized privilege confronts new, globalized privilege. Whether globalization strengthens local stratification, makes the whole world a single stratified space or, in yet another co-constitutive process, restratifies the center while reinforcing local stratification in the periphery remains to be seen.

In any event, status becomes the chief source of identity for all members of the new network society. It also means that honor is reinvested with the emotional and normative significance it once held in Western culture (on the normative significance of honor, see Onuf 1998b). In this time of transition, the human sciences will have the imperatives of status and the mysteries of honor as their subject. Theoretical perspectives will draw on the self-understandings of traditionally stratified societies (see, for example, Lebow 2008a), in the process aiding and abetting the rise of the new network society.

As sites for displaying status and redeeming honor, nations will no doubt take their time in fading away. So will the field of International Relations. Even if International Relations will continue to have a modest vocation as the nation's constitutive guardian, we will have lost a subject called international relations that we can call our own. By putting status and honor to the forefront, a re-envisioned International Relations will join other visions of late modern social relations in making the future, first, by naming the ghost of cultures past and, second, by giving shape to stratification—as a global phenomenon, as a source of identity, as an apparatus of rule, as a warrant for resistance, as a tribute to humanity's deepest needs and urges.

---

9   And so it is for modernization theory. See Lerner (1958) for an especially influential example.

In this time of transition, such modern terms as *center* and *periphery* will atrophy as place dissolves into the space of flows, functional differentiation proceeds, and power reasserts itself in the stratification of proliferating networks. It will matter less and less where theorists come from, where they were trained and where they work because center and periphery will have become theoretically irrelevant. Talk of *elites*, *masses* and *domination* will lose its Marxist coloration and acquire a new status of respectability (for striking evidence, see Castells 2000: 445–7). Those who feel the claims of honor most keenly will speak of it most eloquently.

In a world defined again by status, scholars will feel right at home. In this respect, at least, nothing has changed. The world that we as scholars have made for ourselves has always been stratified. Today, the most prominent status markers in this world are not places—and these matter less and less—or even institutions, but transitional figures such as Grotius and Hobbes, Foucault and Castells, who loom so large in the ontological space that we all share.

BIBLIOGRAPHY

The Aarhus-Norsminde Papers: Constructivism, International Relations and European Studies (1997) collected by K.E. Jørgensen, Aarhus: Department of Political Science, Aarhus University.

Adler, E. (1997) "Seizing the Middle Ground: Constructivism in World Politics," *European Journal of International Relations*, 3: 319–63.

Akashi, K. (1998) *Cornelius Bynkershoek: His Role in the History of International Law*, The Hague: Kluwer Law International.

Alford, C.F. (1989) *Melanie Klein and Critical Social Theory: An Account of Politics, Art and Reason Based on Her Psychoanalytic Theory*, New Haven, CT: Yale University Press.

—— (1991) *The Self in Social Theory: A Psychoanalytic Account of Its Construction in Plato, Hobbes, Locke, Rawls, and Rousseau*, New Haven, CT: Yale University Press.

Alker, H.R. (1996) *Rediscoveries and Reformulations: Humanistic Methodologies for International Studies*, Cambridge: Cambridge University Press.

Althusser, L. (1971) "Ideology and Ideological State Apparatuses (Notes toward an Investigation)," in *Lenin and Philosophy and Other Essays*, trans. B. Brewster, New York: Monthly Review Press, pp. 127–88.

Aristotle (1934) *Nicomachean Ethics*, trans. H. Rackham, Cambridge, MA: Loeb Classical Library.

—— (1999) *Nicomachean Ethics*, 2nd edn., trans. T. Irwin, Indianapolis, IN: Hackett.

—— (2000) *Nicomachean Ethics*, trans. R. Crisp, Cambridge: Cambridge University Press.

Ashley, R.K. (1981) "Political Realism and Human Interest," *International Studies Quarterly*, 25: 204–36.

—— (1984) "The Poverty of Neorealism," *International Organization*, 38: 225–86.

—— (1987) "The Geopolitics of Geopolitical Space: Towards a Critical Theory of International Politics," *Alternatives*, 12: 403–34.

—— (1988) "Untying the Sovereign State: A Double Reading of the Anarchy Problematique," *Millennium: Journal of International Studies*, 17: 227–62.

—— (1989) "Living on Borderlines: Man, Poststructuralism, and War," in J. Der Derian and M.J. Shapiro (eds) *International/Intertextual Relations: Postmodern Readings of World Politics*, Lexington, MA: Lexington Books, pp. 259–321.

——, and Walker, R.B.J. (1990) "Speaking the Language of Exile: Dissidence in International Relations," special issue of *International Studies Quarterly*, 34: 259–417.

Atran, S. (1990) *Cognitive Foundations of Natural History: Towards an Anthropology of Science*, Cambridge: Cambridge University Press.

Austin, J.L. (1975) *How To Do Things with Words*, rev. edn., Cambridge, MA: Harvard University Press.

Baars, B.J. (1997) *In the Theater of Consciousness: The Workplace of the Mind*, New York: Oxford University Press.

Baldwin, D.A. (1993) "Neoliberalism, Neorealism, and World Politics," in Baldwin (ed.) *Neorealism and Neoliberalism: The Contemporary Debate*, New York: Columbia University Press, pp. 3–25.

—— (ed., 1993) *Neorealism and Neoliberalism: The Contemporary Debate*, New York: Columbia University Press.

Barnes, J. (ed., 1984) *The Complete Works of Aristotle*, 2 vol., continuous pagination, many translators (Princeton: Princeton University Press).

Bartelson, J. (1995) *A Genealogy of Sovereignty*, Cambridge: Cambridge University Press.

Barthes, R. (1977) *Roland Barthes by Roland Barthes*, trans. R. Howard, New York: Farrar.

Bauer, H., and Brighi, E. (eds, 2008) *Pragmatism in International Relations*, London: Routledge.

Bay, C. (1958) *The Structure of Freedom*, Stanford, CA: Stanford University Press.

Becker, G.S. (1976) *The Economic Approach to Human Behavior*, Chicago: University of Chicago Press.

Beer, F.A., and De Landtsheer, C. (eds, 2004) *Metaphorical World Politics: Rhetorics of Democracy, War and Globalization*, East Lansing, MI: Michigan State University Press.

Benedict, R. (1946) *The Chrysanthemum and the Sword: Patterns of Japanese Culture*, Boston, MA: Houghton Mifflin.

Benhabib, S. (1998) "Sexual Difference and Collective Identities: The New Global Constellation," *Signs*, 24: 335–61.

—— (2001) *Transformations of Citizenship: Dilemmas of the Nation State in the Era of Globalization*, Amsterdam: Van Gorcum.

—— (2004) *The Rights of Others: Aliens, Residents, and Citizens*, Cambridge: Cambridge University Press.

—— (2006) *Another Cosmopolitanism*, Oxford: Oxford University Press.

Benjamin, J. (1995) *Like Subjects, Love Objects: Essays on Recognition and Sexual Difference*, New Haven, CT: Yale University Press.

—— (1998) *Shadow of the Other: Intersubjectivity and Gender in Psychoanalysis*, New York: Routledge.

Berger, P.L., and Luckmann, T. (1967) *The Social Construction of Reality: A Treatise in the Sociology of Knowledge*, New York: Anchor Books.

Biersteker, T.J., and Weber, C. (eds, 1996) *State Sovereignty as a Social Construct*, Cambridge: Cambridge University Press.

Boghossian, P. (2006) *Fear of Knowledge: Against Relativism and Constructivism*, Oxford: Clarendon Press.

Booth, K., and Wheeler, N.J. (2008) *The Security Dilemma: Fear, Cooperation and Trust in World Politics*, Basingstoke: Palgrave Macmillan.

Bourdieu, Pierre (1977) *Outline of a Theory of Practice*, trans. R. Nice, Cambridge: Cambridge University Press.

—— (1984) *Distinction*, trans. R. Nice, Cambridge, MA: Harvard University Press.

—— (1990) *The Logic of Practice*, trans. R. Nice, Stanford, CA: Stanford University Press.

Bratman, M.E. (1999) *Faces of Intention: Selected Essays on Intention and Agency*, Cambridge: Cambridge University Press.

Bull, H. (1968) "Society and Anarchy in International Relations," in H. Butterfield and M. Wight (eds) *Diplomatic Investigations*, Cambridge, MA: Harvard University Press, pp. 35–50.

—— (1977) *The Anarchical Society: A Study of Order in World Politics*, New York: Columbia University Press.

Burke, K. (1945) *A Grammar of Motives*, New York: Prentice-Hall.

Butler, J. (1997) *Excitable Speech: The Politics of the Performative*, New York: Routledge.

Cameron, L. (1999) "Operationalising 'Metaphor' for Applied Linguistic Research," in C. and G. Low (eds) *Researching and Applying Metaphor*, Cambridge: Cambridge University Press, pp. 3–28.

Carver, T., and Pikalo, J. (eds, 2008) *Political Language and Metaphor: Interpreting and Changing the World*, New York: Routledge.

Castells, M. (2000) *The Information Age: Economy, Society and Culture*, 1, *The Rise of the Network Society*, 2nd edn., Oxford: Blackwell Publishers.

Cavallar, G. (2002) *The Rights of Strangers: Theories of International Hospitality, the Global Community, and Political Justice since Vitoria*, Aldershot: Ashgate.

Certeau, M. de (1984) *The Practice of Everyday Life*, trans. S.F. Rendall, Berkeley and Los Angeles, CA: University of California Press.

Checkel, J.T. (1998) "The Constructivist Turn in International Relations Theory," *World Politics*, 50: 324–48.

Chilton, P. (1996) *Security Metaphors: Cold War Discourse from Containment to Common Sense*, New York: Peter Lang.

——, and Ilyin, M. (1993) "Metaphor in Political Discourse: The Case of the 'Common European House'," *Discourse and Society*, 4: 37–59.

Cicero (1991) *On Duties*, trans. M. Atkins, Cambridge: Cambridge University Press.

Cohen, J.L., and Arato, A. (1992) *Civil Society and Political Theory*, Cambridge, MA: MIT Press.

Critchley, S. (1996) "Prolegomena to Any Postdeconstructive Subjectivity," in Critchley and P. Dews, *Deconstructive Subjectivities*, Albany, NY: State University of New York Press, pp. 13–46.

Davis, J.W. (2005) *Terms of Inquiry: On the Theory and Practice of Political Science*, Baltimore, MD: Johns Hopkins University Press.

Derrida, J. (1996) "Die Gesetze der Gastfreundschaft," lecture given in Frankfurt, June 1996, German trans. B. Vinken, http://www.kuwi.euv-frankfurt-o.de/de/lehrstuhl/lw/westeuropa/Lehrstuhlinhaber/publikationen/rara/Derrida_in_FFO.pdf

—— (1997a) *The Politics of Friendship*, trans. G. Collins, London: Verso.

—— (1997b) *De l'hospitalité*, Paris: Calmann-Lévy.

—— (1999) *Adieu to Emmanuel Levinas*, trans. P.-A. Brault and M. Naas, Stanford, CA: Stanford University Press.

—— (2000) *Of Hospitality*, trans. R. Bowlby, Stanford, CA: Stanford University Press.

—— (2002) "Hospitality," trans. G. Anidjar, in Derrida, *Acts of Religion*, New York: Routledge, pp. 358–420.

Descartes, R. (1960) *Discourse on Method and Other Writings*, trans. A. Wollaston, Baltimore, MD: Penguin Books.

Dessler, D. (1989) "What's at Stake in the Agent-Structure Debate?" *International Organization*, 43: 441–74.

Devitt, M. (1997) *Realism and Truth*, 2nd edn., Princeton, NJ: Princeton University Press.

Dougherty, J.E., and Pfaltzgraff, Jr., R.L. (1996) *Contending Theories of International Relations: A Comprehensive Survey*, 4th edn., New York: Longman.

Drulák, P. (2004) *Metaphors Europe Lives By: Language and Institutional Change in the European Union*, Working Paper SPS No. 2004/15, Florence: European University Institute.

—— (2006) "Motion, Container and Equilibrium: Metaphors in the Discourse about European Integration," *European Journal of International Relations*, 12: 499–531.

Eakin, P.J. (1999) *How Our Lives Become Stories: Making Selves*, Ithaca, NY: Cornell University Press.

Edelman, G. (1992) *Bright Air, Brilliant Fire: On the Matter of the Mind*, New York: Basic Books.

Elliott, A. (2001) *Concepts of the Self*, Cambridge: Polity Press.

Elster, J. (1979) *Ulysses and the Sirens*, Cambridge: Cambridge University Press.

—— (1989) *The Cement of Society: A Study of Social Order*, Cambridge: Cambridge University Press.

Falk, R.A. (1966) "On the Quasi-Legislative Competence of the General Assembly," *American Journal of International Law*, 60: 782–9.

Ferguson, Y.H., and Mansbach, R.W. (1988) *The Elusive Quest: Theory and International Politics*, Columbia, SC: University of South Carolina Press.

Fierke, K.M. (1998) *Changing Games, Changing Strategies: Critical Investigations in Security*, Manchester: Manchester University Press.

Finley, M.I. (1980) *Ancient Slavery and Modern Ideology*, New York: Viking Press.

Finnemore, M. (1996a) "Norms, Culture, and World Politics: Insights from Sociology's Institutionalism," *International Organization*, 50: 325–48.

—— (1996b) *National Interests in International Society*, Ithaca, NY: Cornell University Press.

Fish, S. (1989) *Doing What Comes Naturally: Change, Rhetoric, and the Practice of Theory in Literary and Legal Studies*, Durham, NC: Duke University Press.

Forrester, J.W. (1989) *Why You Should: The Pragmatics of Deontic Speech*, Hanover, NH: University Press of New England.

Foucault, M. (1971) *The Order of Things: An Archeology of the Human Sciences*, trans. A. Sheridan, New York: Pantheon Books.

—— (1972) *The Archeology of Knowledge*, trans. A. Sheridan, New York: Pantheon Books.

—— (1978) *The History of Sexuality*, 1, *An Introduction*, trans. R. Hurley, New York: Pantheon Books.

—— (1980) *Power/Knowledge: Selected Interviews and Other Writings 1972–1977*, trans. C. Gordon, L. Marshall, J. Mepham, K. Soper, New York: Pantheon Books.

—— (2007) *Security, Territory, Population, Lectures at the Collège de France 1977–1978*, trans. G. Burchill, Basingstoke: Palgrave Macmillan.

Freud, S. (1960) *The Ego and the Id*, 1923, trans. J. Riviere, rev. J. Strachey, New York: W.W. Norton.

—— (1961) *Civilization and Its Discontents*, 1930, trans. J. Strachey, New York: W.W. Norton.

Friedel, F. (1947) *Francis Lieber, Nineteenth-Century Liberal*, Baton Rouge, LA: Louisiana State University Press.

Friedman, M. (1953) *Essays in Positive Economics*, Chicago, IL: University of Chicago Press.

Frohock, F.M. (1999) *Public Reason: Mediated Authority in the Liberal State*, Ithaca, NY: Cornell University Press.

Gentner, D., and Bowdle, B. (2008) "Metaphor as Structure Mapping," in R.W. Gibbs, Jr. (ed.) *The Cambridge Handbook of Metaphor and Thought*, Cambridge: Cambridge University Press, pp. 109–28.

Gergen, K.J. (1999) *An Invitation to Social Construction*, London: Sage.

Gibbs, Jr., R.W. (2005) *Embodiment and Cognitive Science*, Cambridge: Cambridge University Press.

—— (ed., 2008) *The Cambridge Handbook of Metaphor and Thought*, Cambridge: Cambridge University Press.

Giddens, A. (1979) *Central Problems in Social Theory: Action, Structure and Contradiction in Social Analysis*, Berkeley and Los Angeles, CA: University of California Press.

—— (1984) *The Constitution of Society: Outline of the Theory of Structuration*, Berkeley and Los Angeles, CA: University of California Press.

Gill, M.L. (1989) *Aristotle on Substance: The Paradox of Unity*, Princeton, NJ: Princeton University Press.

Ginsberg, M. (1934) *Sociology*, London: Thornton Butterworth.

Goddard, S.E., and Nexon, D.H. (2005) "Paradigm Lost? Reassessing *Theory of International Politics*," *European Journal of International Relations*, 10: 9–61.

Gould, H.D. (1998) "What *Is* at Stake in the Agent-Structure Debate?" in V. Kubálková, N. Onuf, and P. Kowert (eds) *International Relations in a Constructed World*, Armonk, NY: M.E. Sharpe, pp. 79–98.

—— (1999) "Toward a Kantian International Law," *International Legal Theory*, 5: 31–42.

Habermas, J. (1973) *Theory and Practice*, trans. J. Viertel, Boston, MA: Beacon Press.

—— (1984) *The Theory of Communicative Action*, 1, *Reason and the Rationalization of Society*, trans. T. McCarthy, Boston, MA: Beacon Press.

—— (1992) *Postmetaphysical Thinking: Philosophical Essays*, trans. W.M. Hohengarten, Cambridge, MA: MIT Press.

Hacking, I. (2002) *Historical Ontology*, Cambridge, MA: Harvard University Press.

Halliday, F., and Rosenberg, J. (1998) "Interview with Ken Waltz," *Review of International Studies*, 24: 371–86.

Hamilton, A. (1961) "The Federalist No. 9," in Jacob Cooke (ed.) *The Federalist*, Middletown, CT: Wesleyan University Press, pp. 50–3.

Hardin, R. (2003) *Indeterminacy and Society*, Princeton, NJ: Princeton University Press.

Harré, R. (1986) *Varieties of Realism: A Rationale for the Natural Sciences*, Oxford: Basil Blackwell.

—— (1993) *Social Being*, 2nd edn., Oxford: Blackwell.

—— (1998) *The Singular Self: An Introduction to the Psychology of Personhood*, London: Sage.

——, and Gillett, G. (1994) *The Discursive Mind*, Thousand Oaks, CA: Sage.

Hart, H.L.A. (1961) *The Concept of Law*, Oxford: Clarendon Press.

Hayden, P. (2005) *Cosmopolitan Global Politics*, Aldershot: Ashgate.

Hayek, F.A. (1944) *The Road to Serfdom*, Chicago, IL: University of Chicago Press.

—— (1967) *Studies in Philosophy, Politics and Economics*, Chicago, IL: University of Chicago Press.

—— (1973) *Law, Legislation and Liberty*, 1, *Rules and Order*, Chicago, IL: University of Chicago Press.

—— (1992) "The Actonian Revival: On Lord Acton (1834–1902)," in P.G. Klein (ed.) *The Collected Works of F.A. Hayek*, Chicago, IL: University of Chicago Press, 4: 216–18.

Hegel, G.W.F. (1991) *Elements of the Philosophy of Right*, trans. H.B. Nisbet, Cambridge: Cambridge University Press.

Hempel, C.G. (1965) *Aspects of Scientific Explanation*, New York: Free Press.

Herman, G. (1987) *Ritualised Friendship and the Greek City*, Cambridge: Cambridge University Press.

Hobbes, T. (1991) *Leviathan*, Cambridge: Cambridge University Press.

Holsti, K.J. (1985) *The Dividing Discipline: Hegemony and Diversity in International Theory*, Boston, MA: Allen & Unwin.

Homer (1900) *Odyssey*, Greek text and S. Butler's translation, http://www.perseus.tufts.edu/cgi-bin/ptext?doc=Perseus:text:1999.01.0135.

Hooghe, L., and Marks, G (2003) "Unraveling the Central State, but How? Types of Multi-level Governance," *American Political Science Review*, 97: 233–43.

Hopf, T. (1998) "The Promise of Constructivism in International Relations Theory," *International Security*, 23: 171–200.

Hovi, J. (1998) *Games, Threats and Treaties: Understanding Commitments in International Relations*, London: Pinter.

Hülsse, R. (2006) "Imagine the EU: The Metaphorical Construction of Supra-Nationalist Identity," *Journal of International Relations and Development*, 9: 396–421.

Hume, D. (1978) *A Treatise of Human Nature*, Oxford: Clarendon Press.

Ikenberry, G.J. (1998) "Constitutional Politics in International Relations," *European Journal of International Relations*, 4: 149–77.

Inayatullah, N., and Blaney, D.L. (1996) "Knowing Encounters: Beyond Parochialism in International Relations Theory," in Y. Lapid and F. Kratochwil (eds) *The Return of Culture and Identity in IR Theory*, Boulder, CO: Lynne Rienner, pp. 65–84.

James, P. (2002) *International Relations and Scientific Progress: Structural Realism Reconsidered*, Columbus, OH: Ohio State University Press.

Jepperson, R.L., Wendt, A., and Katzenstein, P.J. (1996) "Norms, Identity, and Culture in National Security," in P.J. Katzenstein (ed.) *The Culture of National Security: Norms and Identity in World Politics*, New York: Columbia University Press, pp. 33–75.

Jervis, R. (1997) *System Effects: Complexity in Political and Social Life*, Princeton, NJ: Princeton University Press.

Johnson, J. (1993) "Is Talk Really Cheap? Prompting Conversation between Critical Theory and Rational Choice," *American Political Science Review*, 87: 74–86.

Jones, C. (1993) "Rethinking the Methodology of Realism," in B. Buzan, C. Jones, and R. Little (eds) *The Logic of Anarchy: Neorealism to Structural Realism*, New York: Columbia University Press, pp. 169–245.

Jones, D.V. (1992) "The Declaratory Tradition in Modern International Law," in T. Nardin and D.R. Mapel (eds) *Traditions of International Ethics*, Cambridge: Cambridge University Press, pp. 42–61.

Joseph, J. (2010) "Is Waltz a Realist?" *International Relations*, 24: 478–91.

Kant, I. (1965) *Critique of Pure Reason*, trans. N. Kemp Smith, New York: St Martin's.

—— (1991a) "On the Common Saying: This May Be True in Theory, but It Does Not Apply in Practice," in H. Reiss (ed.) *Kant: Political Writings*, 2nd edn., trans. H.B. Nisbet, Cambridge: Cambridge University Press, pp. 61–92.

—— (1991b) "Perpetual Peace: A Philosophical Sketch," in H. Reiss (ed.) *Kant: Political Writings*, 2nd edn., trans. H.B. Nisbet, Cambridge: Cambridge University Press, pp. 93–130.

—— (1996) *The Metaphysics of Morals*, trans. M. Gregor, Cambridge: Cambridge University Press.

Kaplan, M.A. (1979) *Toward Professionalism in International Theory: Macrosystem Analysis*, New York: Free Press.

Katzenstein, P.J. (ed., 1996) *The Culture of National Security: Norms and Identity in World Politics*, New York: Columbia University Press.

Katzenstein, P.J., Keohane, R.O., and Krasner, S.D. (1998) "*International Organization* at Fifty: Exploration and Contestation in the Study of World Politics," special issue of *International Organization*, 52: 645–1061.

Kegley, Jr., C.W., and Raymond, G. (1994) *A Multipolar Peace? Great-Power Politics in the Twenty-first Century*, New York: St. Martin's Press.

Keohane, R.O. (1986) "Realism, Neorealism and the Study of World Politics," in Keohane (ed.) *Neorealism and Its Critics*, New York: Columbia University Press, pp. 1–26.

—— (1989) *International Institutions and State Power: Essays in International Relations Theory*, Boulder, CO: Lynne Rienner.

—— (1990) "Multilateralism: An Agenda for Research," *International Journal*, 45: 731–64.

—— (1993) "Institutional Theory and the Realist Challenge after the Cold War," in D.A. Baldwin (ed.) *Neorealism and Neoliberalism: The Contemporary Debate*, New York: Columbia University Press, pp. 269–300.

—— (ed., 1986) *Neorealism and Its Critics*, New York: Columbia University Press.

Kerby, A.P. (1991) *Narrative and Self*, Bloomington, IN: Indiana University Press.

Kessler, O. (2010) "On Norms, Communication and the Problem of Practice," in Kessler, O., Hall, R.B., Lynch, C., and Onuf, N. *On Rules, Politics, and Knowledge: Friedrich Kratochwil, International Relations, and Domestic Affairs*, Basingstoke: Palgrave Macmillan, pp. 84–101.

King, G., Keohane, R.O., and Verba, S. (1994) *Designing Social Inquiry: Scientific Inference in Qualitative Research*, Princeton, NJ: Princeton University Press.

Klein, M. (1937) "Love, Guilt and Reparation," in *Love, Hate and Reparation, Two Lectures by Melanie Klein and Joan Riviere*, London: Hogarth Press, pp. 55–119.

Knutsen, T. (1997) *A History of International Relations Theory*, 2nd edn., Manchester: Manchester University Press.

Kornprobst, M., Pouliot, V., Shah, N., and Zaiotti, R. (eds, 2008) *Metaphors of Globalization: Mirrors, Magicians and Mutinies*, New York: Palgrave.

Koziak, B. (2000) *Retrieving Political Emotion: Thumos, Aristotle, and Gender*, University Park, PA: Pennsylvania State University Press.

Kratochwil, F.V. (1983) "Is International Law 'Proper Law'?" *Archiv für Rechts- und Sozialphilosophie*, 69: 13–46.

—— (1989) *Rules, Norms, and Decisions: On the Conditions of Practical and Legal Reasoning in International Relations and Domestic Affairs*, Cambridge: Cambridge University Press.

—— (1995) "Contract and Regimes: Do Issue Specificity and Variations of Formality Matter?" in V. Rittberger (ed.) *Regime Theory and International Relations*, Oxford: Clarendon Press, pp. 77–93.

—— (2000) "Theory and Political Practice: Reflections on Theory-Building in International Relations," in P. Wapner and L.E.J. Ruiz (eds) *Principled World Politics: The Challenge of Normative International Relations*, Lanham, MD: Rowman and Littlefield, pp. 50–64.

—— (2008) "Ten Points to Ponder About Pragmatism: Some Critical Reflections on Knowledge-Generation in the Social Sciences," in H. Bauer and E. Brighi (eds) *Pragmatism and International Relations*, London: Routledge, pp. 11–25.

—— (2011) "Making Sense of International Practices," in E. Adler and V. Pouliot (eds) *International Practices*, Cambridge: Cambridge University Press, pp. 36–60.

Kubálková, V., Onuf, N., and Kowert, P. (1998) "Constructing Constructivism," in Kubálková, Onuf, and Kowert (eds) *International Relations in a Constructed World*, Armonk, NY: M.E. Sharpe, pp. 3–21.

Kuhn, T.S. (1970) *The Structure of Scientific Revolutions*, 2nd edn., Chicago, IL: University of Chicago Press.

Kurki, Milja (2008) *Causation in International Relations: Reclaiming Causal Analysis*, Cambridge: Cambridge University Press.

Lacan, J. (1977) *Écrits: A Selection*, trans. A. Sheridan, New York: W.W. Norton.

Laird, N. (2011) "The Triumph of Paul Muldoon," *New York Review of Books*, 58, no. 11: 63–6.

Lake, D.A., and Powell, R. (1999) "International Relations: A Strategic Choice Approach," in Lake and Powell (eds) *Strategic Choice and International Relations*, Princeton, NJ: Princeton University Press, pp. 3–38.

Lakoff, G. (1991) "Metaphor and War: The Metaphor System Used to Justify War in the Gulf," *Journal of Urban and Cultural Studies*, 2: 59–72.
—— (1999) *Philosophy in the Flesh: The Embodied Mind and Its Challenge to Western Thought*, New York: Basic Books.
——, and Johnson. M. (1980) *Metaphors We Live by*, Chicago, IL: University of Chicago Press.
Langlois, R.N. (ed., 1986) *Economics as a Process: Essays in the New International Economics*, Cambridge: Cambridge University Press.
Lapid, Y. (1989) "The Third Debate: On the Prospects of International Theory in a Post-Positivist Era," *International Studies Quarterly*, 33: 235–54.
Lasswell, H.D., and Kaplan, A. (1950) *Power and Society: A Framework for Political Inquiry*, New Haven, CT: Yale University Press.
Lauterpacht, H. (1927) *Private Law Sources and Analogies of International Law (with Special Reference to International Arbitration)*, London: Longmans, Green.
Lebow, R.N. (2008a) *A Cultural Theory of International Politics*, Cambridge: Cambridge University Press.
—— (2008b) "Identity and International Relations," *International Relations*, 22(4): 473–92.
——, and Risse-Kappan, T. (eds, 1995) *International Relations Theory and the End of the Cold War*, New York: Columbia University Press.
Lehmann, W.P. (1976) "From Topic to Subject in Indo-European," in C.N. Li (ed.) *Subject and Topic*, New York: Academic Press, pp. 445–56.
Lerner, D. (1958) *The Passing of Traditional Society: Modernizing the Middle East*, Glencoe, IL: The Free Press.
Lévi-Strauss, C. (1966) *The Savage Mind*, Chicago, IL: University of Chicago Press.
Li, C.N., and Thompson, S.A. (1976) "Subject and Topic: A New Typology of Language," in C.N. Li (ed.) *Subject and Topic*, New York: Academic Press, pp. 457–89.
Lieber, F. (1859) *On Civil Liberty and Self-Government*, enlarged edn., Philadelphia, PA: J. B. Lippincott.
Ling, L.H.M. (2002) *Postcolonial International Relations: Conquest and Desire between Asia and the West*, London: Palgrave Macmillan.
Lipson, C. (1991) "Why Are Some International Agreements Informal?" *International Organization*, 55: 495–538.
Locke, J. (1975) *An Essay Concerning Human Understanding*, Oxford: Clarendon Press.
Luhmann, N. (2002) *Theories of Distinction: Redescribing the Descriptions of Modernity*, many translators, Stanford, CA: Stanford University Press.
MacIntyre, A. (1984) *After Virtue*, rev. edn., Notre Dame, IN: University of Notre Dame Press.
Maoz, Z., and Felsenthal, D.S. (1987) "Self-binding Commitments, the Inducement of Trust, Social Choice, and the Theory of International Cooperation," *International Studies Quarterly*, 31: 177–200.
Marks, M.P. (2001) *The Prison as Metaphor: Re-Imagining International Relations*, New York: Peter Lang.
Marx, K. (1969a) "Thesen über Feuerbach," in Marx and F. Engels, *Werke*, Berlin: Dietz, 3: 5–7.
—— (1969b) "Theses on Feuerbach," in Marx and F. Engels, *Selected Works*, Moscow: Progress Publishers, 1: 13–15.
Mauss, M. (1967) *The Gift: Forms and Functions of Exchange in Archaic Societies*, trans. I. Cunnison, New York: W.W. Norton.
McGinn, C. (1983) *The Subjective View: Secondary Qualities and Indexical Thoughts*, Oxford: Clarendon Press.
Mead, G.H. (1934) *Mind, Self, and Society: From the Standpoint of a Social Behaviorist*, Chicago, IL: University of Chicago Press.
Mearsheimer, J.J. (1995) "A Realist Reply," *International Security*, 20: 82–93.
Meehan, E.J. (1971) "The Concept 'Foreign Policy'," in W.F. Hanrieder (ed.) *Comparative Foreign Policy: Theoretical Essays*, New York: David McKay, 265–94.
Menger, C. (1963) *Problems of Economics and Sociology*, trans. F.J. Nock, Urbana, IL: University of Illinois Press.
Merton, R.K. (1968) *Social Theory and Social Structure*, enlarged edn., New York: Free Press.
Morgan, P.M. (2003) *Deterrence Now*, Cambridge: Cambridge University Press.

Morgenthau, H.J. (1946) *Scientific Man v. Power Politics*, Chicago, IL: University of Chicago Press.

Mühlhäusler, P., and Harré, R. (1990) *Pronouns and People: The Linguistic Construction of Social and Personal Identity*, Oxford: Basil Blackwell.

Mutimer, D. (1997) "Reimagining Security: The Metaphors of Proliferation," in K. Krause and M.C. Williams (eds) *Critical Security Studies*, Minneapolis, MN: University of Minnesota Press.

Naas, M. (2003) *Taking on the Tradition: Jacques Derrida and the Legacies of Deconstruction*, Stanford, CA: Stanford University Press.

Neisser, U., and Fivush, R. (eds, 1994) *The Remembering Self: Construction and Accuracy in the Self-Narrative*, Cambridge: Cambridge University Press.

Nelson, K. (1996) *Language in Cognitive Development: The Emergence of the Mediated Mind*, Cambridge: Cambridge University Press.

Nussbaum, M. (1997) "Kant and Cosmopolitanism," in J. Bohman and M. Lutz-Bachmann, *Perpetual Peace: Kant's Cosmopolitan Ideal*, Cambridge, MA: MIT Press, pp. 25–57.

—— (2001) *Upheavals of Thought: The Intelligence of Emotions*, Cambridge: Cambridge University Press.

Onuf, N.G. (1970) "Professor Falk on the Quasi-Legislative Competence of the General Assembly," *American Journal of International Law*, 64: 349–55.

—— (1987) "Rules in Moral Development," *Human Development*, 30: 257–67.

—— (1989) *World of Our Making: Rules and Rule in Social Theory and International Relations*, Columbia, SC: University of South Carolina Press.

—— (1997) "A Constructivist Manifesto," in K. Burch and R.A. Denemark (eds) *Constituting International Political Economy*, Boulder, CO: Lynne Rienner, pp. 7–17.

—— (1998a) *The Republican Legacy in International Thought*, Cambridge: Cambridge University Press.

—— (1998b) "Everyday Ethics in International Relations," *Millennium: Journal of International Studies*, 27: 669–93.

—— (2001) "The Politics of Constructivism," in K.M. Fierke and K.E. Jørgensen (eds) *Constructing International Relation: The Next Generation*, Armonk, NY: M.E. Sharpe, pp. 236–54.

—— (2005) "Late Modern Civil Society," in R. Germain and M. Kenny (eds) *The Idea of Global Civil Society: Politics and Ethics in a Globalizing Era*, London: Routledge, pp. 47–63.

—— (2007) "In Time of Need: United Nations Reform, Civil Society, and the Late Modern World," *The Global Community: Yearbook of International Law and Jurisprudence 2007*, New York: Oceana, 1: 3–17.

—— (2008) *International Legal Theory: Essays and Engagements, 1966–2006*, London: Routledge-Cavendish.

—— (2009) "Elusive Distinctions, Epochal Changes," in E.A. Heinze and B.J. Steele (eds) *Ethics, Authority, and War: Non-State Actors and the Just War Tradition*, London: Palgrave Macmillan, pp. 231–52.

—— (2010a) "Escavando a 'Comunidade Internacional': Por uma Arqueologia do Conhecimento Metafórico," *Contexto Internacional*, 32: 253–96.

—— (2010b) "Relative Strangers: Reflections on Hospitality, Social Distance, and Diplomacy," paper presented at Griffith University, Brisbane, 7–8 July.

——, and Onuf, P. (2006) *Nations, Markets, and War: Modern History and the American Civil War*, Charlottesville, VA: University of Virginia Press.

Onuf, P., and Onuf, N. (1993) *Federal Union, Modern World: The Law of Nations in an Age of Revolutions, 1776–1814*, Madison, WI: Madison House.

Onuma, Y. (1993) "Agreement," in Onuma (ed) *A Normative Approach to War: Peace, War, and Justice in Hugo Grotius*, Oxford: Clarendon Press, pp. 174–220.

Oppenheim, L. (1955) *International Law: A Treatise*, 8th edn., H. Lauterpacht, New York: David McKay.

Ortony, A., Clore, G.L., and Collins, A. (1988) *The Cognitive Structure of Emotions*, Cambridge: Cambridge University Press.

Parsons, T.C. (1978) *Action Theory and the Human Condition*, New York: Free Press.

Pateman, C. (1970) *Participation and Democratic Theory*, Cambridge: Cambridge University Press.

Patomäki, H. (2002) *After International Relations: Critical Realism and the (Re)Construction of World Politics*, London: Routledge.

Perry, J. (ed., 1975) *Personal Identity*, Berkeley and Los Angeles, CA: University of California Press.

Peters, B.G., and van Nispen, F.K.M. (eds, 1998) *Public Policy Instruments: Evaluating the Tools of Public Administration*, Northampton, MA: Edward Elgar.

Polanyi, K. (1957) *The Great Transformation: The Political and Economic Origins of Our Time*, Boston, MA: Beacon Press.

Polkinghorne, D.E. (1988) *Narrative Knowing and the Human Science*, Albany, NY: State University of New York Press.

Pouliot, V. (2008) "The Logic of Practicality: A Theory of Practice of Security Communities," *International Organization*, 62: 257–88.

President's Commission on National Goals (1960) *Goals for Americans*, Englewood Cliffs, NJ: Prentice-Hall.

Prügl, E. (1999) *The Global Construction of Gender: Home-Based Work in the Political Economy of the 20th Century*, New York: Columbia University Press.

Puchala, D.J., (ed., 2002) *Visions of International Relations: Assessing an Academic Field*, Columbia, SC: University of South Carolina Press.

Putnam, H. (1981) *Reason, Truth and History*, Cambridge: Cambridge University Press.

Reus-Smit, C. (1997) "The Constitutional Structure of International Society and the Nature of Fundamental Institutions," *International Organization*, 51: 555–89.

—— (1999) *The Moral Purpose of the State: Culture, Social Identity, and Institutional Rationality in International Relations*, Princeton, NJ: Princeton University Press.

Ricoeur, P. (1967) *Husserl: An Analysis of His Phenomenology*, Evanston, IL: Northwestern University Press.

—— (1992) *Oneself as Another*, trans. K. Blamey, Chicago, IL: University of Chicago Press.

Riviere, J. (1937) "Hate, Greed and Aggression," in *Love, Hate and Reparation, Two Lectures by Melaine Klein and Joan Riviere*, London: Hogarth Press, pp. 1–53.

Roland, A. (1988) *In Search of Self in India and Japan: Toward a Cross-Cultural Psychology*, Princeton, NJ: Princeton University Press.

Rosenfield, I. (1988) *The Invention of Memory: A New View of the Brain*, New York: Basic Books.

Rostow, W.W. (1960) *The Stages of Economic Growth: A Non-Communist Manifesto*, Cambridge: Cambridge University Press.

Rovane, C. (1998) *The Bounds of Agency: An Essay in Revisionary Metaphysics*, Princeton, NJ: Princeton University Press.

Rowe, N. (1989) *Rules and Institutions*, Ann Arbor, MI: University of Michigan Press.

Ruggie, J.G. (1983) "Continuity and Transformation in the World Polity: Toward a Neorealist Synthesis," *World Politics*, 35: 261–85.

—— (1997) *Constructing the World Polity: Essays on International Institutionalization*, London: Routledge.

Russell, B. (1940) *An Inquiry into Meaning and Truth*, London: George Allen and Unwin.

Rutherford, M. (1994) *Institutions in Economics: The Old and the New Institutionalism*, Cambridge, Cambridge University Press.

Sacks, Oliver (1993) *A Leg to Stand on*, 2nd edn., New York: Harper.

Schelling, T.C. (1960) *The Strategy of Conflict*, Cambridge, MA: Harvard University Press.

Schmalstieg, W.R. (1980) *Indo-European Linguistics: A New Synthesis*, University Park, PA: Pennsylvania State University Press.

Schmitt, C. (1996) *The Concept of the Political*, trans. G. Schwab, Chicago, IL: University of Chicago Press.

Schneewind, J.B. (1998) *The Invention of Autonomy: A History of Modern Moral Philosophy*, Cambridge: Cambridge University Press.

Schofield, M. (1991) *The Stoic Idea of the City*, Cambridge: Cambridge University Press.

Schrag, C.O. (1997) *The Self after Postmodernity*, New Haven, CT: Yale University Press.

Scott, W.R., and Meyer, J.W, and associates (1994) *Institutional Environments and Organizations: Structural Complexity and Individualism*, Thousand Oaks, CA: Sage.

Searle, J.R. (1979) *Expression and Meaning: Studies in the Theory of Speech Acts*, Cambridge: Cambridge University Press.

—— (1992) *The Rediscovery of the Mind*, Cambridge, MA: MIT Press.

—— (1995) *The Construction of Social Reality*, New York: Free Press.

—— (1998) *Mind, Language and Society: Philosophy in the Real World*, New York: Basic Books.

——, and Vanderveken, D. (1985) *Foundations of Illocutionary Logic*, Cambridge: Cambridge University Press.

Shapiro, M.J. (1981) *Language and Political Understanding: The Politics of Discursive Practices*, New Haven, CT: Yale University Press.

—— (1998) "The Events of Discourse and the Ethics of Global Hospitality," *Millennium*, 27: 695–713.

Shotter, J. (1989) "Social Accountability and the Social Construction of 'You'," in Shotter and K.J. Gergen (eds) *In Texts of Identity*, London: Sage, pp. 133–51.

Slaughter, A.-M., Tulumello, A.S., and Wood, S. (1998) "International Law and International Relations Theory: A New Generation of Interdisciplinary Scholarship," *American Journal of International Law*, 92: 367–97.

Slingerland, E.B., Blanchard, E.M., and Boyd-Judson, L. (2007) "Collision with China: Conceptual Metaphor Analysis, Somatic Marking, and the EP-3 Incident," *International Studies Quarterly*, 51: 53–77.

Smith, A. (1976) *The Theory of Moral Sentiments*, Oxford: Clarendon Press.

Sokolon, M.K. (2006) *Political Emotions: Aristotle and the Symphony of Reason and Emotion*, Dekalb, NI: Northern Illinois University Press.

Sprout, H., and Sprout, M. (1965) *The Ecological Perspective on Human Affairs, with Special Reference to International Politics*, Princeton, NJ: Princeton University Press.

Steele, B.J. (2011) "Alternative Accountability after the 'Naughts,'" *Review of International Studies*, 37: 2603–25).

Stern, D.N. (1985) *The Interpersonal World of the Infant: A View from Psychoanalysis and Developmental Psychology*, New York: Basic Books.

Stone, A. (1994) "What Is a Supranational Constitution? An Essay in International Relations Theory," *Review of Politics*, 56: 441–74.

Taylor, C. (1989) *Sources of the Self: The Making of the Modern Identity*, Cambridge, MA: Harvard University Press.

Tocqueville, A. de (1960) *Democracy in America*, New York: Vintage Books.

Todorov, T. (1984) *The Conquest of America: The Question of the Other*, trans. R. Howard, New York: Harper and Row.

Tooby, J., Cosmides, L., and Barrett, H.C. (2005) "Resolving the Debate on Innate Ideas: Learnability Constraints and the Evolved Interpenetration of Motivational and Conceptual Functions," in P. Carruthers, S. Laurence, and S. Stich (eds) *The Innate Mind: Structure and Content*, New York: Oxford University Press, pp. 305–37.

Turner, S. (1994) *The Social Theory of Practices: Tradition, Tacit Knowledge, and Presuppositions*, Chicago, IL: University of Chicago Press.

—— (2002) *Brains/Practices/Relativism: Social Theory after Cognitive Science*, Chicago, IL: University of Chicago Press.

—— (2010) *Explaining the Normative*, Cambridge: Polity Press.

Wæver, O. (1998) "Explaining Europe by Decoding Discourses," in A. Wivel (ed.) *Explaining European Integration*, Copenhagen: Copenhagen Political Studies Press, pp. 100–46.

—— (2003) "Identities, Communities, and Foreign Policy: Discourse Analysis as Foreign Policy Theory," in L. Hansen and Wæver (eds) *European Integration and National Identity*, London: Routledge, pp. 23–47.

Walt, S.M. (1998) "International Relations: One World, Many Theories," *Foreign Policy*, 110: 29–46.

Waltz, K.N. (1959) *Man, the State and War: A Theoretical Analysis*, New York: Columbia University Press.

—— (1967a) "International Structure, National Force, and the Balance of World Power," *Journal of International Affairs*, 21: 215–31.

—— (1967b) *Foreign Policy and Democratic Politics: The American and British Experience*, Boston, MA: Little, Brown.

—— (1975) "Theory of International Relations," in F.I. Greenstein and N.W. Polsby (eds) *Handbook of Political Science*, 8, *International Politics*, Reading, MA: Addison-Wesley, pp. 1–85.

—— (1979) *Theory of International Politics*, Reading MA: Addison-Wesley.

—— (1986) "'Reflections on *Theory of International Politics*: A Response to My Critics," in R.O. Keohane (ed.) *Neorealism and Its Critics*, New York: Columbia University Press, pp. 322–45.

—— (2000) "Structural Realism after the Cold War," *International Security*, 25: 5–41.

Weiler, J. (1998) *The Constitution of Europe: "Do the New Clothes Have an Emperor?" and Other Essays on European Integration*, Cambridge: Cambridge University Press.

Wendt, A. (1987) "The Agent-Structure Problem in International Relations Theory," *International Organization*, 31: 335–70.

—— (1991) "Bridging the Theory-Meta-Theory Gap in International Relations," *Review of International Studies*, 17: 383–92.

—— (1992) "Anarchy is What States Make of It: The Social Construction of Power Politics," *International Organization*, 46: 383–425.

—— (1994) "Collective Identity Formation and the International State," *American Political Science Review*, 88: 384–96.

—— (1995) "Constructing International Politics," *International Security*, 20: 71–81.

—— (1996) "Identity and Structural Change in International Politics," in Y. Lapid and F. Kratochwil (eds) *The Return of Culture and Identity in IR Theory*, Boulder, CO: Lynne Rienner, pp. 47–64.

—— (1999) *Social Theory of International Politics*, Cambridge: Cambridge University Press.

West, R. (1994) *Black Lamb, Grey Falcon: A Journey through Yugoslavia*, New York: Penguin Books.

White, H. (1973) *Metahistory: The Historical Imagination in Nineteenth-Century Europe*, Baltimore, MD: Johns Hopkins University Press.

Wight, C. (2006) *Agents, Structures and International Relations: Politics as Ontology*, Cambridge: Cambridge University Press.

Wight, M. (1968a) "The Balance of Power," in H. Butterfield and M. Wight (eds) *Diplomatic Investigations: Essays in the Theory of International Politics*, Cambridge, MA: Harvard University Press, pp. 149–75.

—— (1968b) "Western Values in International Relations," in H. Butterfield and M. Wight (eds) *Diplomatic Investigations: Essays in the Theory of International Politics*, Cambridge, MA: Harvard University Press, pp. 89–131.

—— (1992) *International Theory: The Three Traditions*, Leicester: Leicester University Press.

Winnicott, D.W. (1971) *Playing and Reality*, London: Tavistock.

Wolff, C. (1934) *Jus gentium methodo scientifica pertractatum*, trans. J.H. Drake, Oxford: Clarendon Press.

Wolin, S. (1980) "Paradigms and Political Theories," in Gary Gutting (ed.) *Paradigms and Revolutions*, Notre Dame, IN: University of Notre Dame Press, pp. 160–91.

Wright, G.H., von (1971) *Explanation and Understanding*, Ithaca, NY: Cornell University Press.

Young, O.R. (1989) *International Cooperation: Building Regimes for Natural Resources and the Environment*, Ithaca, NY: Cornell University Press.

—— (1994) *International Governance: Protecting the Environment in a Stateless Society*, Ithaca, NY: Cornell University Press.

Zehfuss, M. (1998) "Sprachlosigkeit Schränkt Ein: Zur Bedeutung von Sprache in Konstructivistischen Theorien," *Zeitschrift für Internationale Beziehungen*, 5: 109–37.

ACKNOWLEDGMENTS

Chapter 1 "Constructivism: A User"s Manual," in Vendulka Kubálková, Nicholas Onuf and Paul Kowert, eds, *International Relations in a Constructed World* (M.E. Sharpe, 1998), pp. 58–78. Used with permission.

Chapter 2 "Worlds of Our Making: The Strange Career of Constructivism in International Relations," in Donald J. Puchala, ed., *Visions of International Relations: Assessing an Academic Field* (University of South Carolina Press, 2002), pp. 119–41. Reprinted with permission.

Chapter 3 "Fitting Metaphors: The Case of the European Union," *Perspectives: Review of International Affairs*, Vol. 18, No. 1 (2010), pp. 63–76. Published by the Institute of International Relations, Prague. Reprinted with permission.

Chapter 4, in part, in abridged form and in Chinese "Constructivism: A Philosophical Prologue," *World Economics and Politics*, No. 9 (2006), pp. 58–66. Published by the Institute of World Economics and Politics, Chinese Academy of Social Sciences. Reprinted with permission.

Chapter 4, in part "Elusive Distinctions, Epochal Changes," in Eric A. Heinze and Brent J. Steele, eds., *Ethics, Authority, and War: Non-State Actors and the Just War Tradition* (Palgrave Macmillan, 2009), pp. 239–52. Reprinted with permission.

Chapter 5 "Parsing Personal Identity: Self, Other, Agent," in François Debrix, ed., *Language, Agency and Politics in a Constructed World* (M.E. Sharpe, 2003), pp. 26–49. Used with permission.

Chapter 6 "Structure, What Structure?" *International Relations*, Vol. 23, special issue (June 2009), pp. 183–99. The final definitive version of this paper has been published by SAGE Publications, Ltd. All rights reserved. Copyright Nicholas Onuf.

Chapter 7 "Speaking of Policy," in Vendulka Kubálková, ed., *Foreign Policy in a Constructed World* (M.E. Sharpe, 2001), pp. 77–95. Used with permission.

Chapter 8 "Rules in Practice," in Oliver Kessler, Rodney Bruce Hall, Cecelia Lynch and Nicholas Onuf, *On Rules, Politics, and Knowledge: Friedrich Kratochwil, International Relations, and Domestic Affairs* (Palgrave Macmillan, 2010), pp. 115–26. Reprinted with permission.

Chapter 9 "Friendship and Hospitality: Some Conceptual Preliminaries," *Journal of International Political Theory*, Vol. 5, No. 1 (April 2009), pp. 1–21. Published by Edinburgh University Press. Copyright Nicholas Onuf.

Chapter 10 "Institutions, Intentions and International Relations," *Review of International Studies*, Vol. 28, No. 2 (April 2002), pp. 211–28. Copyright Cambridge University Press. Reprinted with permission.

Chapter 11 "Civil Society, Global Governance: One World, Two Views, Three Modes," *Ritsumeikan International Affairs*, Vol. 3 (March 2005), pp. 21–37. Reprinted with permission.

INDEX

Lightning Source UK Ltd.
Milton Keynes UK
UKOW06f0621200516

274640UK00006B/114/P

9 780415 624176